LAURA SHAPIRO has written o[...]
Champagne to Jell-O for the *New York Times*, the *New Yorker*, the *Atlantic*, *Slate*, *Gourmet* and many other publications. She is the author of three classic books of culinary history. Her awards include a James Beard Journalism Award and one from the National Women's Political Caucus. She was a fellow at the Dorothy and Lewis B. Cullman Center for Scholars and Writers at the New York Public Library, where she also co-curated the widely acclaimed exhibition *Lunch Hour NYC*.

Praise for *What She Ate*:

'In this joyful examination of six women's lives in food, Shapiro sets out to excavate the minutiae of domestic routines for insights into the connection between mental state and menu … entertaining and brimming with enticing small details'
Financial Times

'[a] sharp-eyed dietary survey of six famous women … Like a skilled home cook … Shapiro ekes out biographical scarps, turning them into elegant essays sauced with gossip'   *Sunday Times*

'Shapiro sets each woman satisfyingly in her time and social class, giving us food fads, changing tastes and did-they-really-eat-like-that curios. She has a fine eye for the telling detail and choice quote'
The Times

'*What She Ate* is truly original and fascinating; a new and clever form of food writing. Sensuality, sympathy, snobbery, humour and horror – all are here'
Spectator

LAURA SHAPIRO

What She Ate

Six Remarkable Women
and the Food
That Tells Their Stories

4th ESTATE • London

4th Estate
An imprint of HarperCollins*Publishers*
1 London Bridge Street
London SE1 9GF
www.4thEstate.co.uk

First published in Great Britain by 4th Estate in 2018
First published in the United States by Viking in 2017
This 4th Estate paperback edition 2018

1

The author is grateful for permission to quote from letters and other materials held by the following:
The Wordsworth Trust, Dove Cottage, Grasmere; Nancy Roosevelt Ireland and the literary estate of
Eleanor Roosevelt; Justice Michael A. Musmanno Collection, University Archives and Special
Collections, Gumberg Library, Duquesne University, Pittsburgh, PA; the Estate of Barbara Pym;
the papers of Barbara Mary Crampton Pym (1913–80), Bodleian Libraries, University of Oxford;
Julia Child Materials © 2016; Julia Child Foundation for Gastronomy and the Culinary Arts

Photo credits: Dorothy Wordsworth: Artist unknown. Photo by Hugh Thomas. This image has been
reproduced by kind permission of the Wordsworth family, direct descendants of William Wordsworth
and owners of Rydal Mount. Rosa Lewis: Granger, NYC. All rights reserved. Eleanor Roosevelt: Franklin
Delano Roosevelt Library. Eva Braun: Photo by Heinrich Hoffmann. Bavarian State Library Munich/
Hoffmann collection. Barbara Pym: Photo by Mark Gerson. Helen Gurley Brown: Photo by John Bottega.
New York World-Telegram and the Sun Newspaper Collection, Library of Congress.

Portions of this book have appeared, in different forms, in *The New Yorker* and *Food and
Communication* (Proceedings of the Oxford Symposium on Food and Cookery 2015) and on
the website of the Barbara Pym Society.

A catalogue record for this book is
available from the British Library

ISBN 978-0-00-828110-6

Set in Aurelia Com Light

Designed by Francesca Belanger

Printed and bound in Great Britain by
CPI Group (UK) Ltd, Croydon

MIX
Paper from
responsible sources

FSC
www.fsc.org

FSC C007454

For Jack

How many things by season seasoned are . . .

—William Shakespeare,
The Merchant of Venice

Many a non-Chinese has come away from a meal cursing the "inscrutable" Chinese for saying nothing but bland, polite phrases, when the meal itself was the message, one perfectly clear to a Chinese.

—E. N. Anderson and Marja L. Anderson, in
Food in Chinese Culture, edited by K. C. Chang

CONTENTS

Introduction

"Tell me what you eat," wrote the philosopher-gourmand Brillat-Savarin, "and I shall tell you what you are." It's one of the most famous aphorisms in the literature of food, and I thought about it many times as I was probing the lives of the six women in this book. Food was my entry point into their worlds, so naturally I wanted to know what they ate, but I wanted to know everything else, too. Tell me what you eat, I longed to say to each woman, and then tell me whether you like to eat alone, and if you really taste the flavors of food or ignore them, or forget all about them a moment later. Tell me what hunger feels like to you, and if you've ever experienced it without knowing when you're going to eat next. Tell me where you buy food, and how you choose it, and whether you spend too much. Tell me what you ate when you were a child, and whether the memory cheers you up or not. Tell me if you cook, and who taught you, and why you don't cook more often, or less often, or better. Please, keep talking. Show me a recipe you prepared once and will never make again. Tell me about the people you cook for, and the people you eat with, and what you think about them. And what you feel about them. And if you wish somebody else were there instead. Keep talking, and pretty soon, unlike Brillat-Savarin, I won't have to tell you what you are. You'll be telling me.

One of the reasons I began writing about women and food more than thirty years ago was that I was full of questions like these, and I couldn't find enough to read to satisfy my, well,

hunger. Plainly women had been feeding humanity for a very
long time, but for some reason only the advertising industry
seemed to care. History, biography, even the relatively new field
of women's studies weren't producing what should have been
floods of books on female life at the stove or the table. I couldn't
figure it out. Surely women spent more time in the kitchen than
they did in the bedroom, yet everybody was studying women
and sex, and nobody was studying women and cooking except
the companies selling cake mix. Maybe because I was a journalist, not an academic, it struck me as obvious that everyday meals
constitute a guide to human character and a prime player in
history; but I began to see that food was a tough sell in the scholarly world. The great minds were staunchly committed to the
same great topics they had been mulling for centuries, invariably
politics, economics, justice, and power. Today we know that all
these issues and more can be brought to bear on the making of
dinner—those stacks of books that were once missing are piled
high by now—but back then the great minds, not to mention
most of their graduate students, were reluctant to descend to the
frivolous realm of the kitchen. After all, academic reputations
were at stake. Home cooking was associated with women, which
was bad enough, and housework, which was fatal.

Luckily I had come of age writing for the alternative press,
where we made a point of ignoring any precepts set down by the
great minds, so when I began working on my first book there
was nothing to stop me from asking people what they ate and
why. I posed these questions to the dead, primarily—a luxury
unknown in journalism, but I realized that if I thought of myself as a writer of history, I had many more sources available and
none of them could hang up on me. Over the years that followed, as I explored women and food in different eras of Amer-

ican life, I focused chiefly on pacesetters and enthusiasts, the women whose work in the kitchen had made an impact beyond their own lives. Then I had an experience that sent me in a different direction.

One night, bleary with insomnia, I had been staring at a bookshelf for a long time when I finally pulled out a biography of Dorothy Wordsworth. All I hoped to gain from this choice was a short, peaceful visit to the Lake District, where she famously kept house for her brother William—a visit that would lull me back to sleep. Sure enough, here was the calm, sweet record of their years in Dove Cottage: William devoting himself to poetry, Dorothy devoting herself to William, both of them aloft in reveries inspired by the mountains, the clouds, the birds, and of course the daffodils. Then William married, I skipped a few chapters, and Dorothy turned up in a dreary village far from the Lake District, now making a home for her nephew, the local curate. It was winter; she seemed to spend a lot of time trying to improve his sermons, a desultory cook was giving them black pudding for dinner—and suddenly I was wide-awake. Black pudding, that stodgy mess of blood and oatmeal, plunked down in front of Dorothy Wordsworth, the daffodil girl? There had to be a story.

And there was—a story that opened up a startling perspective on a woman I thought I knew. As soon as I was jolted into focusing on how she cooked and ate, the whole picture of her life seemed to shift, like a holographic image that changes as you tilt it. I had always imagined her as a kind of folk heroine of the Romantic movement, enshrined in the imagery of the Lake District until at fifty-seven she began a descent into sickness and dementia. Conventional wisdom sees these later years as a tragedy and leaves them at that, but conventional wisdom isn't looking at the food. The food was telling me something else about Dorothy's long decline, something I found both disturbing and oddly reassuring. Dorothy's food story became my first.

In this book, I take up the lives of six women from different centuries and continents—women who cooked and women who didn't—and in recounting these lives, I've placed the food right up front where I believe it belongs. Food, after all, happens every day; it's intimately associated with all our appetites and thoroughly entangled with the myriad social and economic conditions that press upon a life. Whether or not we spend time in a kitchen, whether or not we even care what's on the plate, we have a relationship with food that's launched when we're born and lasts until we die. As a writer who's been curious for decades about what prompts people to cook and eat the way they do, I've often marveled at the emotional and psychological baggage we bring to the table, baggage we've generally been lugging around since childhood. Cooking, eating, feeding others, resisting or ignoring food—it all runs deep, so deep that we may not even notice the way it helps to define us. Food constitutes a natural vantage point on the history of the personal.

Today, of course, popular culture is on a culinary binge; and so much personal writing is now devoted to gazing back upon the kitchen and the table that we've had to invent a new literary genre, the food memoir, to contain all of it. But this mania is recent. Biography as it's traditionally practiced still tends to honor the old-fashioned custom of keeping a polite distance from food. We're meant to read the lives of important people as if they never bothered with breakfast, lunch, or dinner, or took a coffee break, or stopped for a hot dog on the street, or wandered downstairs for a few spoonfuls of chocolate pudding in the middle of the night. History respects the food stories of chefs and cook-

book writers and perhaps takes note when a painter or a politician happens to be a gastronome as well; but in the published
accounts of most other lives, the food has been lost.

And it really is a loss, because food talks. Food talks whether
the meal is sitting on the table or never leaves the recipe box. In
May 1953 the popular and prolific food writer Nell B. Nichols,
who had a regular column in the *Woman's Home Companion*
called "Nell B. Nichols' Food Calendar," selected May 8 as the
right day to offer a recipe for peanut-butter sandwiches that had
been dipped in an egg-and-milk batter and then fried. We'll
never know the reactions of any family that might have been
offered this surprising variation on French toast. We'll never
even know if a homemaker was inspired to prepare it. What we
do know is that Nell B. Nichols, tapping into the food corner of
the nation's collective imagination, pulled out a culinary artifact
worthy of being titled American Gothic. The food tells us everything. It tells us about our powerful loyalty to peanut butter,
first of all, and our willingness to follow it across any terrain. It
tells us how midcentury American cooks liked to color outside
the lines while holding fast to the coloring book. And of course
it tells us about the national palate, stunned into acquiescence
after decades of gastronomic novelties dreamed up by the food
industry.

Food always talks. The arts patron Mabel Dodge Luhan, who
became friends with Gertrude Stein and Alice B. Toklas, wrote
once that Stein "had a laugh like a beefsteak. She loved beef, and
I used to like to see her sit down in front of five pounds of rare
meat three inches thick and, with strong wrists wielding knife
and fork, finish it with gusto, while Alice ate a little slice, dain-
tily, like a cat." Many, many people wrote about visiting Stein
and Toklas in their famous Paris flat, but we have few descrip-

tions as succinct and revelatory as this one. Luhan noticed the
food.

Food talks—but somebody has to hear it. William Knight,
the philosophy professor who was one of the first and most dedicated scholars of the Wordsworths, read through Dorothy
Wordsworth's journals early on and decided they should be edited for publication. Dorothy had been a close observer of William as he worked, and the two of them were at the center of a
swirl of family and literary relationships important to his poetry. Unaccountably, however, the journals were also littered
with what Knight called "numerous trivial details" of Dorothy's
housekeeping. He couldn't think of a single reason why poster-
ity would ever want to know what Dorothy cooked or sewed,
and it certainly didn't occur to him that the prose devoted to
such chores might be worth reading for its own sake. One gets
the sense from Knight's brief preface to the journals, which he
published in 1897, that he was a little irritated by all the meals
and domestic doings that Dorothy insisted on telling him about,
possibly at the expense of providing more information about the
great Romantic. "There is no need to record all the cases in
which the sister wrote, 'To-day I mended William's shirts,' or
'William gathered sticks,' or 'I went in search of eggs,' etc. etc.,"
Knight explained wearily. He assured readers that he had
snipped out only the material that plainly lacked "literary or biographical value." Later editors put the shirts and the eggs right
back in; and to this day the Grasmere Journal is recognized as a
classic of intimate prose, with a charm that has outlasted a fair
amount of her brother's verse.

This dismissive attitude toward women's domestic lives continued to flourish for another century or so. Indeed, the very
term "trivial" would come to haunt the post–World War II Brit-

ish novelist Barbara Pym, who loved nothing better than to include a mention of tinned spaghetti when she was constructing a character, though she knew such homely references were considered unworthy of serious fiction. "People blame one for dwelling on trivialities," reflects one of her heroines, who can't figure out why the lemon marmalade is taking so long to jell. "But life is made up of them."

Dorothy Wordsworth and Barbara Pym, both irresistible to me precisely because of those "trivial details," were the first two women I chose for this book. Over the next few years they were joined by an Edwardian-era caterer, Rosa Lewis; a First Lady, Eleanor Roosevelt; a notorious mistress, Eva Braun; and an editor, Helen Gurley Brown. Obviously none of these women represents anyone but herself: each stood out dramatically from the female world into which she was born, and each has attracted enough scholarship, journalism, anecdotes, gossip, and downright fantasy over the years to win a secure spot in history. But what struck me as I followed the paper trail through each life was that while extraordinary circumstances produce extraordinary women, food makes them recognizable. If the emotional substance of these food stories rings familiar, it's because they tend to be as messy and discomfiting as our own.

It's easy, it's practically automatic, to associate cooking and eating with our warmest emotions, and to keep that image on permanent pause, with a family forever beaming as Norman Rockwell carries the turkey to the table. Perhaps there are women whose food stories really do land them in such a cozy domestic category. To me it seems more likely that we're just not accustomed to scrutinizing the food as vigorously as we scrutinize a woman's education, or her marriage, or the poetry she writes. What I saw on the surface of each woman's culinary life was never the whole picture. Digging deeper into her food story took me to a more tenuous emotional realm—sometimes I thought of it as the underside of the Rockwell painting—where all those feelings that we're trying not to notice start dribbling down the sides of the bowls and crawling out from under the platters. I don't mean to imply that these women were unhappy; they weren't. By most measures they experienced quite a bit of contentment and success. But in every instance, opening a window on what she cooked and ate cast a different light on the usual narrative of her life. It turns out that our food stories don't always honor what's smartest and most dignified about us. More often they go straight to what's neediest.

Every life has a food story, and every food story is unique. As we move from chapter to chapter in this book, however, we'll find that the themes emerging from each woman's relationship with food not only reflect her own moment, but reach into ours as well. Dorothy Wordsworth, for instance, who starts off the book, appears at first to be something of an outlier, for she was born in the late eighteenth century—so much earlier than the other women that they would have regarded her culinary world as impossibly primitive. But apart from her spelling and capitalization, which of course reflected habits of her time, I found nothing old-fashioned about her descriptions of the meals she shared with William. It's true, she practically ignored the flavor and texture of the food itself, which no food writer today would dream of doing. This is far from the heavy-breathing school of culinary reportage. But the mere presence of William at the table, sometimes lost in poetry as he sat there, was enough to send a wave of ecstasy through her account of the meal. "While we were at Breakfast that is (for I had Breakfasted) he, with his Basin of Broth before him untouched & a little plate of Bread & butter he wrote the Poem to a Butterfly!" she scrawled in her diary, so excited she lost track of the pronouns. "He ate not a morsel," she added, "nor put on his stockings but sate with his shirt neck unbuttoned, & his waistcoat open while he did it." Later in life, too, she exposed her appetites more nakedly than anyone else in this book, at least until we reach Helen Gurley Brown, whose prose also radiated adoration for a man but gave it rather a different spin.

The next chapter introduces Rosa Lewis, the British caterer and social striver, and a food story riddled with the pressures of class. Cooking and eating are always ruled by a tangle of social and economic realities that define a woman's place in her particular world, and in Rosa's time the class implications lodged even in a sandwich could be formidable. According to a food column in *The New York Times* in 1894, only a "day laborer" should be eating a sandwich made from thick slices of bread and stuffed with hefty chunks of meat. For ladies, an appropriate sandwich would measure no more than half an inch, "and its flavoring or filling is delicate and dainty, a suggestion rather than a substantial reality." Nuances like these made sense to Rosa, who grew up in the servant class but escaped it by mastering the rarefied cuisine demanded by her rich and titled clients. White grapes and truffles went into her champagne ices, she told an interviewer; and she used to forage the markets for young, tender vegetables—"What you call 'premier,'" she said, or at least that's how the word was transcribed in the interview. In truth she was using the French term for those baby vegetables—*primeurs*—but the difference had been swallowed up in her brash Cockney accent. These were complicated jousts: the food could climb the social ladder, but sometimes the cook was left behind.

Eleanor Roosevelt comes next, with a food story dominated by her marriage—like class, a persistent theme in women's relationships with food, though clearly Eleanor's marriage was public to a degree that most couples don't have to endure. She and FDR built what many historians have described as a grand political partnership, but it was also a union marked by culinary discords that reverberated into every corner of Eleanor's life. Numerous references to their meals are scattered throughout the voluminous Roosevelt papers, and none speak well for the power of food to bring two hearts together. So far apart were their appetites that when FDR relaxed with a cocktail and a few smoked clams at the end of the day—a ritual he cherished—Eleanor often stayed away. She rarely touched alcohol, and the idea of spending money on a luxury like tinned clams, especially during the Depression, appalled her. George Eliot once remarked that men seemed to get a great deal of pleasure from the "dog-like attachment" of their wives, but this was not Eleanor's approach to marriage. "He might have been happier with a wife who was completely uncritical," she admitted. On many nights, dinner in the White House was served in two different rooms.

Eva Braun's food story, generated as it was by her devotion to Adolf Hitler, might appear to take place strictly within an appalling realm of its own; and to an extent, it does. But despite the moral distance that separates her from everyone else in this collection, there are elements in her relationship with food that we've seen in other chapters. Like Dorothy, she always had her gaze fixed on the man she loved. Like Rosa, she was thrilled by her access to a higher social rank. What emerges most vividly in Eva's relationship with food, however, is her powerful commitment to fantasy. She was swathed in it, eating and drinking at Hitler's table in a perpetual enactment of her own daydreams. For propaganda reasons, she was not allowed to appear in public with Hitler, which meant that she had no truly gratifying forum in which to show herself off as the Führer's chief consort. Only the lunches and dinners he took with members of his immediate circle allowed her to bask in a role for which she had trained by studying movie and fashion magazines. At these meals, her glory visible and her status secure, she treated food as a kind of servant whose most important job was to keep her thin. Indeed, the only aspect of Hitler's life that she found repulsive was his heavy vegetarian diet. When the mashed potatoes with cheese and linseed oil came around, Eva said a firm no.

After Eva, you may be relieved to move on to Barbara Pym—I certainly was—and the warm, jovial relationship with food that she carried on all her life. "Today finished my 4th novel," she wrote in her diary in 1954. "Typed from 10:30 a.m. to 3:30 p.m. sustained by in the following order, a cup of milky Nescafe, a gin and french, cold beef, baked potato, tomato-grated cheese, rice pudding and plums." No, it's not gastronomy. This is friendship. Food was a steadfast companion that nourished everything in Barbara, especially her creativity. If she so much as glimpsed a well-dressed woman in a café eagerly pouring ketchup over a plate of fish and chips, she came away with a character, then a plot, then a novel. Barbara was aware that modern fiction demanded heroines who were having passionate, tormented affairs, not ordering more pots of tea, but she couldn't help herself. All she knew how to do was turn out brilliantly witty novels in her unique style, and when critics lost interest in her books, she just kept going. Barbara loved food and she loved love, and most of all she loved the connection between them, which was writing.

Last we meet Helen Gurley Brown, the only woman here whose life extended into the twenty-first century. Helen's relationship with food, like all her relationships, was dominated by men, or more precisely by what feminist art historians have called "the male gaze." As the editor of *Cosmopolitan* she promoted full equality for women, but she did so in a spirit better exemplified by *Playboy*. Yes, women could be senators, stockbrokers, cabdrivers, and firefighters, but there was no higher calling for any woman than to attract a man. And Helen was adamant on how to attract men: it started with being thin. Rigorous self-denial at the table was the first of her ten commandments for women; in fact, it was all ten of them. The reward would be love and marriage, she promised, and she always displayed her own story as proof. Nevertheless, when she and David Brown were at home in the evening, they ate the way the Roosevelts did— separately.

Pursuing these women through their own writing, through their biographers, through the archives, pouncing on every clue that might help me figure out what they cooked or ate or thought about food, has been just the sort of research I love. It's like standing in line at the supermarket and peering into the other carts, but with the rare privilege of complete freedom to pry. (Quinoa, miso soup, *and* four cans of tomato paste? What on earth are you making?) In the archives, happily, there's no such thing as a rude question. Now that I've assembled each of these portraits, however, I can see that even though I've always worked within the facts, the facts alone are just the scaffolding. It's the writer who comes up with the story. And I'm quite sure that none of these women would have written her food story the way I did. This became clear when I began assembling the epigraphs that appear at the top of each chapter. The idea was to introduce every woman with a meal that I found in the records of her life—a meal that summed up for me the complications inherent in her story. I can already hear the six of them objecting to my choices.

Dorothy is wondering a little nervously why I didn't focus instead on one of those nice gooseberry tarts she used to make.

Rosa is demanding a rewrite: she wants an elegant French entrée that will assure her the place she deserves in gastronomic history.

Eleanor is lecturing me, patiently, on the progressive rationale behind her luncheon menu.

Eva is insulted that I'm describing her life in terms of food instead of, say, showcasing one of her handsome evening gowns.

Barbara, who loved finding out what people ate in real life, can't imagine why I didn't use one of her own recipes, especially since there were several among her papers.

Helen alone understands why I chose her particular meal, but she's making it clear that a better writer would have recognized it as a triumph.

Ladies, I'm listening. What I've learned is that everyone's a critic, even after death, and that any biographer who dares to think she's getting the last word is sure to end up eating it.

Dorothy Wordsworth

(1771–1855)

Dined on black puddings.

—Diary, January 13, 1829

Ever since the publication of the Grasmere Journal, a luminous record of some three years spent keeping house for her brother William in one of the loveliest regions of England, Dorothy Wordsworth has been a cherished figure in the history of Romantic poetry. As a person separate from her famous brother, however, she's been notoriously difficult to assess. Here was a smart, spirited, well-read woman who threw herself into a life of ardent service to her brother—so ardent she came to resemble one of those present-day political wives whose gaze is permanently fixed on a godlike husband. Then William married, and Dorothy withdrew any claim on his heart except the appropriate one of a sister. Yet she passed out cold on his wedding day, and her profound distress on that tumultuous morning leaps from the Journal like a frightened animal. Scholars have been wondering for years what to make of it.

There have been countless warring interpretations of the Grasmere Journal and of Dorothy's life. Was she as happy as a robin in the sunshine of family love? Or was she tormented by incestuous passion for William? Does the Journal prove, tragically, that she might have become a great writer if she hadn't dedicated herself to William and then his family? Or does the Journal prove, triumphantly, that she became a great writer any-

way, working within the modest scope available to her? It's a
murky life with an uncertain moral, but it's also a life that beautifully demonstrates the way food speaks up even when a very
private, very conflicted woman prefers to say nothing.

As I noted in the introduction, it was Dorothy's encounter
with a dinner of black pudding that prompted me to start my
search for the food stories in women's lives. But it was her
writing—the spark in her perceptions, the great washes of emo-
tion, the pleasure she took in the mundane—that made it clear
why she belonged in this book, indeed right at its front door. By
virtue of her wide-open senses and a passion to record, she was
creating a perfect context for the idea of culinary biography. To
be sure, she kept a great deal of herself hidden even when she
was being effusive, and it's impossible to know how much of her
own silent editing went into her journals and letters. Thomas
De Quincey, who met her at Dove Cottage in 1807, five years
after William's marriage, was struck by her eyes—"wild and
startling"—but said she seemed nervous in company and spoke
with a slight stammer. He attributed this to what he called "self-
conflict"—an ongoing struggle between her instinctive intelligence and the sense of social propriety that quickly clamped
down on it.

I thought about De Quincey's reaction to Dorothy when I
came across a letter she had written thirteen years before they
met. Dove Cottage, her journals, William's marriage—all of it
was still ahead. Here was Dorothy at the very beginning, a
twenty-two-year-old woman who had fled convention to seize
her own future in a blaze of love and poetry. I've gone back to
that letter many times in the course of pondering Dorothy and
her well-kept secrets, and I'm introducing it now, at the outset of
her story, because I can't imagine a stammer in this prose. She

A miniature portrait by an unknown artist
showing Dorothy Wordsworth
as a young woman.

was writing in a powerful, deliberate voice quite different from the more impressionistic Grasmere Journal. Dorothy wanted to be understood in this document. It was her declaration of independence. And she chose the language of food.

It was the spring of 1794, and she and William had embarked on one of those arduous, exhilarating walks across country that he loved and Dorothy was just discovering. After years spent apart and months of secret plotting—secret for reasons that will be clear in a moment—the two of them had finally managed to meet, and they were determined to live together as soon as they could assemble some kind of home. Now they were tramping side by side in rain and mud, with Dorothy in bliss at every step. They passed Grasmere, where years later they would settle, and then stopped to visit friends in a mountainside farmhouse overlooking the town of Keswick. There, gazing at a landscape so spectacular she exclaimed that it was "impossible to describe its grandeur," she received a letter from an aunt she particularly disliked, scolding her for "rambling about the country on foot" in the face of dreadful but unmentionable risks.

She didn't have to spell out the dangers; Dorothy knew what she meant. During a recent stay in France, William had had an affair with a Frenchwoman and fathered a baby girl. Now he was in disgrace with his family, and nobody considered him a fit companion for his maiden sister—nobody, that is, but Dorothy herself. She had been stunned by the news, but a conflict between conventional morality and the actions of her brother was no conflict at all; her loyalty never wavered. She even pulled together her French and took over the necessary correspondence with his ex-mistress. "I consider the character and virtues of my brother as a sufficient protection," she told her aunt coolly, and she added that spending time with William was turning out to be a fine way to expand her education. "I have regained all the knowledge I had of the French language some years ago." Her aunt would not have missed the subtext.

But when she picked up her pen to compose this rejoinder, the first thing Dorothy wanted to establish—even before she launched into her defense of William—was what she was eating. "I drink no tea . . . my supper and breakfast are of bread and milk and my dinner chiefly of potatoes by choice," she wrote. It was a diet practically biblical in its simplicity, a perfect stand-in for the dignity of her new commitment. Dorothy maintained strong family ties all her life, but the food of this trek—inscribed in the letter as if it were a placard to be carried overhead—proclaimed her allegiance. She was William's sister, and it was not just a relationship, it was a calling. She would live as she chose.

The Grasmere Journal is full of food; in fact it's so voluble on the subject that Dorothy has gained a culinary reputation as well as a literary one. Today, when tourists visit the Wordsworth home that's come to be known as Dove Cottage, they can see where Dorothy kneaded bread and rolled out pie dough; they can envision the large open fireplace with pots and pans hanging above it (the space is now occupied by a Victorian-era range); they can go into the garden and imagine her gathering broccoli, potatoes, radishes, and spinach. Afterward they can wander through Grasmere and stop at the very shop, more or less, where Dorothy went on a cold Sunday looking for the "thick" ginger-bread that William preferred.

Unfortunately for culinary sleuths, however, the trail grows cold here. Apart from the Grasmere Journal, surprisingly little in Dorothy's extensive written archive—letters, travel journals, more diaries—touches on what she cooked or ate. There are enough scattered passages, especially in her travel writing, to remind us that she was in the habit of paying attention to food. But only during the Grasmere Journal years did she make a point of writing about it regularly. At first glance, then, her food story seems to begin and end in those pages. But if you look more closely, and take into account some of her later journals, which have never been published, it turns out that Dove Cottage gives us only the first act of her food story. There was a second act, which took place twenty-five years later in a distant village called Whitwick; and a third, back in the Lake District, during which she gradually, sometimes cheerfully, lost her mind.

Dove Cottage was a whitewashed house on the busy road between Ambleside and Keswick, a cluster of six dark rooms that were cold and nearly empty when Dorothy and William moved in just before Christmas of 1799. He was twenty-nine, burning to be a great poet; she was a year younger and burning to help him. They examined the place as best they could without much light. The main sitting space downstairs lacked a proper ceiling— it was merely the floorboards of the room above—and the room they thought to use as an upstairs sitting space filled with smoke as soon as they tried to light a fire. Privacy was going to be impossible; the slightest noise bounded from room to room. Dorothy had never seen inside the house before she walked through the door, but she had been dreaming for years about finding a simple dwelling where she could make a home for William. She used to furnish it in her mind; sometimes she set the table for tea and planned what they would talk about. Now she knew exactly what she was looking at: here was paradise.

And it was, but there's always a serpent. This one bore the

much-loved face of a family friend from Yorkshire named Mary Hutchinson. She arrived for a visit two months after they moved in, stayed five weeks, and by the time she departed William knew he was in love with her. In the middle of May he set out on a walk to her home in Yorkshire, taking his brother John with him. Dorothy, who normally relished these marathon treks across country, stayed back this time: she didn't want to be there when William proposed. On the day he left, her emotions were on such a rampage she burst into tears the moment he was out of sight; and that evening she opened a notebook.

> *May 14 1800.* Wm & John set off into Yorkshire after dinner at 1/2 past 2 o'clock—cold pork in their pockets. I left them at the turning of the Low-wood bay under the trees. My heart was so full that I could hardly speak to W when I gave him a farewell kiss.

She cried for a long time, she wrote, and then went out for a chilly walk by the shore of the lake, which looked "dull and melancholy." She described the berries and wildflowers she had seen, and she named them. She remarked on the stirring views, she said she had encountered a blind man "driving a very large beautiful Bull & a cow," and she recalled that she kept stopping to sit down despite the cold. Her eyes had always been sharp, and she had an artist's instinct for focus; now she would put those gifts to work. "I resolved to write a journal of the time till W & J return, & I set about keeping my resolve because I will not quarrel with myself, & because I shall give Wm Pleasure by it when he comes home again."

"I will not quarrel with myself." This vow set the tone, not only for what became the Grasmere Journal, but for the way

Dorothy would live from that day on. Long ago she had chosen her future without hesitation: she would be William's sister, the word "sister" going round and round in her imagination until it blossomed into the glory of a life's work. She would care for him, cook for him, and be the handmaiden to his poetry. Now, caught up in the trauma of William's departure, she returned to that commitment and strengthened it: she would permit no flicker of dissatisfaction, unease, or resentment. She knew precisely the degree of happiness she could expect, and she was determined to want no more. William was going to marry, she told herself; his bride would join their household, and Dorothy would give her whole heart to the new configuration—she would, she would, she would. "Arrived at home with a bad head-ache. . . . Oh! that I had a letter from William!"

Writing the journal, which she kept on doing even after her brothers returned from Gallow Hill, was what sustained her during the two and a half years of William's engagement. All day she gathered up impressions as greedily as a bird pecking about in a newly planted field. Then she opened her notebook and filled page after page with her quick scrawl, describing the crows and ravens, the colors of the lake, the twigs and catkins and clouds and moonlight. She recorded the walks she and William took, their visitors, their illnesses, their quiet evenings, their work in the garden and orchard. And, continuing as she had started with her very first sentence, she wrote about food. Assembling the ingredients and preparing their simple meals was a process that went on continually, and it comes up in these pages over and over like the gently recurring rhymes in a sonnet. She picked peas from the garden, she took apples from the orchard. Their neighbors brought them gooseberries and she turned out pies and tarts and puddings. She bought bacon from another neighbor and gingerbread from the blind man down the street. They caught fish from the lake. She baked bread, she made broth, she bottled rum, she boiled eggs. After years in which her letters and journals said little about food, now it's everywhere.

Why this sudden attention to their meals? They hardly constituted a novelty: Dorothy had been cooking for William for years. But the notes on food served a different purpose from the other jottings in her journal. When she wrote about the clouds and flowers, the beggars and the gypsies, she was writing for William. She liked to feel that she was his companion, perhaps his inspiration, anytime he might need a bit of support in the lonely work of writing poetry. Her observations on the world around them were there for him to use as he wished. The notes on food, by contrast, spoke directly to Dorothy herself. They reminded her, though she was hardly in danger of forgetting, that everything about Dove Cottage mattered. It was all sacred. She had eaten gooseberry tarts before living in Dove Cottage and she would eat them afterward, but to eat them there was to feed on the very time, the very place, the very love that sustained her.

Cooking, moreover, was wifely. Far more than a chore, in Dorothy's world it was an aspect of identity. Even if a married woman didn't do the cooking herself, she was judged on her ability to manage the food of the household. Dorothy was no amateur: she had kneaded and chopped and stirred in many kitchens before she began preparing meals in Dove Cottage. But only now did she seem intent on keeping a written record of how she fed William and their guests, as if to shore up her right to a role she wouldn't dream of claiming openly.

More than two centuries later, it's impossible to gauge the

quality of Dorothy's cooking. We'll never know, alas, whether William used to get up from the table hungry and go out hoping to find a couple of fallen apples in the orchard. Dorothy's habit of jotting down only cursory notes about the food makes it difficult to analyze the success of her efforts. But inadequate cooks generally know all too well how inadequate they are, especially if they have to cook every day, and there's nothing in the Journal to suggest that Dorothy lacked confidence in the kitchen. On the contrary, those brief, habitual notations sound as though she accomplished her cooking with practiced efficiency. If she suspected that William didn't like what she was serving, she would have noticed—he was the object of her intense daily scrutiny—and the anxiety would have pursued her from page to page the way she was pursued by her various illnesses and, occasionally, "my saddest thoughts."

What we do know about the food of paradise is, first of all, that it was practical. She and William were trying to live as stringently as possible on their small income, and she was accustomed to setting a thrifty table. In the morning they liked a bowl of mutton broth, with bread and butter. For dinner, the most substantial meal of the day, there was often a savory pie filled with veal, rabbit, mutton, giblets, or leftovers. Supper was pretty casual—broth again, or else they just ate whatever appealed to them. One evening that meant tapioca for Dorothy, an egg for Mary, and cold mutton for William.

But there was something wonderfully idiosyncratic about the way they approached mealtime itself. She and William arranged their days exactly as they pleased, and meals took place when they felt like eating them. Nobody was ever dragged in from a beautiful lakeside ramble merely because it was the proper hour for tea. One day she stayed in bed, just because she wanted to, until one p.m.; then she went down to breakfast. Dinner was understood to be a midday event, but in actuality it wandered across the afternoon, sometimes happening as late as five p.m. Tea and supper had to fit into whatever time was left before bed. And if a meal disappeared entirely, nobody seems to have missed it. "We had ate up the cold turkey before we walked so we cooked no dinner," she reports. On another occasion, "We got no dinner, but Gooseberry pie to our tea." Home cooking in this era meant that somebody was going to be home, cooking, much of the time; and Dorothy noted more than once that she stayed behind at the oven while others went outdoors. But she wouldn't allow the steady march of mealtimes to exert any more control over the day than necessary.

What springs most vividly from Dorothy's food writing is her tone of voice. If the words themselves tended to be dispassionate, there was a glow about them that belied their brevity. "Writing" is almost the wrong term for what she was doing; it seems too effortful. Whenever a pie or a roast or a bag of peas from the garden rose to her consciousness, she simply dropped the image into place among the rest of the day's incidents, as if she were adding a tiny square of marble to a boundless mosaic of the quotidian.

> Wm was composing all the morning—I shelled peas, gathered beans, & worked in the garden till 1/2 past 12 then walked with William in the wood.

> Coleridge obliged to go to bed after tea. John & I followed Wm up the hill & then returned to go to Mr Simpsons— we borrowed some bottles for bottling rum. The evening somewhat frosty & grey but very pleasant. I broiled Coleridge a mutton chop which he ate in bed.

I baked pies & bread. Mary wrote out the Tales from Chau-cer for Coleridge. William worked at The Ruined Cottage & made himself very ill. I went to bed without dinner, he went to the other bed—we both slept & Mary lay on the Rug before the Fire.

Priscilla drank tea with us—we all walked to Ambleside—a pleasant moonlight evening but not clear. Supped upon a hare—it came on a terrible evening hail & wind & cold & rain.

We had Mr Clarkson's turkey for dinner, the night before we had broiled the gizzard & some mutton & made a nice piece of cookery for Wms supper.

We had pork to dinner sent us by Mrs Simpson. William still poorly—we made up a good fire after dinner, & William brought his Mattrass out, & lay down on the floor I read to him the life of Ben Johnson & some short Poems of his which were too *interesting* for him, & would not let him go to sleep.

I made bread & a wee Rhubarb Tart & batter pudding for William. We sate in the orchard after dinner William fin-ished his poem on Going for Mary. I wrote it out—I wrote to Mary H, having received a letter from her in the eve-ning.

I threw him the cloak out of the window the moon over-cast, he sate a few minutes in the orchard came in sleepy, & hurried to bed—I carried him his bread & butter.

Cooking, for Dorothy, was inextricable from her life with William: to serve him food was to reinforce all the emotions that bound them. We can almost feel the way the air around them takes on color and sensibility when she sets down the bread and butter or gazes at him as he sits over his bowl of broth. Food transforms the two of them, at least in Dorothy's mind, to a single glowing entity. Once, when he was away from Grasmere for a few days, she tried frantically to fend off despair by throwing herself into housework, working in the garden, and sending herself on long walks. It was difficult for her to believe in the relationship unless they were together, and the symbol of their shared presence was always food. "Oh the darling! here is one of his bitten apples! I can hardly find it in my heart to throw it into the fire." On that occasion he returned a day earlier than she expected—"How glad I was"—and she gave him a beefsteak while they sat at the table, "talking & happy."

Thursday, July 8, 1802, was Dorothy's last day in paradise. She spent much of it copying out 280 lines of William's recent work on "The Pedlar," and in the evening the two of them went out to gaze at the moon. "There was a sky-like white brightness on the Lake. The Wyke Cottage Light at the foot of Silver How. Glow-worms out, but not so numerous as last night—O beautiful place!" The next morning they embarked on a three-month journey that would culminate in Yorkshire, where Mary was arranging the wedding. Dorothy scribbled frantically in her journal as long as she could, recording each blessed sight around her. Everything would be there when the three of them returned, but everything would be different; this was a painful good-bye. "The horse is come Friday morning, so I must give over. William is eating his Broth—I must prepare to go—The Swallows I must leave them the well the garden the Roses all—Dear creatures!! they sang last night after I was in bed—seemed to be singing to one another, just before they settled to rest for the night. Well I must go—Farewell.—"

The Grasmere Journal was discreet on many topics, but when she wrote about the wedding, Dorothy tore her heart open. She and William arrived ten days before the ceremony was scheduled to take place. Dorothy took note of the garden, with its asters and sweet peas, and reported, not very convincingly, "I looked at everything with tranquillity & happiness." The next day she fell sick and remained sick right up until the morning of the wedding when, she wrote, she woke up feeling "fresh & well." Just before he left for the church, William came upstairs to see her. "I gave him the wedding ring—with how deep a blessing! I took it from my forefinger where I had worn it the whole of the night before—he slipped it again onto my finger and blessed me fervently." There is some debate about Dorothy's exact wording here. In her definitive edition of the Grasmere Journal, the Wordsworth scholar Pamela Woof points out that the wedding-ring passage has been heavily inked over, probably by Dorothy. Examined under infrared light the words are fairly legible, and Woof believes that instead of "and blessed me fervently" Dorothy may have written "as I blessed the ring softly."

Fervently, or perhaps not, then, William went off to the ceremony, while Dorothy stayed behind in her room, fighting off her agitation. "I kept myself as quiet as I could, but when I saw the two men running up the walk, coming to tell us it was over, I could stand it no longer & threw myself on the bed where I lay in stillness, neither hearing or seeing anything." Mary's sister, who had been downstairs preparing the wedding breakfast, came up to tell her that the newlyweds were approaching the house, and Dorothy swam back to consciousness. "I moved I knew not how straight forward, faster than my strength could carry me till I met my beloved William & fell upon his bosom." With the help of one of Mary's brothers, William got Dorothy back into the house, "& there I stayed to welcome my dear Mary."

After breakfast, all three departed on a wedding trip home to Grasmere. Dorothy filled page after page of the Journal with details of their sightseeing—"Dear Mary had never seen a ruined Abbey before except Whitby"—and wrote with passion about how her own heart "melted away" as they neared Grasmere, traveling through a landscape she had first encountered with William three years earlier. Only upon reaching home did she suddenly fall silent. "I cannot describe what I felt, & our dear Mary's feelings would I dare say not be easy to speak of."

In the weeks following their return Dorothy recorded several cozy scenes. She and Mary baked cakes and had all the neighbors in for tea; Mary read Chaucer aloud one cold day; the three of them went off on their usual rambles. But Dove Cottage was not an ideal home for newlyweds plus one. Everything was audible everywhere, and William worried that the noises of lovemaking were distressing to Dorothy. She never made so much as an oblique reference to any such tensions, but as the months passed she seemed to lose her zeal for the Journal, and by January she was writing hardly at all. On January 11 she took note of the date—"Again I have neglected to write my Journal"—recognizing how thoroughly she had fallen away from the practice of daily observation and note taking. From that day forward, she resolved, she would write more regularly, and she would even try to improve her handwriting. It was a new year and a new life, she was determined to make the best of both, and she would open a "nice" clean notebook as soon as the current one was full.

It never happened. Less than a week later, she made what would be the last entry in the Grasmere Journal. "Intensely cold," she began. "Wm had a fancy for some ginger-bread." She went on to describe how she had bundled up and gone to visit Matthew Newton, the blind man who sold gingerbread from his house. William liked thick pieces of gingerbread, but Matthew Newton had none that day, only the thinner sort, baked in slabs. She decided to make her own instead but couldn't bring herself to tell this to Matthew and bought sixpence' worth of the slabs just to be charitable. The next day, while she was baking, his wife appeared at the door—she had managed to obtain a supply of thick gingerbread. Dorothy felt obliged to buy some, despite the fact that her own was under way, and took two pennies' worth. She always enjoyed telling stories about their encounters with the locals, and this one had a mix of generosity and misunderstanding that appealed to her. She also liked what Matthew Newton said about trying to obtain more thick gingerbread for her and transcribed his exact phrase: " 'We'll *endeavour* to get some.' " The next day she opened the notebook and started to write the date—Monday, January 17—but something distracted her and she put down her pen even before finishing the word. The Journal ends, disconcertingly, with "Monda."

Dorothy continued cooking, of course, even when she wasn't writing about it. But the emotional ingredients that went into each meal changed, now that she was no longer the only woman who broiled a steak for William or gathered the scraps of left-over dough to make him a wee tart. The domestic center of gravity in Dove Cottage shifted to Mary. Talented cook, efficient housekeeper, diligent copier of William's drafts—she could do everything Dorothy was doing and quickly topped her maiden sister-in-law by becoming a mother. John was born eight months after the wedding, Dora a year later, then Thomas, Catharine, and finally William Jr.

Now we come to the second act of Dorothy's food story, which unfolds during the winter of 1828–1829. By this time she had been the all-purpose spinster in the Wordsworth family for a quarter century, and what was once a hectic round of domestic responsibilities had largely disappeared. William had become prosperous, and the family was living in one of the grandest houses in the area: Rydal Mount, just down the road from Grasmere. Servants took care of the spacious, well-appointed rooms; there was a full-time cook; the children had grown up. At fifty-six, Dorothy was as energetic as ever, but she was no longer crucial to the smooth running of the household, and when she spied a sudden opportunity to be useful again, she snatched it. Her favorite nephew, John Wordsworth, was about to start his first job in the church: he was going to be the curate in a poor Leicestershire village called Whitwick. William couldn't hear the name without a groan—"There are not many places with fewer attractions or recommendations than Whitwick"—but Dorothy was elated. She would spend the winter there, a "fireside companion" to brighten his home and make the evenings less lonely. It would be Dove Cottage all over again. She wouldn't have William across from her at the table, but she would have his eldest son, a perfectly good surrogate. John even had trouble with his eyes, as William did, and couldn't read very long by candlelight. He needed help, he needed conversation, he needed support in his new endeavor. Dorothy would be indispensable.

According to an early nineteenth-century description of Whitwick, the village was set "in a sharp and cold situation" and

had no pleasant features worth noting apart from nearby Charn-
wood Forest and a trout stream. The main source of employment among the villagers was framework knitting, an industry
that produced stockings and was so notorious for low wages that
the expression "poor as a stockinger" had been a familiar one for
decades. The work was done on huge knitting machines, which
families kept in their cottages, running them all day and, if they
could afford the candles, into the night. John's parish also included the neighboring village of Swanington, which had been
given over to coal mining for the last two hundred years. Poverty and a grim physical landscape were the most prominent
features of Dorothy's new surroundings.

A handful of Dorothy's letters survive from the winter of
1828–1829; but more important, she was also keeping a diary.
She had started it four years earlier, an irregular record of her
walks, travels, visitors, and household activities, quite different
from the expansive, emotional conversation with herself she had
carried on in the pages of the Grasmere Journal. This time it was
as if she simply wanted to gather up whatever scraps of the day
had fallen like dry leaves across her memory. So she remarked
on an encounter with a villager, an arresting view, a round of
laundry, a visit to a neighbor. Her style was nondescript, the
content was irrelevant to William's poetry, and to a modern eye
her speedy scrawls are barely legible. Hence these later journals
have attracted far less attention than her other writing and have
never been transcribed or published in full. But thanks to a few
scholars, in particular Robert Gittings and Jo Manton, who scru-
tinized these jottings in the course of preparing their biography
of Dorothy, we can start to guess what it was like for Dorothy to
live in Whitwick. The version in her diary didn't always match
what she was telling friends in her letters.

Take the weather. "Five weeks have I been here, and not a single rainy day," she announced to her close friend Jane Marshall right after Christmas. Yet the diary for her second week at Whitwick tells a different story: "A gloomy morning. Slight rain. . . ." "Blustering dark morning—Light Rain. . . ." "Dreary and damp. . . ." "Very slight rain before church—gloomy only. . . ." Or take the habit of vigorous walking that was still important to her. In Whitwick she headed out onto a bare, pitted terrain or followed a road busy with cartloads of coal. "It may be called a good country for walkers," she told Jane brightly. In the letters she says little about her day-to-day activities; her diary, by contrast, tells us that much of her time went to housework. Cleaning went on constantly, for instance, because of the soot and coal dust in the area. Laundry, too, was more onerous. In the evenings she helped John with his sermons—apparently they were not very stirring—and rarely entertained visitors. But her letters say nothing of drudgery or tedium. Over and over she indicated that she had found the best possible place to be, and that was at John's side. "I am more useful than I could be anywhere else."

The blissful certainty that John needed her was the sun that greeted her each morning in Whitwick, no matter the weather. Dorothy's rose-colored letters from Whitwick were not efforts to hide or disguise reality; on the contrary, they offered a picture closer to her emotional experience than the plain facts in the diary. Jotting down what she did each day reminded her of how she really lived. Then she closed the notebook and surrendered for a while to her heart, which was trying to reassemble Dove Cottage from the unpromising materials around her. But unlike the Grasmere Journal, her Whitwick diary says almost nothing about food, and the absence is noteworthy. No sacred moments over a basin of broth, no tears over a bitten apple. Only on a couple of occasions did something about a meal prompt Dorothy to jot down what they had eaten—and to do so in the diary, her outlet for truth telling.

John's cook was a woman named Mary Dawson, who had worked for the Wordsworths back at Rydal Mount. Dorothy called her "an honest good creature, much attached to her Family," but missing from this testimonial was any praise for Mary Dawson's skill in the kitchen. In fact, she had worked chiefly as a maid until the Wordsworths, eager to replace a terrible Rydal Mount cook, moved Mary Dawson into the position. The family needed a talented cook just then, because Mary Wordsworth was recovering from an illness and could not be persuaded to eat. In order to tempt the invalid, Dorothy had asked Mary Dawson to prepare "all sorts of nice things"—a challenge evidently beyond her, because she, too, was soon replaced. But for John's purposes, Mary Dawson appeared to be the perfect choice. He was living on a very small salary, and there would be no call for "nice things." The virtue of Whitwick cuisine would be its economy. As Dorothy put it, "She will be a right frugal housekeeper."

And so she was, which explains one of the most startling notes on food in any of Dorothy's journals. She jotted it down on a frosty January day in Whitwick: "Dined on black puddings."

That's all she wrote, and it's possible, of course, that I'm reading too much into it. Perhaps black pudding was a perfectly ordinary dinner for the Wordsworths, one that William, Mary, Dorothy, and the children had eaten happily for years; and on this particular January day Mary Dawson simply continued the tradition. But I don't think so. Nothing about the nature of black pudding—and nothing about the Wordsworths—suggests that this was the case. I believe Dorothy found it extraordinary to dine on black pudding and that the few words she said about it said everything.

Dorothy made only two remarks about food in the Whit-wick diary: this note about black pudding and an earlier note in which she mentioned Christmas dinner. Her birthday was December 25, so Christmas dinner was always doubly festive, and the family typically put her favorite dishes on the menu. This year the celebratory meal was simple but just right, and she scribbled it down: "Rabbit pie & plumb pudding." She and William had dined constantly on savory meat pies when they were living together, and plum pudding was a holiday icon she had long relished. The Christmas menu, in other words, was a taste of her beloved past. Black pudding was the opposite: it was a taste of Whitwick.

Pretty much everything about black pudding signals that this menu originated not with Dorothy but with Mary Dawson—"our homely Westmoreland housemaid," as Dorothy called her. It's true that the Wordsworths ate plenty of pork in all forms, and for a time they even owned pigs. Yet black pudding never appeared anywhere else in Dorothy's journals; it never showed up in her letters, and there's no mention of it in the family's recipe collections. A look at how the dish was made, and the class connotations that were packed into the casings along with the blood and oatmeal, may help to explain why.

Here's a typical recipe, from Hannah Glasse's authoritative kitchen bible, *The Art of Cookery, Made Plain and Easy,* first published in 1747. Before killing your hog, she instructs, boil a peck of groats for half an hour. As soon as the hog is dead, collect two quarts of the warm blood and stir it constantly until it cools. Then stir in the groats and add salt, a mixture of cloves, mace, and nutmeg, and a few chopped herbs. The next day, clean the intestines of the hog and fill them with the blood mixture, adding an abundance of chopped fat as you go. "Fill the skins three parts full, tie the other end, and make your puddings what length you please; prick them with a pin, and put them into a kettle of boiling water. Boil them very softly an hour; then take them out, and lay them on clean straw."

Plainly, there wasn't much margin for error. The blood had to be fresh and warm or it would coagulate; the oats had to be fully cooked beforehand so they would be ready at the right moment; the intestines had to be scrubbed absolutely clean, and they couldn't be overfilled or they might burst. As a vicarage cook, Mary Dawson wouldn't have made her own black puddings; she would have purchased them, and we don't know where. What we do know is that she was a penny-pinching housekeeper with no instinct for good food—a terrible combination of character traits for someone buying this particular product. Provenance was key. Like all sausages, a black pudding of unknown origin was suspect by definition. The cookbook author Mary Radcliffe, writing in 1823, advised her readers that they could safely eat the ones offered by respectable farmers and country gentlemen, but not the ones for sale in the butcher shops of London. These, she cautioned, were "so ill manufactured . . . as to form a food by no means very inviting."

Cheap and ubiquitous, with a phallic shape irresistible to humorists, black puddings often appeared in the popular press as the favorite food of petty criminals, rascals, serving wenches, fools, and assorted lowlifes. "Merry Andrew," the archetypal eighteenth-century buffoon, carried a black pudding, and "Moggy," a dunce of a girl who couldn't answer the simplest questions of the catechism, angrily pulled a black pudding out of her dress and smacked the parson in the face with it. But by the early nineteenth century more dignified sources were also acknowledging the lowly class standing of black pudding. The author of a Victorian-era glossary of North Country words and expressions called the dish a "savoury and piquant delicacy" but added that it was mostly seen "among the common people of the North." At the large breakfasts set out for upper-class families, black pudding continued to make an appearance; but eventually the dish lost even its morning cachet. "Black puddings are not bad in their way, but they are not among the things we would make to set before our friends," ruled Georgiana Hill in *The Breakfast Book,* published in 1865.

Why, then, did it show up that January day? Dorothy wouldn't have enjoyed such a meal under any circumstances, for she suffered from what was probably colitis or irritable bowel syndrome and had been reporting painful attacks for years. Black pudding, heavy and notoriously indigestible, would have looked to her like intestinal agony on a plate. And she was the de facto mistress of the house; Mary Dawson would have consulted her on the dinner menu. Dorothy could have raised an objection. She didn't.

Dorothy didn't object to anything at Whitwick. She accepted all of it and simply translated her experience into the language she preferred, the language of happiness and satisfaction. She approved of frugal cooking and had done it herself, joyfully, at Dove Cottage, where her simple meals had been woven into the fabric of each day's blessedness. When she made broth, it was for William's breakfast; when she broiled a mutton chop, she served it to Coleridge in bed. "Wm & John set off into Yorkshire after dinner at 1/2 past 2 o'clock—cold pork in their pockets," she wrote on the first page of the Grasmere Journal. It was she who had roasted the pork and wrapped the cold scraps for travel; that's why she put it in the Journal. The very words bound her together with William. Now she was gazing at her dinner in John's lonely house and seeing all she had lost. The food was foreign, it belonged nowhere, and neither did she. So she translated it. Like the gloomy weather, black pudding went into the diary undisguised; the words were plain and truthful. But the meal as she chose to taste it was sweet.

Dorothy had been in Whitwick for only a few weeks when John received news that the prospects for his future had brightened. Another opening for a curacy had turned up, this one in Moresby—a more prosperous and appealing town, located on the west coast of England not too far from Grasmere. He accepted the offer gratefully and made plans to move by summer. In this congenial new post, he would have no further need of his aunt's companionship. Dorothy would stay with him for the rest of the winter, but the fantasy of extending her term of service indefinitely—winter after winter, central to John's life and first in his heart—was abruptly shut down. As always, she expressed only happiness; but paradise was about to disintegrate once again. Dorothy had arrived in Whitwick in perfect health. As she assured a friend, "I can walk 15 miles as briskly as ever I did in my life." When she left, she was an invalid.

It's hard to know what precipitated her collapse that April, but one day, after she had nursed her nephew through a bad week of influenza, Dorothy was seized with intestinal pain and spent two long days in what William described later as "excruciating torture." This may have been an attack of gallstones or possibly a dramatic worsening of her usual colitis. The family was terrified that she might die. An "obstruction" was removed, and afterward she was so feeble she couldn't move or speak. Mary sped to Whitwick to take care of her, and slowly she became stronger, but that summer she had a relapse. When she finally returned to Rydal Mount in September, she found that even a two-mile walk was too much for her. Increasingly she felt exhausted and confused. Her symptoms—violent pain in her bowels, nausea and vomiting, and debilitating weakness—were not unfamiliar to her. She had recorded similar attacks from time to time in the Grasmere Journal (much to the displeasure of William Knight, the Journal's first editor, who didn't like the bowel references any better than he liked the food references). But after Whitwick, a pattern set in: she would collapse in agony, recuperate and gain a bit of strength, then fall back once more.

The standard treatment for pain was laudanum, a tincture made from opium mixed with wine or brandy. Dorothy had taken it regularly in the past for toothaches. Now she was relying on it for her frequent intestinal attacks, and the worse they became, the more heavily she was dosed. The drug, of course, was addictive; it also affected the brain, and by 1835 Dorothy was showing signs of mental disintegration. Gradually illness stripped her of nearly everything that made her recognizable. Once she had been sharp-minded, vigorous, and perpetually curious, always ready for a trek or a project, always eager for conversation. As her body and mind deteriorated she became trapped ever deeper in what Mary called a "child-like feebleness," given to outbursts of rage, hilarity, babbling, and profanity. Helpless and homebound, she became the focus of constant worry and round-the-clock nursing. Yet in one way or another, using language when she had it and other means when she

didn't, she continued to tell her food story. In fact, it was all she
wanted to talk about.

The third act of Dorothy's food story takes place during the
twenty-six long years of her illness, which among other gifts and
heartbreaks left Dorothy with a new body. She had always been
thin, even gaunt, but after the onset of her dementia she started
complaining of "faintness and hollowness," as William described
it. He said she constantly craved "something to support her."
More and more, that something was food. She wanted to eat, she
demanded to eat; her pleas became incessant. For the first time
in her life she grew fat, then very fat: it took two people to hold
her up if she decided to "walk" by pushing her feet along the
floor. She told William she was happy only when she was eating.

But much as she craved food, it was a metaphor for something she craved even more desperately. No, not love—she knew
she was loved; William never left her in the slightest doubt
about that. One day at Dove Cottage she broke a tooth and realized she was well on the way to losing all of them. "Let that
pass," she wrote calmly in the Grasmere Journal. "I shall be
beloved—I want no more." But in the wake of her first breakdown at Whitwick, she had experienced a novel sensation. As
she recuperated, she became aware that her illness had prompted
an outpouring of tenderness, sympathy, and worry from numerous friends and family members. She was deeply moved to hear
from so many people. For the first time in her life, she was able
to bask in the warmth of simultaneous attention from just about
everyone she knew. "It drew tears from my eyes to read of your
affectionate anxiety concerning me," she wrote to an old friend.
"In fact it is the first time in my life . . . in which I have had a

serious illness, therefore I have never before had an opportunity of knowing how much some distant Friends care about me—Friends abroad—Friends at home—all have been anxious."

Selfless devotion to others had long been Dorothy's vocation. She had taken care of William, she had tended to Coleridge, she had helped raise children, she had poured attention on the lonely and the needy, and whenever it seemed that she might run out of work, she managed to find more—until illness opened up another way to live, and she slipped right in. By 1835 she had discovered self-pity. That year William and Mary made a trip to London, leaving Dorothy and their daughter Dora, who was also chronically sick, in the care of the Rydal Mount servants. Dorothy was still able to write in her diary at that point, so we have an account of her reaction; apparently she had begged them not to go. "Wm & Mary left us to go to London. Both in good spirits till the last parting came—when I was overcome. My spirits much depressed. . . . More than I have done I cannot do therefore shall only state my sorrow that our Friendship is so little prized & that they can so easily part from the helpless invalids." Never in her life had she expressed herself in those terms—"poor me, poor me" was simply not the way she responded to trouble or deprivation. But she was whining now, feeling sorry for herself as assiduously as if she had decided to make up for lost time.

"It will please Aunty if one of you will write to her,—for she often tells us nobody takes notice of her," Mary reported to a niece, adding, "She has been very cross lately." Dorothy complained often that she was neglected by her family; she said she was "ill-used" and needed protection, and she begged for signs of affection. The arrival of a birthday gift sent her into cries of delight: "You see, I *have* good friends who care for me, tho' you do not," she declared to a Rydal Mount servant who had been attending her faithfully. When the man of letters Henry Crabb Robinson, an old friend, was planning a Christmas visit to Rydal Mount, William wrote to tell him Dorothy was demanding a present. She fancied a box of the winter apples known as "Norfolk Beefins" and had been asking for them over and over, saying "she was sure if Mr Robinson knew how she *longed* for them, you would send her some."

Responding to Dorothy's pleas and outbursts was a tiring job, and responding to her physical needs was even worse. Dorothy's symptoms included incontinence and bouts of violent diarrhea, as well as racking pains, chills, fever, and perspiration. She and her bedclothes had to be cleaned up repeatedly. She could not be left alone. Sometimes she moaned, chattered gleefully, or let out a wild shriek; when she was in a fury she struck out wildly at the women caring for her, and on occasion she horrified the family by bursting into profanity. When guests stayed overnight in the house, they had to be given rooms as far as possible from Dorothy's lest she frighten or unnerve them. Yet there were also periods of clarity when she seemed almost her old self. "If I ask her opinion upon any point of Literature, she answers with all her former acuteness; if I read Milton, or any favourite Author, and pause, she goes on with the passage from memory," William observed wonderingly. She was able to write a letter occasionally or sit in the garden contentedly. Then suddenly she became a spoiled child again, hurling demands. All year round she insisted on having a fire in her room, saying the warmth was the only thing that made her feel better. In summer her room was so hot nobody else could bear sitting in it, but if the fire was allowed to die down, she went into one of her rages until it was restored to full strength. The ever-sweltering bedroom drove Mary to the edge of her patience. "This is an *in-*

tolerable experience," she complained in a rare burst of open frustration. She was thinking in part about the amount of money they were spending on coal in the middle of August.

Physically dependent, mentally beyond responsibility, the object of constant and devoted care, the center of attention whenever she chose—Dorothy in illness was reborn. Even during the periods when she felt relatively strong, she never objected to the restrictions on her activity imposed by the doctor and her family, and she calmly accepted the pampering. "I have been perfectly well since the first week in January—but go on in the invalidish style," she reported to a friend in April 1830, two years after her initial breakdown in Whitwick. "Such moderation I shall continue for another year. . . . My spirits are not at all affected."

But of course her spirits were affected. They were transformed. She had entered a realm of greed without guilt, insisting on more heat than anyone else could bear, more attention than her weary caregivers could muster, more gestures of love than she had ever received before. And, incessantly, more food. In all the many pages of her diaries and letters over the years, she rarely mentioned an instance of feeling hungry. Now she was never satisfied. One Christmas Jane sent a gift of freshly killed fowl—a turkey and two chickens—and Mary brought them to show Dorothy. "I wish you could have but seen the joy with which that countenance glistened at the sight of your never-to-be-forgotten present," Mary wrote later. "Every sensation of irritation, or discomfort vanished, and she stroked and hugged the Turkey upon her knee like an overjoyed and happy child—exulting in, and blessing over and over again her dear, dearest friend. . . . The two beautiful lily white Chicken were next the object of her admiration, and when Dora said it was a pity that such lovely creatures should have been killed, she scouted the regret, saying 'What would they do for *her* alive . . . and she should eat them every bit herself.' "

William fought desperately with her about food. The Dove Cottage days of quietness and harmony over lovingly prepared bowls of broth were long gone. Dorothy was clamoring for all sorts of rich foods, and her anguished brother was terrified to give them to her, certain they would make her "bilious" and bring on another agonizing attack. "I feel my hand-shaking," he wrote to Robinson after a bout of her screaming and frustration. "I have had so much agitation to-day, in attempting to quiet my poor Sister. . . . She has a great craving for oatmeal porridge principally for the sake of the butter that she eats along with it and butter is sure to bring on a fit of bile sooner or later."

"I will not quarrel with myself." Dorothy held firm to her vow for twenty-nine years, but after her collapse at Whitwick she lost control. Everything came out, unseemly and uncensored. From time to time she experienced intervals of remarkable lucidity, writing letters and remembering her favorite poems in a manner that reminded everyone of the person she used to be. "She is . . . for a *short space* her own acute self, retains the power over her fine judgment and discrimination—then, at once, relapses," Mary reported. "But she *has no delusions*." Dorothy did retain a grasp of her environment even when her personality disappeared, so in that sense she had no delusions; yet she was meeting the world afresh. She took to singing when she felt like it; she made friends with a bird that flew in her bedroom window. In 1837, amid some of the worst years of her illness, she woke up one day feeling momentarily clearheaded and wrote a letter to her niece Dora. "Wakened from a wilderness of dreams, & rouzed from Fights & Battles, what can I write, do, or think?—

To describe the *past* is impossible—enough to say I am now in my senses & easy in body." She was in her senses, she was at ease in her body; that was all she could say, and it was enough.

There are different ways to read a life, and Dorothy's long decline, most often described as tragic, perhaps had moments of triumph as well. Consider, for instance, the image that will serve to conclude her food story—Dorothy in her chair, round and imperious as royalty, demanding porridge so that she could eat the butter.

Rosa Lewis

(1867–1952)

"Do you know King Edward's favourite meal? Let me whisper. It was boiled bacon and broad beans. He loved them."

—*Daily Sketch*, June 13, 1914

O f all the women in this book, Rosa Lewis should have been the one whose food story was already right there in full view. She was a cook by profession, her meals were famous in her own time, and she worked for herself. Surely she wrote down recipes, drafted menus, scribbled shopping lists, saved receipts from the fishmonger and the greengrocer, and kept notes on the likes and dislikes of her clients. What's more, she was a public figure, one of the best-known caterers in Edwardian London, sought out by many of the most revered families in the aristocracy, and a favorite of King Edward himself. Newspapers called her "England's greatest woman chef" and "the greatest woman cook that the world has ever known" and reported on her death and funeral.

Yet the written record is mostly scraps and gaps, gossip and anecdotes. We do have the newspaper stories, as well as a sampling of Rosa's menus and a few recipes. Occasionally she shared culinary home truths with reporters ("When you cook a quail or a plover, make it taste like a quail or a plover, not like something else"). We know when she bought the Cavendish Hotel on Jermyn Street, we know when she died, and we know the impressive size of her estate—£123,000, the equivalent of around $340,000 at the time, not including the Hepplewhite chairs, Regency tables, free-standing marble staircase, and quantities of rugs and pictures, all from the hotel and sold at auction after her death. But for a woman whose life has inspired five books and *The Duchess of Duke Street,* a thirty-one-episode public television series, there is surprisingly little that can be verified, apart from some of the food that made her famous. The truth and the legends about Rosa Lewis have been intertwined for so long that it's impossible to separate them. Which was just the way she liked it.

Plenty of young girls learned to cook professionally in Edwardian England, but Rosa had a more complicated ambition. She wanted great cooking to open the doors of the most exclusive houses in London, and she had her sights on the drawing room as well as the kitchen. It wasn't about marrying up or discarding her origins; it was about being exactly who she was— "Rosa Lewis, cook!"—whether she was wearing an apron or a Paris gown. There were no role models for such an accomplishment. Auguste Escoffier, the most lionized chef in London, came close, but he was a man, he was French, he ran lavish restaurants, and he hadn't started out as a Cockney scullery maid.

Most of what has been written about Rosa has borrowed heavily from the first book published about her, which appeared in 1925. The author, an American journalist named Mary Lawton, had heard about Rosa from the theatrical designer Robert Edmond Jones, who urged her to do a story on a woman he called one of the most extraordinary characters in London. "She began life as a scullery maid and became one of the greatest cooks in England—a friend of the King as well as his cook," he told Lawton—a capsule biography that would always be the best line in Rosa's résumé. Lawton persuaded the editor of the popular monthly *Pictorial Review* to give her an assignment, then traveled to London and asked Rosa if she would consent to a series of interviews. Rosa was in her fifties. She had outlived the grand culinary style that made her famous; indeed, she no longer did much cooking of any sort, and the war had done away with the culture of affluence and entertainment in which she had been something of an adored mascot. Here was an opportunity to resurrect a lost world and give life to memories she treasured. She agreed to talk, according to Lawton, and allowed a stenographer to take down every word. *Pictorial Review* ran a four-part series based on the interviews in the spring of 1924, under the byline "Recorded by Mary Lawton." A year later the series was published in book form as *The Queen of Cooks—And Some Kings (the Story of Rosa Lewis)*. Written entirely in the first person, the text conveys the impression of a comfortable, loquacious raconteur looking back on a remarkable life and thoroughly enjoying every moment she pulled from the past. ("Once, when I went out to cook a big dinner in a very smart house, one of the maids said—'Hello! are you one of Mrs. Lewis' cooks?' 'Yes,' I replied. Then she said—'How long have you been with her? Does she still drink?' I said—'Yes'm, just a little.' 'Does she still use bad language?' 'Oh, yes, quite a lot,' I answered.") Famous names were scattered liberally across the pages—lords and ladies, politicians and actors, a handful of American millionaires—and although Lawton didn't attempt to re-create Rosa's Cockney accent, it practically bounces off the page.

As soon as she saw the book, Rosa indignantly called it a "travesty" and threatened to sue. She denied that she had participated in the project. Lawton had come to see her, she acknowledged, and eventually she had agreed to a brief interview, but—"only 20 minutes," she insisted. She accused Lawton of begging "typists, book-keepers and personal servants" for gossip and chasing down "well-known Americans, who are among my

*Rosa Lewis, right, with friends and staff members
at the Cavendish Hotel, 1919.*

friends," for material. Maybe so, but this long, rambling narra-tive, with its reminiscences piled haphazardly one on top of the other, does have the sound of a word-for-word transcript that's been loosely edited for coherence. The tone of voice is consistent, and the anecdotes have the well-worn patina of tales often told—vague chronology, fuzzy details, vivid moments of triumph. For all her outrage at what she claimed were lies and distortions, moreover, Rosa spent the rest of her life telling the same stories in the same raucous, irreverent style. We don't know if the sto-ries are true, but I've drawn on them here because at least we know that Rosa herself was telling them—a degree of credibility missing from some of the later biographies, which tended to bulk up Lawton's account with occasional helpings of the au-thors' own fantasies.

Rosa Ovenden grew up in the village of Leyton, just outside London, the fifth of nine children born to a watchmaker-turned-undertaker. The family was able to keep Rosa in school until she was twelve, but after that she had to work; and for a girl her age the only choice was the lowest rung of domestic service. She became the "general servant" in a nearby household, a job so grim that even Mrs. Beeton, who published the first edition of her soon-to-be-indispensable *Book of Household Man-agement* in 1859, felt sorry for anyone forced to take such em-ployment. "Her life is a solitary one, and, in some places, her work is never done," she wrote with a candor unusual in nineteenth-century domestic manuals. "She is also subject to rougher treatment than either the house or kitchen-maid, espe-cially in her earlier career; she starts in life, probably a girl of thirteen, with some small tradesman's wife as her mistress, just a step above her in the social scale; and although the class contains among them many excellent, kind-hearted women, it also contains some very rough specimens of the feminine gender." If Rosa's mistress ran her home according to Mrs. Beeton's rules for proper domestic service, it's probable that Rosa started her day at dawn by lighting the fire in the kitchen stove, cleaning the hearth in the dining room, dusting the dining room, cleaning the front hall, cleaning the boots, preparing the family's breakfast—"if cold meat is to be served, she must always send it to table on a clean dish, and nicely garnished with tufts of parsley"—and then quickly eating her own breakfast so that she could run upstairs and air out the bedrooms while the family was still at table. She then cleaned the house, prepared and served dinner, cleaned up after the meal, ate her own dinner, cleaned the scullery, prepared and served tea, cleaned up after tea, and finally sat down to "a little needlework for herself," spending two or three hours making and repairing her clothes before bed.

It's not clear how long Rosa lasted in this situation. She told Lawton that at the age of thirteen—that is, around 1880—she took a job at Sheen House, in Richmond, where the Comte de Paris, an heir to the French throne whose succession had been halted by the revolution of 1848, was living in exile with his family. Hired as a lowly "washer-up" in the comte's kitchen, she said she began helping his French chef and was soon assisting at dinners served to visiting royalty from all over Europe. The chef put her in charge of the kitchen when he was away, and other family members borrowed her to cook in their various houses in England and in France. "I worked in their family for many years," she asserted, and gave notice at the end of 1887 only because it had become so difficult for her to share the kitchen with an increasingly jealous French chef. ("For an Englishwoman to try to be their equal—it was impossible for me.")

Unfortunately this chronology makes no sense. The date of her departure in 1887 can be verified, for Rosa showed Lawton a note written by the comte's secretary acknowledging Rosa's decision to leave and offering a reference if she needed one. But records indicate that the comte didn't move to Sheen House until 1886. Rosa would have had less than two years to transform herself from . . . a thirteen-year-old scullery maid to a twenty-year-old master chef? One of her biographers, Daphne Fielding, who came to know Rosa in the 1920s, says that she went to work for the comte at sixteen; but that would still put her in Sheen House three years before the comte leased it. (There's never been a lot of fact-checking when the subject is Rosa, and having tried with little success to track her through libraries and archives, I can understand why.) Nonetheless, there's truth in the big picture: Rosa did find work in one or more French-run kitchens in the 1880s, which made it possible for her to learn the principles and techniques of the most exalted cuisine in high-society England.

High-society England was what she wanted. Throughout her life she talked jubilantly about her friendships in the aristocracy, and she tried hard to keep a supporting cast of the rich and titled within reach at all times. As a girl working at Sheen House, she told Mary Lawton, "I learnt to think . . . that it was not a stupid thing to cook. I saw that the aristocracy took an interest in it, and that you came under the notice of someone that really mattered." Other girls her age chose factory work, but what was a factory girl? "Just one of a number of sausages!" Cooking offered a way to stand out, to win the attention of the sort of people who counted. "My family did not know what Lords or Ladies or Earls or Dukes meant," she said. "I knew it by being a Cook."

So it was as a cook that she made her way to the most fashionable dinners in London and the countryside. One of her first employers after Sheen House was Lady Randolph Churchill, the American-born mother of Winston. How she and Rosa connected is unknown, but Rosa's culinary training at Sheen House would have made her an excellent candidate for a job in a high-class kitchen, and Lady Randolph's kitchen was among the highest. Her in-laws were the Duke and Duchess of Marlborough; with that flawless credential, as well as the fortune she brought from America, she had become one of the leading hostesses of an obsessively social era. The most important of her dinner guests was the Prince of Wales, who would become King Edward VII after Victoria's death in 1901. A warm friend and admirer of Lady Randolph's, rumored to be her lover as well, the prince was also a prodigious eater who genuinely appreciated fine food. Rosa's cooking pleased him, and from the moment he first complimented one of her dinners, her future was assured. (There are many anecdotes describing this turning point, mostly along the lines of "And the Prince was so impressed by the food that he asked to meet the chef, whereupon a slim young girl dressed in white appeared at the door and hesitantly . . ." etc., etc.) No matter how the prince and the cook discovered each other, Rosa's career soon flowered. Society ladies who were distinguished enough to entertain the prince but nervous about whether their kitchens were up to the task hired Rosa for the evening. Other ladies, who couldn't hope to bring the prince to their tables but aspired to put on luncheons and dinners and late suppers in the best style of the time, hired her as well. Abundant gossip suggesting that Rosa was one of the prince's many lovers—she never confirmed or denied—did its own part to heighten her desirability as a caterer.

In 1893, just six years into her career as an independent caterer, Rosa married a butler named Excelsior Lewis. She told Lawton she cared nothing for him and married only because her family insisted; but since her parents barely register in her life story apart from this sudden spark of influence, she very likely had other reasons. Describing the wedding to Lawton, she made it sound like a comic song in a music hall: "I went off to church, and we were married. I had nothing on but a common frock. I told the parson to be quick, and get it over with, and he said— 'Why, what a funny woman you are. I'd like to know where you live.' So we were married, then I threw the ring at him at the church door and left him flat." But she didn't leave him flat, not yet. Though she showed no interest at all in children or a conventional domestic life, marriage moved Rosa into a zone of respectability that was very useful to her: with her own home, and a husband attached to her name, she could go from mansion to mansion working wherever she pleased. After the wedding the two of them lived together for nearly a decade while she went right on with her cooking.

Over the next twenty years, Rosa built up her catering until she was managing a staff of six, eight, sometimes twelve women, all uniformed in white, who accompanied her to one wealthy home or another to stage the glamorous luncheons and dinners that were her specialty. "I took *full* charge," Rosa told Lawton. "I had complete authority—as though it were my own house, like a general in command." England had a profligate upper class in the decades preceding World War I, and lavish entertainments were at the center of the London season, which ran from May through July. At a time when a High Court judge was earning £5,000 a year, Rosa said she used to make more than £6,000 during the three-month season alone. She loved talking about her glory years. "I used to go down to Mr. Waldorf Astor's place, Hever Castle, nearly every week-end. . . . I did dinners for Lady Millicent, Duchess of Sutherland. . . . I did the Ascot Races and the Goodwood Races. . . . Everybody of any note, politicians and famous people, Lords and Ladies, everybody in the aristocracy and in the great London world, had me for their dinners and luncheons." Sometimes, for families living in the country who wished to entertain in London, she not only prepared the food but rented and decorated an entire house—a service nobody else in the catering business could match, she emphasized. "I furnished the linen and silver and everything and my linen had no names on, silver had no names and my muslin curtains came from the Maison de Blanc in Paris. I would get all the curtains and new carpets from Paris, and then I would go and hire all the best rugs I could find, and all the best furniture I could find, and the whole house would then look as though it were lived in, and not a rented place." According to Rosa, the other caterers were left in the dust, teeming with jealousy.

Although Edward officially became king in January 1901, his formal coronation with its elaborate ceremonies and entertainments didn't take place until the summer of 1902. So the spring of coronation year, packed with formal dinners, balls, and house parties, was especially lucrative for Rosa. She would have made a fortune from the supper balls alone: multicourse dinners followed by multicourse late suppers verging into breakfast, and she told Lawton she did twenty-nine of them in six weeks. That same year she learned that the Cavendish Hotel on Jermyn Street, a fashionable enclave near Piccadilly, was up for sale. She promptly bought the place.

The plan was to let her husband run the hotel while she kept on with catering. But Lewis proved inept as a hotel keeper: the hotel deteriorated, guests stopped frequenting it, and the bills went unpaid until he had run up a debt of £5,000. At that point she threw him out of the hotel and out of her life. She called it a divorce, but she may have simply banished him without the trappings of a legal procedure. She told Lawton that once she was rid of him, she took charge of the hotel and was able to re-store its former high standard while keeping up the catering business and paying Lewis's debts in full—all this in sixteen months, by virtue of hard work and scrimping. Rosa was very fond of this story. "So I put my shoulder to the wheel and did everything—only kept a few servants, went to market myself, bought quail at fourpence, and sold them at three shillings, bought my game and vegetables in the open market, loaded them on the wheelbarrow, and pushed the barrow home myself, back to the hotel. . . . I paid that £5,000 on tea and toast, never had anything else to eat, never had a new dress, never even took a bus if I could avoid it. No, I never had a new frock or a stitch of clothing until I had paid every farthing of the £5,000."

With the Cavendish as her anchor, Rosa had no need any longer for even a symbolic husband: the hotel became her home, her social life, and the center of her business empire. She gave the place the intimacy of a private club, filling it with the pedigreed furniture she found at auction whenever the contents of a great English estate went up for sale. The hotel had no public restau-rant at first: the guests dined at graciously arranged tables in their suites, and she took charge of many private parties at the behest of socialites, politicians, and theater people. In the kitch-ens, a staff of women whom she selected with care and trained herself were cooking for the hotel and also for her catering busi-ness, which was busier than ever once Edward was on the throne. As a favored chef of the king, she was hired to prepare formal dinners at the Foreign Office and the Admiralty; and when the kaiser visited England in 1907, spending three weeks at Highcliffe Castle in Dorset, Edward asked Rosa to take charge of all the cooking for his stay. ("One King leads to another, what? . . . He would eat ham, partridges, very fond of game, and salad, but must always have fruit with everything.") The *Daily Telegraph* published an admiring feature on one of the governmental dinners she staged at Downing Street—"Woman Cook's Triumph"—and her reputation took another leap. "I was at the top of the tree," she told Lawton, and she stayed at the top until World War I shook the branches.

George Bernard Shaw's play *Pygmalion* opened in London in 1914, the last year of Rosa's reign. The play, which later became the Broadway musical *My Fair Lady,* has an obvious overlap with Rosa's story—so obvious that a bit of gossip flutters through a scene in the television series *The Duchess of Duke Street* to the effect that Shaw based the character of Eliza Doolittle on Rosa. Perhaps, but the differences were in many ways more striking than the overlap. In the play, the Cockney flower seller Eliza Doolittle decides that in order to get ahead in life, she has to get rid of her accent and learn to speak like a lady. She goes to Henry Higgins, a professor of phonetics, who takes her on as an experiment: can he transform this guttersnipe into someone who can pass as a duchess? Eliza is coached in speech, dress, and deportment; and then Higgins introduces her to society—first at an afternoon garden party and later at a dinner party followed by the opera. Eliza conducts herself perfectly everywhere, never revealing a trace of her origins, and not a soul doubts that she belongs among the well-born.

It's tempting to think of Rosa sitting in the audience on opening night. By her own account she was a close friend of the star, the renowned actress Mrs. Patrick Campbell, although "Mrs. Pat" ran off with Lady Randolph's second husband that same year, which would have tested Rosa's loyalty since she adored Lady Randolph. At any rate, if Rosa saw the play, she certainly would have deemed herself a greater success than Eliza, whose despairing cry "What is to become of me? What is to become of me?" rings out during the fourth act. After her triumph in society, Eliza realizes that she has been successfully uprooted but now belongs nowhere. She can't go back to selling flowers in the street, and since she has neither the money nor the family associated with her new class identity, she can't see a path forward. In the play, Shaw deliberately left her future vague.

Rosa would have found the whole quandary pathetic. She had conducted her own climb up the ladder very differently, and with a different goal in mind. It was as Rosa herself, Cockney born and kitchen raised, that she demanded to be made welcome in the highest ranks of society—defiantly flaunting her Cockney accent all the way. Back when she was a young servant in the household of the Comte de Paris, she had developed a passion she would nurture for the rest of her life—not for a man, but for an entire class, starting with the comte's family. "I was overwhelmed with admiration for them," she told Lawton. He was "marvellous," his wife "the most interesting woman in the world," their marriage "the most perfect match in the world." She had no such language of superlatives for her first employers, an undistinguished family at 3 Myrtle Villas in Leyton, but everything that went on at Sheen House entranced her. All the family members used to visit her in the kitchen, she said. "If you had a round back, when the Comtesse passed through, she would give you a whack and tell you to stand up straight. She told me to keep my back straight just as she told her daughters—

with a whip!" To have been disciplined exactly as if she were a noblewoman's daughter was still making her proud some forty years later.

Lady Randolph Churchill was a similar paragon in Rosa's eyes, despite an obvious penchant for awkward marriages. (Randolph reportedly died of syphilis; George Cornwallis-West left her for Mrs. Pat; and Montagu Porch, whom she married at sixty-four, was three years younger than Winston.) "She was one of the most perfect women . . . that I have ever met," Rosa declared. Another figure in her personal pantheon was Thomas Lister, Lord Ribblesdale, who lived at the Cavendish for years and became a genuine friend. Ribblesdale was lord-in-waiting to Queen Victoria and also master of the buckhounds, a post that chiefly required him to display the grandeur of British high birth as he led the royal procession at the opening of Ascot. By all accounts he did this superbly. John Singer Sargent's portrait of Ribblesdale, showing him swathed in the magnificent cape, breeches, and boots of a nobleman ready for a day's hunting, hangs in the National Gallery. Rosa was devoted to him and treasured her copy of the painting. (In fact, she said it was she who urged him to present the original to the museum.) "Lord Ribblesdale was the most wonderful man in the world," she told Lawton. "His voice and manner and everything about him was just charming. He was a very, very great gentleman—a great specimen of an English gentleman."

By contrast, she wanted nothing to do with what she called "boughten" nobility. "I don't like the people who buy their titles," she told Lawton. "I don't like the man who makes sugar or the man who gives a few thousands to a hospital having a title, I only like titles which are inherited." Back in olden times, she went on, "people used to lie under the table drinking and drive a four-in-hand and go swash-buckling around, but they did those things like *gentlemen* and aristocrats and on certain occasions only—not every day in the week like the *nouveau riche* hooligans do now. . . . Now it is all vulgar, because the people who do it are vulgar. . . . They are aping their betters."

The arrivistes were doing badly what Rosa was determined to do perfectly. Coming of age when she did, in the midst of a long, frantic spree of social mobility generated by the Industrial Revolution, she could see that new money was disrupting many of the verities that had long ruled Britain. People whose parents had never dreamed of such advancement were gaining access to education, opportunity, and wealth; and the most conservative among the old-money classes had to close ranks sternly if they wanted to avoid associating with the wrong sort. Then as now, there was no simple way to define social class in Britain—birth, education, accent, manners, taste, and income all contributed, and only the first of these was immutable. Who belonged? Who didn't? More nerve-racking still, who might belong next week or next year, given a little luck or the right fiancée? Rosa knew, just as Henry Higgins did, that anybody could slip into the upper ranks by acting the part properly. But she also believed that the true greatness of aristocracy was beyond imitation, a state of grace bestowed only upon the well-bred, and that all others would fall short sooner or later. One of the stories she loved telling about herself was tantamount to her own version of *Pygmalion:* she described the time she arrived at a country estate to arrange a dinner and decided to go in the front door instead of the back. "I was smartly dressed and very good looking in those days, so the lady of the house was almost kissing my lips when I said—'Oh, it is only Mrs. Lewis, the cook. I know my way to the kitchen.' Oh, you should have seen their faces! . . . Lady Paget or Lady Randolph Churchill would have seen the joke, but these people couldn't, they not being exactly tip-top. It's only a thoroughbred that does the right thing instinctively."

Rosa believed with all her heart that she had won a special place among the thoroughbreds. "Although I was a servant as you might say, and went out and cooked for them, they didn't regard it so," she explained, distancing herself from the word "servant" even as she was forced to use it. "They found other things in me than my capacity to cook. They seemed to enjoy being with me, and I have always associated with them on equal terms." Her rich clients visited her in the kitchen, she often said, and she in turn dropped into their drawing rooms—their dining rooms, too— whenever she felt like it. "And I was always welcome," she stressed. "I trotted in to see everybody at these dinners." Sometimes she borrowed a gown from a Bond Street dressmaker, along with gloves and a fan—"dressed myself up like a Duchess and gone to the dinner. Then between the courses I would slip down into the kitchen if anything was going wrong, and sometimes bring up a dish in my own hands—and why not?"

One of the photographs she gave Mary Lawton for the book showed the head cook at the Cavendish, "Mrs. Charlotte," dressed in a simple but beautifully styled evening gown, with her hair piled high in fashionable waves and puffs. She was posed in an upholstered chair, one hand positioned palm-up on her lap, the other holding a book, her gaze off to the side, her expression slightly nervous and frozen into place. "My cook photographed in evening dress looks as good as anybody—as good as a Duchess," Rosa declared. The occasion for the picture was the annual ball that Rosa staged for her staff and dozens of other cooks, maids, butlers, and doormen from London establishments. She borrowed clothes from shops and from ladies' maids who passed along gowns from their employers; and she taught the women how to fix their hair and apply a little powder. She hired musicians, she brought in flowers, she put on a splendid supper. "Then I made all the gentry come to these balls and dance with them," she said. "I made the gentry wait on them, too." What she wanted to do, she said, was show these servants "the other side of life." If they could experience it, they would do a better job providing it for others—"with graciousness."

Rosa could dress the part, and she had an honorary seat at some of the best tables in town; but she knew very well that a former scullery maid was never going to be accepted as an equal in the highest circles, no matter how cheerily everyone socialized with her. Hence she never tried to pass. Once she went with a party of top-drawer friends to dinner at the Carlton, the finest French restaurant in London. At a table across the room she saw half a dozen gentlemen and a lady ("very ugly") whom she recognized—they were representatives of Pommery, the champagne house, and quite surprised to see her there. One of them asked, loudly, "Isn't that Mrs. Lewis, the Cook?" Rosa called back across the room, "Yes, it *is* Mrs. Lewis. I've sold all my cutlets, how are you getting on with your champagne?"

To get a sense of the full force of this remark, it's crucial to remember that Rosa made a point of announcing her class identity with a flourish every time she opened her mouth. She never discarded her Cockney accent—precisely because she knew as well as Eliza Doolittle that it was the most damning of all the accidents of birth and upbringing that kept a flower seller on the street in rags. There were a good many disreputable accents strewn across England—indeed, only one was safely beyond criticism, and that was the style of speech known in the mid–nineteenth century as "pure and classical parlance" and later as

BBC English. But Cockney had no rival as the most widely despised of the incorrect accents. Phonetics experts ruled it ugly, offensive, and "insufferably vulgar," and women in particular were warned to take strict care of their h's, for ladylike speech was perceived as the outward manifestation of both status and virtue. Manuals on correct pronunciation were popular among those who hoped to climb the ladder, and it was widely believed that a diligent student could shake off poor habits of speech just as he or she could learn from an etiquette manual not to slurp the soup. Rosa could have cleaned up her accent, but she made a choice to retain the speech she had been raised with and deliberately lavished it with slang and profanity. A barrage of impassioned Cockney became her trademark, and everybody who encountered her received a direct hit. American reporters loved to quote her in full color, with every lurid expression intact. In the British press, however, she was invariably quoted in standard English. It would have been impossible for print to convey the impression of a respectable woman if the reporter had ladled a Cockney accent over everything she said.

To be treated with respect, to be treated exactly as one would treat a lady—despite the apron, despite the accent—was what she demanded of the world. When she chose cooking as her life's work, she made a point of choosing haute cuisine, the most expensive and socially competitive cooking of its time. If food was going to be her shield and her weapon, she would deploy it at such an exalted level that nobody could look down on her. It was a smart choice for a young cook of that era, because wealthy British families were preoccupied not only with setting a fine table, but with using that table to reflect their own rarefied place in society. If Rosa had indeed been in the audience at *Pygmalion*, she would have scoffed at Shaw's decision to send Eliza Doolittle to a garden party to test her skills. What a paltry victory! The truly treacherous social occasion of her time was a formal dinner. Rosa, whose longtime vantage point from behind a full-length apron gave her a perspective that Shaw lacked, would have sent Eliza straightaway to the dining room.

"Nothing more plainly shows the well-bred man than his manners at table," wrote the anonymous author of *How to Dine, or Etiquette of the Dinner Table*. "A man may be well dressed, may converse well . . . but if he is, after all, unrefined, his manners at table will be sure to expose him." And if his manners passed scrutiny, his conversation might trip him up. One reason a dinner party was "one of the severest tests of good breeding" was that a proper host would have made sure that all his guests came from similar backgrounds. "They need not necessarily be friends, or all of the same absolute rank," explained Lady Colin Campbell in *The Etiquette of Good Society*, "but as at a dinner people come into closer contact one with the other than at a dance or any other kind of party, those only should be invited to meet one another who move in the same class or circle." In other words, an upstart at a garden party could chat for a moment and move on. At a dinner, by contrast, the upstart had to understand all the references that bubbled along in the conversation and even contribute a few. (It may not have occurred to Shaw that there was a more exacting test for Eliza's initial outing than a garden party. He was a vegetarian and also hated getting dressed up, so he made a point of refusing most invitations to formal meals.)

But Rosa understood what was at stake at the dinner table. She knew why people anxiously studied books like *How to Dine*, which was published in 1879, around the time she first went out to work. "Soup will constitute the first course, which must be noiselessly sipped from the side of a spoon," counseled the author. "Fish usually follows soup. It is helped with a silver fork, and eaten with a silver fork, assisted by a piece of bread held in the left hand." Less than a decade later, "Fish should be eaten with a silver fish knife and fork," ruled the handbook *Manners and Tone of Good Society.* "Two forks are *not* used for eating fish, and one fork and a crust of bread is now an unheard-of way of eating fish in polite society." Only the cognoscenti could hope to make their way through a fashionable meal flawlessly. When Rosa chose high-class cookery as her future, she was gaining access not only to a cuisine, but to all the social behaviors associated with it. She was learning the secret handshake.

Rosa's remarkable ascent took place at a time when wealth, fashion, and ambition were making extraordinary demands not only upon manners but upon food, which was constantly radiating signals that confirmed or dispelled the status of the householder. The human appetite itself had to be retrained to accommodate the stress. "No age, since that of Nero, can show such unlimited addiction to food," recalled Harold Nicolson, the diplomat and writer, who was obliged to attend innumerable weekend house parties during the Edwardian era. Four massive meals a day were the rule, he wrote, with a fifth, slightly less massive, at midnight. The author of *Party-Giving on Every Scale,* published in the 1880s for the benefit of hosts and hostesses who were rightly nervous about this challenge, set out in detail what guests expected to be served at a top-of-the-line dinner. Two soups, to start, one clear and one thick; and the guests would choose whichever they preferred. Two kinds of fish came next, and again the guests made their choices, although there was an important nuance here—"A guest never eats but of one fish, with the exception of whitebait." Whitebait, a tiny fish caught in the Thames amid much seasonal acclaim, was so definitively British and celebratory that it was the moral equivalent of a separate course and did not have to compete with the other fish on the menu. Then came at least three entrées, a term that did not yet mean "main course" but suggested more of a side attraction, sometimes called a "made dish." These could be cutlets, croquettes, fricassees—lighter than a roast or a joint, often in a sauce. One or two "removes" then appeared, substantial roasts of beef, lamb, or ham. If there were two removes, it was decreed that the second must be chicken. Then two rotis, or game dishes, arrived, followed by a slew of the pretty, sometimes fanciful dishes known as *entremets*. Again, this was a term difficult to translate, but they could include savory preparations such as aspics or oysters au gratin and sweets such as jellies, creams, and sweet soufflés. Vegetables were served at different stages of the meal; often there was a salad course; occasionally there was a respite for ices; and sometimes one or two "piquant savories" of cheese, anchovies, or caviar were offered after the last of the sweet *entremets*. Finally the table was cleared for dessert, typically an array of fruits, ices, cakes, and preserves. No wonder there was an occasional voice pleading for restraint. "Ample choice, so as to allow for the differences of taste, is necessary, but there should be a limit," urged Lady Colin Campbell. "The perpetual repetition of 'No, thank you,' to the continuous stream of dishes handed to you becomes wearisome."

Just as wearisome were overlong evenings at the table. During the season many of the rich attended formal dinners nearly every night, often sitting next to the same person each time, since places at the table were assigned strictly according to social rank. Depending on one's regular dinner partner in the course of a particular season, the meals could drag on with excruciating tedium. King Edward was an especially difficult guest in this regard: he got bored very quickly as course after course plodded along. In the royal household he insisted that dinner last no more than an hour, and the new timetable became fashionable across society, at least as an ideal. Hostesses tried their best to keep the courses moving steadily, though having paid huge sums for truffles, foie gras, imported game, and hothouse fruits, they now found themselves nervously watching out for guests who were enjoying a dish so much they threatened to linger over it. "I still remember my intense annoyance with a very greedy man who complained bitterly that both his favourite fish were being served and that he wished to eat both," recalled Consuelo Vanderbilt Balsan, the American-born wife of the Duke of Marlborough. "I had to keep the service waiting while he consumed first the hot and then the cold, quite unperturbed at the delay he was causing." Lady Colin Campbell set down the rule: No second helpings of the soup or the fish, ever. Second helpings of the other courses were permissible, but only at a small and forgiving family meal.

It wasn't easy to navigate a safe route through British haute cuisine: traps for the unwary were set everywhere. Anthony Trollope, that excellent authority on Victorian class anxiety, made a point of identifying it with culinary anxiety in his novel *Miss Mackenzie,* published in 1865. As novelists so often do, he sent several characters to a dinner party, this one at the home of the heroine's sister-in-law, Mrs. Mackenzie. Eager to stage the affair properly, she had hired a butler named Mr. Grandairs to supervise the food and service, and chose the increasingly fashionable *service à la Russe*—the food to be offered in courses rather than set out on the table all at once. Each course was a disaster. The soup, purchased from a shop and laden with Marsala, arrived at the table cold. The fish, "very ragged in its appearance," was also cold; and the melted butter had become "thick and clot-ted." Then came three ornate little entrées—"so fabricated, that all they who attempted to eat of their contents became at once aware that they had got hold of something very nasty." While these were under way, champagne went around the table but quickly ran out since Mrs. Mackenzie had economized by order-ing only one bottle. "After the little dishes there came, of course, a saddle of mutton, and equally of course, a pair of boiled fowls." These were badly carved, and nobody got any of the sauces since they didn't appear until the course was nearly finished. "Why tell of the ruin, of the maccaroni, of the fine-coloured pyramids of shaking sweet things which nobody would eat . . . the ice-puddings flavoured with onions? It was all misery, wretched-ness, and degradation."

And yet, as Trollope emphasized, Mrs. Mackenzie was not trying to better herself with that pretentious dinner. This was not an instance of an upstart aiming at a higher class than she deserved. "Her place in the world was fixed, and she made no contest as to the fixing. She hoped for no great change in the direction of society." She had staged such a dinner simply be-cause that was how well-bred people were supposed to entertain, and since she didn't have the money or the experience to do it properly, she had done it badly. At this point Trollope, who had clearly eaten more than his share of misbegotten dinners, broke out of his narrative and addressed his readers directly. Why, oh why, he demanded, couldn't "the ordinary Englishman" with a middle-class income simply offer his friends a little fish and a leg of mutton?

But such a familiar, comfortable solution was inconceivable for Mrs. Mackenzie, and for hosts and hostesses far more sophis-ticated than she was. Everyone knew that it was the French who occupied the highest realms of cuisine, while the very notion of traditional British cuisine was, as the London chef Charles Elmé Francatelli put it, "a by-word of ridicule." By the time Rosa began catering, thousands of French chefs were working in British homes, clubs, hotels, and royal palaces, drawn across the English Channel by the opportunities beckoning from a prosperous, bustling nation that was ready to enjoy the unexpected laurel of culinary prestige. Escoffier himself moved to London in 1890 and spent the rest of his career there, in charge of renowned restaurants first at the Savoy Hotel and then at the Carlton. In 1913, when he was president of the London branch of the Ligue des Gourmands, an international association of distinguished French chefs, London had sixty members—the largest branch in the world. Paris came in second, with forty-three. London had become one of the great capitals of French cuisine, and British-born chefs needed French training if they hoped to reach the height of their profession.

Everything about Rosa made her a doomed candidate for advancement in this culinary world. She was British, she lacked formal training in a restaurant kitchen, and worst of all, she was female. The French prejudice against women in professional kitchens had long ago settled over England in a fog of misogyny that wouldn't lift until decades after her death. For a woman with culinary ambitions there was only the National Training School of Cookery, founded in 1874 to funnel women into careers as cooking teachers and household cooks. Neither of these futures appealed to Rosa, nor was she interested in any of the school's other diploma programs, which included Housewifery, Needlework, and Laundry. At the time, the most successful woman in the British food world was Agnes Marshall, whose accomplishments would have made her a phenomenon in any age. She ran a cooking school, wrote four successful cookbooks, published a weekly paper called *The Table,* and sold an extensive line of packaged ingredients, including Marshall's Curry Powder, Marshall's Icing Sugar, and Marshall's Finest Leaf Gelatine. We don't know whether she and Rosa ever met, or if Rosa saw her as any sort of inspiration, but Rosa chose a very different path. She didn't teach, she didn't write, she didn't sell; she simply cooked, at a professional level that the leaders of her profession refused to recognize. After she bought the Cavendish, she made a point of staffing her kitchens entirely with women and took every opportunity to tell the press why she was doing so: "A good woman cook is better than a man any time."

Nonetheless, she was careful to work the way every ambitious male cook in London was working: they all kept an eye on the restaurants run by Escoffier. His innovative techniques and recipes, rooted in classic cuisine but refining and refreshing it, constituted the new gold standard for anyone aspiring to work in the best kitchens. There was no escaping his influence, especially after his comprehensive *Guide Culinaire,* packed with instructions for every dish in his repertoire, was published in French in 1903 and four years later in English. Escoffier's best-known principle was *"Faites simple"*—"Simplify"—but even so, he raised the glamour stakes with every major dinner he created. When a group of Englishmen who had won handsomely at Monte Carlo wanted to celebrate at the Savoy, Escoffier created a red-and-gold dinner dripping with excess, its colors carried out in every course from the smoked salmon and pink champagne to the final *"Mousse de Curaçao,"* which was covered with strawberries and displayed inside an ice sculpture modeled after the hill of Monte Carlo and decorated with a string of red lights. (Only a chicken stuffed with truffles forced the chef to depart, briefly, from the color scheme.) "M. Escoffier holds that things which are beautiful to the taste should be fair to the eye," wrote Nathaniel Newnham-Davis, the most prominent restaurant reviewer of the day. He singled out a dessert he called "typical" of the great chef's work: *"Baisers de Vierge,"* or "Virgin's Kisses"— "twin meringues, the cream perfumed with vanilla and holding crystallised white rose leaves and white violets. Over each pair of meringues is a veil of spun sugar."

Rosa was acquainted with Escoffier; in fact, she called him "one of the few Frenchmen I ever had any respect for," which suggests that Escoffier did her the honor of treating her as a professional equal—unlike the other French chefs in town, who would have regarded her with the undisguised contempt they had for all female cooks except their mothers. But what she valued in Escoffier's work, or perhaps learned in the kitchen of the Comte de Paris, wasn't so much the color schemes and the spun sugar; it was a very French fixation on ingredients. Quality began with the raw materials, Escoffier emphasized in the *Guide Culinaire,* and whenever interviewers asked Rosa how she cooked, she liked to tell them how she shopped. "I did the buying myself for all those dinners," she told Lawton. "I selected everything. . . . I would quarrel with every tradesman in the town. . . . And I would turn over sometimes sixteen legs of mutton until I got just the right one. . . . And I used in those days to go to Covent Garden Market and pick out all my own fruit and game, and wheel it back on a barrow myself." She bought hundreds of quail at a time, scrutinizing each one; and although even Escoffier approved of buying turtle soup ready-made from a reputable source, Rosa purchased live turtles, killed them, and made the soup from scratch. Once, choosing the woodcocks for a Foreign Office dinner at a time when the game birds were scarce, she stayed in the shop while each one was plucked and trussed, to make sure not a single inferior bird was slipped into the order. "Whatever I got, I paid the top price, but had the best there was," she told Lawton.

Rosa didn't consider her habits extravagant, she considered them essential. No steps in cooking were unimportant; every contribution from every ingredient mattered. "What I have always done (which no other cook ever does) is to cook the potatoes, and the beans, and the asparagus *myself*," she told Lawton. "I do not give these to the charwoman or the scullery maid—or a person without brains." The potatoes were treated "just the same as if they were gold." And when she had gold, she let it shine unadorned. One of her specialties, the essence of understated luxury, was a whole truffle, boiled in champagne or Madeira and served in a napkin, one truffle per guest. King Edward was fond of this dish, she told a reporter from *The New York Times:* he hated being served truffles all cut up into little pieces.

The few existing menus that can be attributed to Rosa are all written in French, and to read them is to envision one classic dish after another parading down the runway: *Consommé Princesse, Médaillons de Soles à la Joinville, Suprêmes de Volaille à la Maréchale, Selle d'Agneau à la Chivry.* But despite the high-style dinners she turned out for the most impressive names in Britain, she was never invited to join her male colleagues in the Ligue des Gourmands. She wasn't even invited to join her male colleagues in the Réunion des Gastronomes, a dining club for the owners and managers of London's leading hotels and restaurants, despite the fact that she owned the Cavendish. This snub from Britain's French establishment may have been one reason why she refused to swoon over the ineffable glories of French cuisine when she was interviewed. She wouldn't even admit that French cooking was superior to all other cooking the world had ever known, which was the mildest form of appreciation acceptable in her profession. "Good cooking really came from France," she conceded, but she made it clear that the French had outlived their own success. "A Frenchman couldn't make a simple quail pudding, for instance. He would not think it was right. He would want to chop it all up and mess it all over with something." She thought the French used too much wine in cooking and that they overdid garlic: "You don't want to know it's there," she protested. "When you use it as the French do, it kills the taste of what you are eating." If you're cooking for the English palate, she emphasized, beef should taste like beef and mutton should taste like mutton—a degree of simplicity she felt the French would never stand for. "And I don't like anything to *look* like something else, either—I don't believe in covering anything just to change it. If it is a sole, I don't like it all curled up like a lobster—let it remain in its proper shape. Messing things up, is like putting a silk patch on a leather apron—unnecessary and stupid."

At the same time, however, she acknowledged that a great deal of British cooking was terrible, and she had very specific advice on that subject for home cooks. "Englishwomen seem to be decided on 'killing' taste!" she exclaimed. "If the average Englishwoman would only braise her meat, instead of doing so much roasting in her little oven! She ought to braise her vegetables with the meat, in the same pot. It would give better results, and it would save considerable expense." And, she added, they would not have to keep buying "sundry bottles of sauces, which are always expensive." But the problem, as she saw it, was the low status of cookery in Britain, not some grim national predilection for overboiling vegetables. "To cook, to a Frenchman, is to be an artist," she told the *Daily Sketch*. "To cook, to an English-man, is to be a menial. We have simply got our standards of the kitchen wrong." Think of the kitchen as an artist's studio, she urged, or a lawyer's office, or a surgeon's consulting room. Encourage a "better class of people" to take up cooking. "There is only one remedy," she concluded. "You must make cooking a profession, and you must cease calling cooks servants." This last, of course, was at the heart of her entire career.

The best cooks of all came from America, she used to say—an opinion so heretical not even Americans shared it, but Rosa had her reasons. "Your American darkies . . . are wonderful cooks," she told Lawton. "It was a darkey cook from Savannah who taught me to cook rice." And not just rice: Rosa also discovered Virginia hams, canvasback ducks, waffles, maple syrup, sweet potatoes, corn on the cob, peanuts, and bell peppers. Her tutor was Mosianna Milledge, one of the best-known cooks in Savannah, Georgia, and the only one of her peers whom Rosa praised by name. They met when Rosa first went out catering. Mosianna had worked for the Gordons, a prominent Savannah family, for many years; and when their daughter Juliette married and moved to England, Mosianna followed to see to the cooking. Juliette and her husband, William Low, became part of the social set around Lady Randolph Churchill and began hiring Rosa to help Mosianna with dinner parties. There was no way to obtain in England the Southern specialties Juliette wanted to serve, so she had them shipped from home; and Mosianna introduced Rosa to new foods and a different way of cooking. Within a few years the Lows' marriage disintegrated: he became infatuated with another woman, which set off a long, ugly battle over divorce and money that didn't end until after his death in 1905. (Seven years later Juliette Gordon Low returned to Savannah and founded the Girl Scouts.) But Rosa kept the new Southern foods in her repertoire. The Americans in her clientele loved them, and the British were so enthusiastic that Jacksons of Piccadilly, the luxury food shop, began stocking Virginia hams and brandied peaches.

Rosa said that she invented most of her recipes and that she carried them in her head; she never acknowledged looking in a cookbook. But every time she planned a menu, put on an apron, and went into the pantry, she was aware of the most famous appetite in Britain. The Prince of Wales had transformed her career from hired cook to sought-after caterer, and his seal of approval made it possible for her to earn enough money to buy the Cavendish. She cooked with him in mind, whether or not he was going to be at the table. There's no reliable evidence for a love affair here: much has been hinted, but little has been footnoted. Rosa called him "the most wonderful person in the world . . . so appreciative of everything," and assured Lawton that he had given her many presents, including a great deal of jewelry, which unfortunately had all been stolen. Whatever the scope of the relationship, she grew up as a cook in response to his tastes; they animated her own, and she expressed devotion to him all her life.

Unlike his dour, reclusive mother, Queen Victoria, Edward was an unabashed sybarite who reveled in the culinary privileges heaped upon royalty. "There is probably no man in England who has mastered the art of dining so completely as the Prince of Wales," ran an admiring article in the journal *Food and Cookery*. That was one way of putting it. Historians, by contrast, described Edward's appetite as so relentless it frightened his wife and doctor. He stuffed himself mercilessly at every meal, and by the summer of his coronation he was so fat that he refused to get on a scale. (One of his biographers has pointed out what was possibly "an unconscious mockery" in the words to Edward Elgar's "Land of Hope and Glory," first performed in honor of the new king: "Wider still and wider shall thy bounds be set; / God, who made thee mighty, make thee mightier yet.") Nonetheless he was a very popular monarch who won the affection of the British in part because of the obvious delight he took in good living. Even relatively simple meals served to the royal family were vast, including the suppers held behind the royal box at the Royal Opera House. Up to a dozen courses were hauled to the Opera House along with the silver, the linens, and the gold plate, for a meal to be devoured at intermission. Whenever Escoffier had the honor of preparing a banquet in Edward's honor, the great chef did not hold back: he poached the quails in Château d'Yquem and stuffed the chickens with both truffles and foie gras.

But Rosa took a different approach to pleasing the most influential man in her life. When she cooked for Edward, she cooked in English. "Do you know King Edward's favourite meal?" she asked a reporter in the course of an interview four years after the king's death. "Let me whisper. It was boiled bacon and broad beans. He loved them." This was hardly a secret, especially after she told it repeatedly, but Edward's fondness for old-fashioned British home cooking was genuine. All haute cuisine all the time was a lot of haute cuisine even for him. At his command Buckingham Palace instituted the custom of serving roast beef and Yorkshire pudding on Sunday nights. He also relished a plate of salt beef—beef that had been brined and boiled—with its homely sides of dumplings and carrots. Most of the chefs who were invited to cook for the king when he visited a restaurant or a private house wouldn't have dreamed of boiling carrots for him, not when they had a chance to do their extravagant best. Even Rosa, catering a society dinner where he was the guest of honor, could hardly send out a whole menu of plainspoken English fare. But she could slip one or two of his favorites into the meal and soothe for a moment that frantic appetite. Rosa understood his hunger.

Edward died in 1910, but his influence on Rosa's cooking—or, more accurately, the glow of the royal imprimatur on her cooking—lasted for years. He was certainly in the room two or three years after his death when she served one of the most important lunches of her career. Nathaniel Newnham-Davis, the widely read food writer, had asked to interview her over lunch at the Cavendish, and Rosa agreed. She was in the full bloom of her success, and critical recognition from Newnham-Davis would mean far more than the praise she had received from the daily press. Well-born and cosmopolitan, Newnham-Davis retired from the military in 1894 and took up a second career in journalism, pursuing a longtime passion for good food and wine. He had already published two collections of his reviews by the time he met Rosa—*Dinners and Diners* and *The Gourmet's Guide to Europe*—and he was at work on a third. His reviews were always positive, his writing style always genial, and he was endlessly fascinated with the style and atmosphere that made each restaurant noteworthy. His accolades counted, and he heaped them all over Rosa. When *The Gourmet's Guide to London* appeared in 1914, it featured his story about the Cavendish among reviews of more than three dozen other restaurants, including all the most renowned. The book was small and easy to carry around, with only a few illustrations, but two of the city's chefs were honored with photographs, and they were Rosa Lewis and Escoffier.

Rosa looked very demure in the picture, dressed in a simple shirtwaist and gazing modestly away from the camera. She had made a brilliant success of Newnham-Davis's visit, in part by closely reading his reviews beforehand and gaining a sense of his personality. Newnham-Davis often mentioned his preference for shorter, lighter meals, for instance, and said outright that he skipped courses whenever he was served more than he wanted to eat, no matter how great the chef. So she planned a succinct little lunch and invited a few other guests whom she handpicked to flatter both herself and the journalist. "Into the tea-room came a slim, graceful lady with a pretty oval face and charming eyes, and hair just touched with grey," wrote Newnham-Davis. "She was wearing a knitted pink silk coat, and one of those long light chains that mere men believe were intended to support muffs. She was arm in arm with one of the prettiest of the young comediennes of to-day, and when she told me that amongst the people she had asked to lunch was an ex–Great Officer of the Household, a young officer of cavalry, and an American editor, I began to feel that at last I was moving in Court circles."

Sure enough, Newnham-Davis was delighted when he could see a relatively simple meal coming his way. "Mrs. Lewis lays it down that three dishes are the right number at any lunch, for she, like all other really great authorities on gastronomy, is opposed to a long menu," he reported with much gratification. He didn't even chastise her for slipping in a fourth dish this time— she was merely breaking her own rule, "as great authorities sometimes do." The first course was grilled oysters and celery root on skewers, and then came "one of those delicious quail puddings which are one of Mrs Lewis's inventions and for which King Edward had a special liking." Quail in any form was a specialty of Rosa's, and quail pie (as he termed it later in the story) had become her signature. "There was a whole quail under the paste cover for everyone at table, with a wonderful gravy, to the making of which go all sorts of good things and which when it has soaked into the bottom layer of paste makes that not the least delicate part of the dish." After this she served breaded chicken wings and kidneys and concluded the lunch with what Newnham-Davis described as "pears and pancakes, an admirable combination."

Rosa had taken the daring step of serving the city's most renowned food writer an entirely British meal. In fact, her disavowal of cookbooks notwithstanding, she may have taken her recipe for quail pudding right out of Charles Herman Senn's *New Century Cookery Book,* a well-known British manual published in 1901, which called the dish *"Pouding de Cailles à l'Anglaise* (Quail Pudding)." We have her recipe, because she shared it with a reporter from the *Daily Mail* in 1909, and her procedure was the same as Senn's: she lined a pudding basin with a suet pastry, filled it with quails and thin slices of beef, topped them with seasonings and stock, added a pastry cover, and boiled the pudding. This was a classic boiled pudding with nothing French about it except the regulation French name that had been tacked on to give the dish a properly high-class identity. But Newnham-Davis showed no surprise or displeasure at being served such a lunch—quite the contrary. Like everyone else in London's elite circles, he knew the late king's preferences at table: Edward's passion for grilled oysters was as famous as his devotion to Rosa's quail pudding. Rosa had prepared a not-so-subtle homage to her great patron, and Newnham-Davis understood exactly who was gazing down upon the lunch table with a pleased expression on his royal face.

The admiring story about Rosa that went into *The Gourmet's*

Guide to London was the first account of her to be published in book form and a significant source for all the books and articles that followed. Rosa herself may have consulted it when she was talking to Mary Lawton ten years later, or perhaps it was Lawton who lifted bits and pieces of the article in the course of assembling her book. Yet Newnham-Davis and Lawton could have been writing about two different women. Newnham-Davis described someone charming, modest, and ladylike, a stellar cook who deserved, he said, to be seen as the female equivalent of Escoffier. His attitude was one of delight and honest respect. As a journalist, he was a gentleman. Mary Lawton also professed great admiration for Rosa, but as a journalist, she was a journalist, and she wanted a story with a vivid character at the center. The rambling, name-dropping monologue in an all-but-audible Cockney accent, swaggering across the pages of Lawton's book, would have been inconceivable coming from the genteel Mrs. Lewis who presided over Newnham-Davis's account. Ultimately it was Lawton's version that became immortal, not only because it made better copy, but because it was true. After 1914, the Rosa who had so impressed Newnham-Davis disappeared into the harsh sorrow of the war years. When she returned, she was another creature.

"Life became the War and the War only," Rosa told Lawton. "Every year it got worse." She was forty-seven when it began; she had been mingling with the British elite for more than twenty-five years, and each day brought word of another young man she knew, killed in battle. His father had stayed at the Cavendish, or his mother had hired her to cook, or he had come to parties at the hotel with his university friends. She cut out the war stories and the obituaries and pinned them up on the walls of the Cavendish. The hotel itself was requisitioned: she housed ninety

British troops at a time and fed some two hundred Belgian refugees in the garage. Wounded soldiers who had been released from the hospital stayed at the Cavendish until they could return to the front, so many of them crammed into each room that some of them were sleeping on the floor. Crutches were stacked all over the hotel. "Every man who left for France always had a package," she told Lawton. "If it was not pies or cakes, or suet puddings, it was cocktails, eau de Cologne, listerine, ham, chicken, cheese." British officers traveled with servants, whom Rosa knew as well as she knew the officers, and every time she sent a food parcel to someone at the front, she sent another to his servant. Lord Ribblesdale's son Charles Lister, who was wounded at Gallipoli, wrote to Rosa asking for "a nice, damp plum-cake. If made damp and packed in tins they keep splendidly." Soon after writing, he died on a hospital ship; he was twenty-seven, and Rosa grieved with his father. Any soldier who had nowhere to stay on leave, or who decided to stop at the Cavendish for a few days on the way home, was made welcome with a bed, brandy, champagne, and, according to long-lasting rumor, feminine company if he wished it. Rosa never presented a bill to a soldier or an officer. Civilian guests at the Cavendish, including politicians, businessmen, and foreign diplomats, might find a few extra charges on their bills that they didn't recognize. If they wanted to remain on good terms with Rosa, they paid quietly.

After the armistice, she repaired and refurbished the Cavendish and tried to run it as usual. But the Britain of wealth and frivolity, the Britain that had shaped her imagination and inspired her ambition, was gone. Everything she relied upon to furnish her identity as the remarkable Rosa Lewis, that wonderful cook who was friends with lords and ladies—the borrowed gowns, the foie gras in aspic—was unobtainable or out of style.

How on earth was she to prepare *Médaillons de Soles à la Joinville* for a party of twenty, or even six? The supply of young women she once trained to poach slices of sole in a fish stock, arrange them around a display of shrimps, mushrooms, and truffles, coat them lightly with a sauce, and garnish each with a sliced truffle had disappeared into offices or factories. "I can not get the servants that I used to have—nobody wants to do anything in the way they used to do it," she complained. As for the ingredients—"There is nothing left," she said flatly. "I would not do a dinner now if you gave me a hundred pounds to walk into the kitchen." Once, in the 1920s, a duchess begged and begged: would Rosa please prepare a dinner? She finally went out and tried to buy partridges, found a few she wouldn't have dreamed of accepting before the war, and cooked them. But she wouldn't take any money. If the duchess was going to complain about the food, Rosa didn't want to listen.

Meals at the Cavendish became skimpier and more erratic, and the catering business shut down entirely. Perhaps if she'd been younger, she could have updated her recipes to suit the new economy and a new generation. But she couldn't scrap the habits of a lifetime, and she didn't have much respect for the rising rich. "The young bloods of today haven't tasted that other sweet world," she told Lawton. "They are an awful lot!" The more money they had, the worse they were at spending it, especially on food. "The only thing that appears to matter is the jazz band. I think people who require jazz music to eat by are short of their intelligence." So she let it all go.

She had cooked her way to the top; now the top was gone and so were the meals that had given her access to it. She was still vigorous, still dropping all the best British and American names. But without food as her fixed point, she was adrift, with nowhere to fix her attention except the past. Her culinary reputation survived in memory only, and gradually she took on a new identity that would be her refuge for the rest of her life. She became an eccentric, one of those dimly alarming characters who have been wandering through English letters for centuries. By the 1920s she had stopped taking visitors downstairs; she had no staff dressed in white to show off and no decent food to serve. When people arrived, she entertained them in a back parlor she called the Elinor Glyn room. Glyn was the notorious author of *Three Weeks*, a novel published in 1907 that scandalized its avid readers by depicting a clearly sexual affair between a young man and an older woman. (King Edward, whose sense of morality was much stronger in public than it was in private, once furiously shut down a dinner table conversation about *Three Weeks* because there was a young girl within hearing distance.) Glyn had no association with the Cavendish, but Rosa loved playing off the lingering aura of the novel. It suited the vaguely racy, vaguely bohemian, vaguely lunatic image she was assembling, the one she wore wrapped around herself like the furs she insisted on calling her "Sables of Sin." Whenever she couldn't pay her bills, she said, she put on her sable coat and went to her creditors with half of what she owed. One look at the fur and they were fully persuaded she could come up with the rest.

Writers began portraying her as a Miss Havisham figure, locked in the tattered remnants of the past, "wearing a bile-green coat and skirt, twenty years out of style, and an amber chain that bumped her knees gently," as *The New Yorker* put it in a profile published in 1933. The novelist Anthony Powell, who described Rosa in his memoir *Messengers of Day*, said she might have passed for the wife of a civil servant were it not for a distinctly raffish look suggesting that this particular wife "had suddenly

decided to have the most reckless of nights out." The backdrop
was always the Cavendish, which became more and more of a
shambles over the years, with its uncertain plumbing, dusty tap-
estries, and antique furniture piled about haphazardly. A handful of old-timers continued to check in; others used to stay there
for the low rates. Looming out of a dim interior an ancient waiter
might be glimpsed—"an irascible, scowling old man who mut-
tered angrily to himself," recalled Daphne Fielding—though he
had little to do but pour champagne most of the day and long
into the evening. Rosa was never without what she called a
"cherrybum"—a jeroboam—and she wandered around the hotel
making sure no glass was empty. As in the war years, she always
charged the champagne to the wealthiest guest on hand. Fielding, who had been one of those freewheeling roisterers of the
1920s known as "the Bright Young Things," said her friends
sometimes dropped in at the Cavendish for a lark and had late-
night champagne with Rosa. Once—"after a court ball at Buckingham Palace," she wrote—they showed up and roused Rosa
from bed. She came downstairs in a nightgown, wrapped in her
sables, and sat in a daze of champagne and reminiscences until
dawn.

Invariably, the accounts of Rosa in these years dwelled on
what it was like to carry on a conversation with her. Especially
after a glass or two, she liked to spin a surreal monologue featuring random names from the past—socialites and aristocrats, ladies of loose morals, kings and prime ministers—who bobbed
about like chairs and bureaus and bedposts on the floodwaters
of memory. "You don't know how much I've helped some of
these young men," she announced at a lunch with Powell. "Look
at the way Jack Fordingbridge wanted to marry Ivy Peters. He
wanted to *marry* her. Set on it, he was. The Duke was almost off

his head about his son and heir. I introduced Fordingbridge to Frieda Brown, and he dropped Ivy Peters like a hot potato. People forget all the good I've done." Joseph Bryan III, who wrote the *New Yorker* profile of Rosa, quoted her rambling on and on in unfettered Cockney, sounding a good deal more demented than picturesque, and there was no mistaking the pathos wrapped around the working-class accent. When people congratulated her on the story, Rosa said she hated it.

She hated nearly everything written about her. One exception was a novel by her old friend the diplomat and writer Shane Leslie, who slipped Rosa into *The Anglo-Catholic* as Louisa Rose, proprietor of the Sackville Hotel. Leslie's loyalty to Rosa could not be shaken, and he described the food at the Sackville just as her cooking used to be described everywhere: very French, utterly resplendent, the cuisine of monarchs, famed all over London. Few other writers had anything good to say about the food at the Cavendish in these years. Theodora FitzGibbon, who stayed at the hotel during World War II and later became a prolific cookbook writer, remembered an appalling dish she called "Game Pie" being served three times a day. She said she had once been served an unusual breakfast dish—"it was a chunk of smoked haddock, which tasted like fish flannel"—after which the pie didn't seem so bad. Still, these amused accounts of the ramshackle state of the Cavendish and its owner had no sharp edges: all the writers were fond of Rosa personally, and their stories were affectionate, if comic. Bryan, in *The New Yorker*, called her "the most remarkable woman in England." (He even praised the food, calling it "delicious," either because he hoped to remain on good terms with Rosa or because the story wasn't fact-checked.) But Rosa didn't care about their good intentions. As soon as she saw herself re-created in print, she exploded in fury. The persona she had created, costumed, and given voice to belonged to her, and nobody else had the right to appropriate it for their own purposes—not even in an article about Rosa Lewis.

The writer she hated most was Evelyn Waugh, and she hated him with a ferocity that became legendary. Waugh's *Vile Bodies*, a satire on life among the Bright Young Things, was his second novel and the one that secured his fame. Published in 1930, just five years after the garrulous, slightly unhinged portrait in Lawton's book had appeared, *Vile Bodies* featured a garrulous, slightly unhinged character named Lottie Crump, owner of Shepheard's Hotel. We first meet Lottie when she ushers a new guest, Adam Symes, into her sitting room at Shepheard's, where residents of the hotel seem to spend most of their time.

> "You all know Lord Thingummy, don't you?" said Lottie.
>
> "Mr. Symes," said Adam.
>
> "Yes, dear, that's what I said. Bless you, I knew you before you were born. How's your father? Not dead, is he?"
>
> "Yes, I'm afraid he is."
>
> "Well, I never. I could tell you some things about him. Now let me introduce you—that's Mr. What's-his-name, you remember him, don't you? And over there in the corner, that's the Major, and there's Mr. What-d'you-call-him, and that's an American, and there's the King of Ruritania."
>
> "Alas, no longer," said a sad, bearded man.
>
> "Poor chap," said Lottie Crump, who always had a weak spot for royalty even when deposed.

After Adam has been staying at the hotel for a while—and taking his meals there—he receives an invitation to lunch at a London restaurant and leaps to accept. Waugh explains why: "The food at Shepheard's tends to be mostly game-pie—quite black inside and full of beaks and shot and inexplicable verte-brae." Like Theodora FitzGibbon, who was still recoiling from the game pie more than a decade later, Waugh had never tasted Rosa's signature dish when it was the pride of her table and the delight of a king, when it was praised by the discerning Newnham-Davis and sought after by all the best hostesses. Now it was a joke, and so was Rosa.

Rosa always believed she knew exactly where she stood in rela-tion to the rich and famous, but she may not have grasped the precarious nature of her footing. She was aware that the gentle-men who dropped by the kitchen to chat with her wouldn't have dreamed of proposing to the pretty caterer, and she understood that the ladies who gave her a cup of tea in the drawing room had no intention of including her in their "at home" afternoons, when they welcomed their real friends. Rosa and the upper classes could enjoy a good-natured game of equality precisely as long as her betters remained in the upper class and Rosa re-mained a cook. But she altered her part of the arrangement when she dropped the cooking. Now all she brought to the game was a decrepit hotel and the bizarre behavior she brandished about her. Food had been the passport allowing her to travel freely in and out of other social worlds. Without the food, her relationships with those she once called "the greatest people of that time" became as rickety and uncomfortable as the dusty old sofas at the Cavendish. She was like a devoted governess who had outlived her pupils and her place at the family dinner table but refused to be put aside. Fielding recalled that it was a custom among the Bright Young Things to gather at the Cavendish on their way to a royal wedding. As they piled back into their cars,

Rosa would wave from the door, looking envious. She would have loved an invitation to a royal wedding. No such invitation was ever going to appear. And like many an eccentric whose charm was fading, she was getting to be a nuisance.

A letter written in 1937 by a young American woman in London suggests, discomfitingly, what it was like to maintain a connection with Rosa in her years of increasing frailty and desperation.

Isabella Gardner was twenty-two at the time and had just moved to London to study acting. She came from one of the distinguished Boston families that Rosa would have categorized approvingly as "your American aristocracy." Her great-great-aunt was the art collector Isabella Stewart Gardner, and her father, George Peabody Gardner, had been a favorite of Rosa's when he stayed at the Cavendish years earlier. Rosa loved dropping his name, and when she did it was always "Peabo," the nickname his friends used. Despite these ties, Isabella was not staying at the Cavendish while she looked for a flat. She was writing to her parents from her room at the Hyde Park Hotel in Knightsbridge to report, guiltily, that Rosa was driving her crazy. "I *wish* I hadn't but I . . . went down to see her and took her out to supper. I thought then I probably wouldn't see her again for a month or so. But ever since she has pursued me—in the *kindest way imaginable* but making it terribly difficult for me. I *know* that she only wants me to meet the 'best people' and to give me fun and do the right thing by 'Peabow' and I can't *bear* to hurt her feelings . . . but I can't go down there except once in a *great* while and it's embarrassing to have her telephone me constantly, write me incessantly—send me flowers etc." Isabella went on to say that Rosa had discovered her one evening about to dine with friends at Prunier, a fine French restaurant, and "dragged us out of our seats and back to the Cavendish where she proceeded to tell Paul how she 'ated the 'Inchingbrookes—the Hinchin-brookes being Paul's Aunt and Uncle that didn't go down so well. . . ."

Isabella wasn't creating a character for literary or sentimental purposes; she was describing somebody she knew: an old woman with an abrasive accent who couldn't bear to make a graceful exit from other people's lives. Rosa was surely aware that if she implored Isabella and her friends to go back to the Cavendish for champagne, they would say yes out of politeness, and she also knew it would constitute a poor victory. Underneath Isabella's acquiescence there would have been . . . irritation? Pity? Contempt? Whatever it was, Rosa heard it, just as she could always hear her own accent.

One of the stories Rosa most enjoyed telling was about going to supper at the fashionable Berkeley Hotel with a few of her upper-crust friends during the years when food was still her calling card. "We were supposed to have duck or teal—all smothered over with orange, but it was only a damned plover. That's all it was. You couldn't fool me, though. I couldn't sit down at a restaurant and be fooled at my time of life. So I sent it back and said—'I would rather have a piece of cold ham than a fake plover any day!' Give you a rabbit for a chicken! Not me! Not Rosa Lewis, cook!"

As long as she could proclaim her profession, she could flaunt all the contradictions of her life with glee. But no matter how desperately she tried to celebrate herself during her last decades, those who knew her best understood that they were witnessing a caricature. It took death to restore her to dignity. Rosa always wanted her funeral to be held at St. James's, Piccadilly, where she occasionally attended Sunday services wearing a large diamond brooch. When she died at eighty-five, St. James's presided over her farewell just as she had requested. But what would have pleased her even more was the funeral cortege, as resplendent as if she had summoned it herself, and perhaps she did. Four cars made their way majestically through Piccadilly heaped high with roses, gardenias, and orchids sent by a roster of brilliant names, including the Earl of Strathmore, the Earl of Sandwich, the Marquess and Marchioness of Bath, Lady Milbank, and—as the *Daily Mail* put it—"many other families who were her friends." How gratified she would have been to read that last word.

Eleanor Roosevelt

(1884–1962)

Hot Stuffed Eggs with Tomato Sauce
Mashed Potatoes
Whole Wheat Bread and Butter
Prune Pudding
Coffee

—Lunch at the White House, March 21, 1933

Eleanor Roosevelt didn't care what she ate. She had no palate, she wasn't interested in food, it gave her no pleasure—or at least people have been saying these things ever since she became a public figure in the 1920s. "Victuals to her are something to inject into the body as fuel to keep it going, much as a motorist pours gasoline into an auto tank," her son James once declared, and nobody among her friends or relatives seems to have disagreed. Eleanor herself joined the chorus: she used to say she was incapable of enjoying food. It's too bad, then, that she never had the chance to study her own paper trail. It's as long and rich as you might expect from one of America's most prominent political activists, and it would have surprised her by delivering quite a different verdict. An intense relationship with food ran right through Eleanor's life, darting into her work, her feminism, and her deepest relationships. "I am sorry to tell you that my husband and I are very bad about food," she wrote in response to a query from the *Ladies' Home Journal* in 1929. "I do not know of any particular dish which he likes unless it is wild duck." FDR did like wild duck; he also loved steak, lobster, heavy cream, caviar, and cocktails, but she wasn't about to admit any of that to the *Journal*. Instead, she chose to lie, which was sometimes her favorite way to discuss matters of appetite—especially, as we'll see, FDR's appetite. But the art of the cover-up, which Eleanor practiced diligently all her life, was difficult to maintain when it came to cooking and eating. Eleanor wrote so often and so copiously about herself, in memoirs and letters and articles, that the truth had a way of spilling out. Over the years, she became a reliable source on a subject she would have insisted she knew nothing about—her own food story. And it isn't a story about a woman with no palate for pleasure.

Still, it's easy to see how Eleanor acquired her bleak culinary reputation. By all accounts, the food in the Roosevelt White House was the worst in the history of the presidency. Longtime White House staff began noticing a change right after FDR's inauguration in 1933. Eyeing the luncheon buffet Eleanor had ordered, the chief butler called the table "sick-looking"—it featured two kinds of salad, bread-and-butter sandwiches, and vast quantities of milk. A few weeks later California senator Hiram Johnson was invited to dinner and told his son afterward that the most ordinary meal they had at home was "infinitely superior" to what he had been served at the White House. "We had a very indifferent chowder first, then some mutton served in slices already cut and which had become almost cold, with peas that were none too palatable, a salad of little substance and worse dressing, lemon pie, and coffee." Mutton was not on the menu that night; Johnson had been eating dark, dry, overcooked lamb. Ernest Hemingway, invited to dinner in 1937, told his mother-in-law it was the worst meal he had ever eaten. "We had a rain-water soup followed by rubber squab, a nice wilted salad and a

Eleanor Roosevelt posing in her inaugural gown at the White House, January 16, 1937.

cake some admirer had sent in. An enthusiastic but unskilled admirer." The visit had been arranged by the journalist Martha Gellhorn, who was a good friend of Eleanor's and often stayed overnight at the White House. As they waited for their flight in the Newark airport, Hemingway was surprised to see Gellhorn intently eating sandwiches, three of them, and asked her what on earth she was doing. She said everyone in Washington knew the rule: When you're invited to a meal at the White House, eat before you go.

Formal dinners prompted more elaborate menus and the best White House tableware, but the same desultory cooking. "I suppose one ought to be satisfied with dining on and with a solid-gold service, but it does seem a little out of proportion to use a solid-gold knife and fork on ordinary roast mutton," wrote Secretary of the Interior Harold L. Ickes in his diary after the 1934 cabinet dinner. Again, he was eating lamb. Guests who had arrived in black tie and evening gowns for the first state dinner of the new administration found themselves sitting down to an early Thanksgiving. Stuffed celery, roast turkey and cranberry sauce, sweet potatoes with marshmallows, frozen pineapple salad, and ice cream with a product called "rubyettes"—grapes that had been colored and flavored to resemble cherries—made up what *The New York Times* politely referred to as a "traditionally American" menu. *The Washington Post* was more blunt: "Gentlemen, let us adjourn to a coffee-shoppe!"

Even the return of wine to the White House table, announced for the 1934 cabinet dinner after the long drought of Prohibition, didn't offer much by way of festivity. The American wine industry was a shambles after fourteen years of neglect, with vineyards lost and wineries ruined. French wines were available—Elizabeth Farley, the wife of the postmaster general, treated herself to a glass of imported champagne at the Mayflower Hotel before the dinner—but Eleanor didn't want the public to think that the new administration was staging some sort of bacchanal in the midst of the Depression. She decided that two "light American wines" would be served and ordered a California sherry and a New York State sparkling wine, limiting the hospitality to one glass of each. As it turned out, overindulgence was not a problem. "The sherry was passable, but the champagne was undrinkable," Ickes wrote in his diary. He could see Mrs. Farley reacting to her first sip: she nearly grimaced. Eleanor's consultant on the wines had been Rexford Tugwell, the undersecretary of agriculture, who was born in upstate New York and remained loyal to its struggling vineyards. Late the next evening, Ickes and a few friends joined FDR in his study for an impromptu get-together, and the president, laughing about how awful the cabinet dinner champagne had been, ordered up a couple of bottles of the real thing. They all drank convivially until midnight. Eleanor wasn't there.

Everyone who ate in the White House seems to have complained about the food—FDR, his aides, the family, old friends, Washington insiders. Even the women in the press corps, who flocked to the all-female press conferences Eleanor held every week and were devoted to her, whispered that a press lunch had been "abominable." Yet now and then a positive report surfaces. Louis Adamic, for instance, a prolific writer on issues of American immigration and diversity, was invited to come for dinner with his wife one evening in January 1942. Because FDR rarely socialized outside the White House—he disliked being seen in public in his wheelchair—Eleanor made a point of bringing new people into his orbit when she thought they might interest him. Adamic said later that he had been far too nervous to pay attention to the menu, but his wife told him afterward what they had eaten: rare roast beef, Yorkshire pudding, string beans, salad, and a trifle for dessert, along with wine, champagne, and brandy. She said it was all very good, and she was probably right—since Winston Churchill had arrived unexpectedly. No wonder Adamic couldn't focus on his plate. The original menu, planned without the prime minister in mind, had been baked fish stuffed with bread crumbs, and a marshmallow pudding.

Serving appetizing food in the White House was hardly an impossible challenge, and previous administrations had managed very well. The Hoovers, unpopular though they were, never had to field criticism about the menus or the cooking. On the contrary, Lucius Boomer, manager of the Waldorf-Astoria, had lunch at the White House after Hoover was trounced in 1932 and said he had never tasted food so delicious. (Ava Long, the housekeeper at the time, whom Eleanor replaced, pointedly included this anecdote in her reminiscences.) But the fact that a decent meal for Churchill could be summoned on such short notice makes it all the harder to understand why the typical state of White House food should be so dreary. Nobody expected the White House to serve roast beef and champagne every night during wartime, but Churchill didn't just get a special menu, he was treated to careful cooking as well. The Roosevelts were accustomed to dry, leathery roasts; Churchill's was properly rare.

What happened in 1933? Why did the food deteriorate so spectacularly? Most historians blame Eleanor and what they assume to be her indifference to matters of the table. After the election, according to this theory, she quickly hired a housekeeper and a kitchen staff for the White House and then threw herself into what mattered far more to her—civil rights, women's equality, poverty, housing, employment, and the war. She was the busiest, most public, most productive First Lady in history, and complaints about dinner just didn't register.

But this explanation ignores nearly everything else we know about Eleanor, beginning with her extraordinary talent for friendship. Warm, charismatic, genuinely sympathetic, and invariably thoughtful, she was the one who always remembered to ask the timely question, send the flowers, write the note. All year she kept an eye out for possible Christmas presents, so she could be sure of having just the right gift ready for each person on her long list. Stories abound of guests arriving for lunch or dinner at the White House and feeling desperately nervous until Eleanor, comfortable and welcoming, drew them into the room and put them at their ease. What's more, as she wrote in her memoir of the White House years, she was impressed early on by the awe and affection Americans felt when they visited 1600 Pennsylvania Avenue, either as tourists or as invited guests. It was a powerful symbol not only of the nation, but of American hospitality, and she strongly believed that as First Lady she personified that hospitality. It's hard to imagine that such a woman could read caustic newspaper stories about the terrible White House food and do nothing about it just because she cared more about unemployment. In truth, what was happening at the White House table didn't reflect Eleanor's disdain for food, it reflected a welter of complicated feelings about being First Lady at all—a job she had never wanted and the public face of a marriage that tormented her.

During FDR's first term, Eleanor happened to read a popular new novel called *Time Out of Mind,* by Rachel Field. She was so taken by the portrait of the heroine that she wrote about the book in her syndicated column, "My Day." The novel is set in a village on the coast of Maine, at the end of the nineteenth century, and features a woman whose crushing disappointments in love have left her profoundly detached not only from others, but from herself as well. In Eleanor's words, the heroine is "absolutely self-forgetful," as if her own humanity has fled. She puts in hours of hard, physical work each day and hopes to think of nothing else. "The description of the times when she tried to be just hands and feet, a mechanical automaton that moved and yet was numb, is very poignant," Eleanor wrote. "For one reason or another, many of us can remember times like that in our lives." Eleanor certainly could—the word "automaton" was one she used about herself more than once; and "times like that" extended over much of her life. It was during those times that she cultivated a detachment from the ordinary pleasures of eating and drinking. "How I wish I could enjoy food!" she cried out in a letter once. And yet she did enjoy food, as we'll see, when the place and the people were right. They were never right in the White House.

Early in their marriage, the Roosevelts established a Sunday-night ritual that featured Eleanor playing the part of a cook. She and Franklin invited friends to come for supper, and when everyone was gathered around the table, she sat down at her place and made scrambled eggs in a chafing dish. Fashionable from the late nineteenth century until well into the 1950s, the chafing dish was widely recognized as a vehicle for what women's magazines called "dainty cookery," for a hostess could prepare an entrée or dessert in full view of her company without wearing an apron or putting her hands into a lot of raw, messy food. Any prep work necessary, such as cutting up meat or sautéing onions, could be done in the kitchen beforehand. At the Roosevelts' table, the chafing dish was already warming up when the guests took their seats, and the ingredients were arrayed in front of Eleanor: a bowl of eggs, a dish of butter, a pitcher of cream, the salt and pepper. She began by dropping a chunk of butter into the pan and letting it melt. Then she cracked each egg directly into the pan, added the cream, the salt, and the pepper, and beat the mixture with a fork until the eggs were done. There was more to the meal—bacon or sausage, hash browns, sometimes cold cuts, and cake or pudding for dessert—but all these came from the kitchen, where the real cook was at work as usual.

Eleanor clung to this tradition throughout the forty years she was married. It was the only version of homemaking she felt she was good at: everybody liked the eggs and the convivial atmosphere, and nobody questioned the casting. Otherwise she struggled hard with the role of wife and mother; nothing about it came easily. Her own mother had been cold and disapproving; her father, whom she adored, drank himself to death; and Eleanor, an orphan from the age of ten, had been raised mostly by a grandmother who had few instincts for bringing up children. Discipline was constant and irrational. "She so often said 'no' that I built up a defense of saying I did not want to do things in order to forestall her refusals and keep down my disappointments," she wrote in *This Is My Story*, the first of her three memoirs. When she married her distant cousin Franklin, she was deeply in love but anxious and ignorant, captive to what she later called "an almost exaggerated idea of the necessity for keeping all one's desires under complete subjugation."

Like all their friends and relatives, Eleanor and Franklin had a house full of servants. Both of them had been brought up with cooks, maids, and nurses and wouldn't have known how to live any other way. But looking back on those early years, Eleanor regretted that she hadn't been thrown into homemaking unassisted for a few years to acquire "knowledge and self-confidence." Had she gained some practical skills, she believed, "my subsequent troubles would have been avoided and my children would have had far happier childhoods." These "subsequent troubles" ran deeper than the mishaps she recorded in her memoir, such as the time their cook quit the day before a dinner party ("I was simply petrified, because I knew nothing about preparing a meal"). Eleanor had the bad luck to enter married life with another woman hovering right at her shoulder—Franklin's widowed mother, Sara Delano Roosevelt, who had raised her son with ferocious care. He was still bound to her, loyally if uneasily, especially since he never tried to live within his income and depended on his mother for financial support. Sara had every domestic skill that Eleanor lacked, not to mention the confidence of a long-seated monarch; and she imposed her wisdom ruthlessly on the Roosevelt household. Grateful at first, Eleanor soon began to squirm and finally to resist, but combat rumbled along in one form or another until Sara's death more than thirty years later.

Shortly after Eleanor and Franklin were married, they moved into a town house on East Sixty-Fifth Street in New York—built for them by Sara, with a twin town house adjoining it for herself. The two houses were connected with sliding doors on every floor, to permit easy access back and forth. Eleanor hated living that way, but she didn't know how to object. When she burst into tears of frustration one day, telling Franklin the house wasn't hers and didn't represent her taste or her wishes in any way, he was astonished. "He thought I was quite mad and told me so gently," she wrote later. After that she retreated into self-enforced docility.

Nor did she ever feel at home during the long stretches of time they spent at Springwood, the lavish estate in Hyde Park where Franklin had grown up. He was deeply attached to the house and its farmland, woods, stables, and gardens, and Springwood became the family's permanent second home. During his presidency he retreated there often, not least because in his mother's house he could be assured of getting a good meal. Sara was renowned for her fine table: she wrote out her menus in French, kept first-rate cooks, and put considerable time into planning meals and supervising the kitchen. The fresh produce, milk, and eggs came right from the estate, and sometimes Sara herself went into town to do the shopping. This was the culinary background that had shaped FDR's gourmandise, and Eleanor grew to despise it. She was always uncomfortable staying in Sara's house, and she was especially irked by the dinner table. Sara made a point of arranging it around herself and Franklin, so that mother and son presided over the meal at opposite ends of the table. After dinner, mother and son occupied the two easy chairs set before the fire. No special seat was ever planned for Eleanor.

Even more distressing was the fact that Sara appropriated Eleanor's role as mother. Eleanor spent the first eleven years of her married life having babies—six of them, including a boy who died at seven months. She blamed herself for the loss. Anxiety pursued her through motherhood; she was never at ease taking hands-on care of her children. Discipline was easier for her to dispense than hugs and treats. Sara, by contrast, indulged her grandchildren freely, often reversing Eleanor's decisions—to the children's delight. "What she wanted was to hold onto Franklin and his children; she wanted them to grow up as she wished," Eleanor wrote many years later. "As it turned out, Franklin's children were more my mother-in-law's children than they were mine."

Thirteen years into the marriage came the now famous crisis that would slam down a permanent barrier between husband and wife. They were living in Washington, D.C., comfortably outside Sara's immediate orbit for once, and both of them were thriving. President Woodrow Wilson had given a boost to Franklin's political career by appointing him assistant secretary of the navy, and Eleanor was hurtling through a schedule tightly packed with wartime volunteer work. Raising money for the Red Cross, visiting the wounded, staffing a canteen for waves of troops passing through the city—she was discovering that jobs like these were far more satisfying than supervising the household help or making the seating charts for official dinner parties. Then, in 1918, Franklin returned from a trip to Europe with pneumonia, and while he was recuperating Eleanor sorted through his mail. To her horror, she came across letters from a pretty young woman named Lucy Mercer, who had worked for Eleanor as a social secretary four years earlier. Lucy and Franklin had been a semisecret couple for some time, as many Washingtonians in her circle knew; but if Eleanor had suspected anything, she kept her worries far below conscious awareness. Now the truth flew directly at her, and she was devastated.

Eleanor's personal commitment to the role of wife was absolute. It was the heartbeat of her identity: she was Mrs. Franklin D. Roosevelt, nothing else. Now the man whose existence made her whole had slipped away and left her standing alone. As she told a friend much later, the bottom fell out of her world. But despite the scandal and humiliation that would accompany a divorce, despite the five children who would suffer, despite the bleak uncertainty of the future, she was willing to end their marriage. As far as she was concerned, it was over anyway. She told Franklin that if he wanted to leave her, he was free to go. Sara, however, was horrified at the possibility of a divorce in the family and told her son she would cut off his financial support if he left Eleanor. This was a serious threat to a man who spent as freely as he did, but worse was knowing that he would have to give up a future in politics. He had been mapping his road to the White House for years, and in 1918 a divorce would have put an end to any such dream. He promised Eleanor he would never see Lucy again, and Eleanor agreed to keep the family intact. But she knew very well that it was ambition, not love, that drove the decision.

"Few pictures from these years . . . show ER with her face to the camera," Blanche Wiesen Cook has written in her multi-volume biography of Eleanor. "She rarely smiled; she was depressed. . . . She felt profoundly tired, suffered headaches, and had days when she wondered about her will to live." Eleanor was eating very little and often threw up whatever she had managed to get down. She quarreled with Sara, then frantically apologized. Though she went to church as she had always done, something stopped her from taking Communion. According to Joseph Lash, another insightful biographer and a friend of Eleanor's for many years, "Religion was of the utmost seriousness to her and prayer a kind of continuing exchange with God, a way of cleansing the heart and steadying the will." The wild incoherence of her heart, mind, and moral core was tearing away at her, Lash wrote; she felt "cut off from divine grace." Perhaps to reach communion of a different sort, she began driving out to Rock Creek Cemetery every few days, to sit on a bench in front of the statue by Augustus Saint-Gaudens known popularly as *Grief*. Commissioned by Henry Adams in memory of his wife, Clover, who committed suicide in 1885, the statue is a long, slim figure of a seated woman, draped and hooded. Her face is visible but in shadow, her expression is tranquil, one hand is raised to her chin, and she projects a calm strength that appears to have outlasted her suffering. Eleanor gazed at this figure often, not only during her own period of anguish, but on visits that continued for the rest of her life. She used to bring friends out to the cemetery with her, as a way of opening herself up and sharing with them her own darkest time.

In 1920 the Roosevelts returned to New York, and as soon as they were back home, Eleanor arranged for cooking lessons. Twice a week she went to her teacher's apartment and prepared a dinner, leaving the meal for the woman's family to eat and criticize. Did she ever taste her own cooking? She didn't say in the memoir, but it's doubtful that this was an exercise in gastronomy. The goal was to acquire practical skills: she knew she would never be without a hired cook, but she wanted to understand the nature of female independence. In the same spirit, she took lessons in typing and shorthand. Up until then, she wrote later, "I looked at everything from the point of view of what I ought to do, rarely from the standpoint of what I wanted to do. In fact, there were times when I think I almost forgot that there was such a thing as wanting anything." Now she launched a crash course in being her own person. A year later Franklin was stricken with polio, and she cared for him around the clock throughout the worst of his illness. He went on to spend most of the 1920s focused on physical therapy and recuperation, traveling often to the South for the warm-water swimming he believed would strengthen him. This left Eleanor relatively free to pursue whatever challenges appealed to her, and increasingly these were out of the house and political. The 1920s became the most exhilarating decade of her life.

Franklin's closest adviser, Louis Howe, who lived with the Roosevelts and had earned Eleanor's trust and affection, was determined to see Franklin return to public life, even if he had to do so as a paraplegic. Partly to keep Franklin in touch with political events, partly to keep the Roosevelt name in play, and partly because he was sure Eleanor would take to it, he urged her to get involved in women's Democratic Party politics. He was right; Eleanor turned out to be very good at organizing, strategizing, and fund-raising. By the time of the 1924 Democratic convention, she was chair of the women's platform committee, responsible for an array of progressive planks including equal pay and endorsement of the League of Nations. The women's proposals were dismissed without so much as a hearing, but she was gaining widespread recognition as a popular and effective new player on the scene.

Eleanor loved the work, but what turned her life around was the women she was meeting. They were very different from her friends in Washington, the obedient political wives doing their duty by volunteering at the Red Cross. These new friends had fought for suffrage, they had won, and now they were determined to use the vote to advance women's interests. They did not define themselves by their achievements as wives. Their zeal, their brains, their integrity, the inspiring vision they brought to politics—all of it was thrilling to Eleanor. The activists she met in the 1920s became her tribe.

They were also her teachers—indeed, it's possible to say they invented her. Contrary to everything she represents as a historical figure today, Eleanor was not a natural-born radical. The bold and eloquent progressive principles that became her personal manifesto were acquired over time; she didn't think that way at first. She had been raised with all the bigotry considered acceptable in her social world, and she retained it longer than she knew. Well into the 1930s she was using the word "darky" and warmly recalling the tales of old plantation days told by her Southern relatives. Similarly, it was almost impossible for her to talk about Jews without summoning stereotypes. "I think much can be done to overcome anti-Semitism in this country," she wrote in 1941. "Jewish people themselves can help by trying to be as natural and unself-conscious as possible . . . trying not to be too aggressive or too ingratiating. . . ."

Most surprising of all, Eleanor was not a born feminist. Women had been fighting for the vote since 1848, but she had never paid much attention to the battle and neither had Franklin. She was "shocked," she wrote, when he came out in favor of women's suffrage in 1911. "I took it for granted that men were superior creatures and still knew more about politics than women," she recalled. Dutifully she adopted the same position as her husband but did not become an active suffragist. Many women her age remembered for the rest of their lives the day they cast their first vote; Eleanor didn't even include it in her memoirs. But in the course of the 1920s, as she worked with her new colleagues on the wide-open frontiers of feminism and progressivism, she began to understand what the struggle for the vote had been all about. Nobody talked about "consciousness raising" back then, but that's what was happening to her. She delved into the Women's Trade Union League; she cofounded a political journal called the *Women's Democratic News* and became its editor; she worked on child labor laws, unsafe housing, minimum-wage legislation, and world peace; and she recognized that all these were women's issues. What she gained from her feminist friends was an outlook on moral and political activism that helped her grow into leadership and thrive for decades to come.

Franklin did not feel the same way about Eleanor's friends—he called them "she-males"—which may be why it took Eleanor a little time to completely shift her allegiance. Writing to him from the second national convention of the League of Women Voters in April 1921, she reported on a flock of women speakers and concluded, "I prefer doing my politics with you." Two days later, however, she saw the great suffrage leader Carrie Chapman Catt push aside a prepared text in favor of an impromptu speech that shook the hall. President Warren Harding had just declared his opposition to the League of Nations, and Catt was livid. "You have heard politics all day," she told the delegates. "I can't help saying something I feel I must. The people in this room tonight could put an end to war. . . . It seems to me God is giving a call to the women of the world to come forward, to stay the hand of men, to say: 'No, you shall no longer kill your fellow men.'" Here was a cause, and a call to women, that sprang right from Eleanor's own soul. She continued doing politics with her husband—it was one of their few lasting bonds—but she was coming into her own. "During this time ER relinquished the old 'puritan' habits of social duty that had prevented her from enjoying spontaneous fun and the most casual pleasures," wrote Blanche Wiesen Cook. "She embraced the countryside. . . . She could outwalk anybody. She enjoyed swimming and riding. She loved to drive, and she drove fast." To her family's astonishment, she and one of her women friends showed up one day in matching British knickerbockers and jackets—Eleanor had had them specially made. The she-males were in her life for good.

But there was one cause she embraced far more fervently than her new friends did. Remember, this was a woman who jump-started her decade of personal liberation by taking cooking lessons. Eleanor was never going to be a feminist who railed against domesticity; what she longed to do was conquer it. So when she discovered that there was an entire political movement dedicated to the home and woman's place in it, she was enthusiastic—and she was enthusiastic instantly. No learning curve, no gradual dismantling of old prejudices. Home economics was the first reform movement that fired up her passion from the moment she heard about it.

There is every possibility that Eleanor had never washed a floor or even a dish in her life. But the proponents of home economics, which generations of schoolgirls have experienced as a simple-minded curriculum in cooking and sewing, originally set out to design a far grander and more serious enterprise in women's education. Eleanor discovered the movement at a time when its rhetoric was echoing through academia, the press, and, increasingly, her own world of politics—which is where she encountered it. In 1925, the New York State Legislature was considering a bill to make the School of Home Economics, founded as part of Cornell University's College of Agriculture, into the New York State College of Home Economics—still within Cornell, but a change that would confer the stature and dignity of autonomy. Martha Van Rensselaer and Flora Rose, pioneers in the field who had been building up the Cornell department since 1907, were eager to put home economics on this new footing; but the bill had been introduced year after year since 1920, only to be defeated each time. Finally they wrote to Eleanor Roosevelt. Would she help lobby for the bill? Eleanor had campaigned hard for Governor Al Smith's reelection, and she had excellent connections in the state legislature. A month later the bill was signed into law.

Everything she heard about home economics made sense to Eleanor. The women promoting it wanted to peel back the sentiment wrapped around domestic life, dismiss its old-fashioned trappings, and free the American home to take its rightful place in the modern world. Under the rubric of home economics, or so its founders dreamed, all women would study the science involved in cooking, cleaning, and child care; and those who wished to study further could earn an academic degree representing their intellectual fitness for the job of wife and mother. Feminists who had been struggling to establish women's colleges with classical curricula on a par with Harvard's were disgusted at the notion of recasting housework as a career. But home economists saw it differently, focusing on the good that a woman could do for her family and her nation, once she had been trained in hygiene, child psychology, nutrition, and economics. Male educators, too, could see the value of home economics—not only as an all-female academic discipline, but as a wonderfully convenient solution to the problem of what to do with the women trying to pursue higher education. Surely they could be funneled directly into the home economics department, especially the ones who showed up at school hoping to train for a career in chemistry or biology. Some such students did, in fact, welcome the prospect of working in a field especially designed for women; others resented it; few escaped. Flora Rose, who became one of Eleanor's cherished friends, had earned a master's degree in nutrition and decided there was no better way to put it to use than in home economics. "I would not be in this field if I did not believe it to be the most important one in women's education," she wrote to Eleanor years later. "To me it represents the thinking which women have done about their own needs, interests and activities. . . . I regard it as the one original contribution which women have made to education." She herself administered food relief programs in World War I, conducted nutrition and health surveys, and did considerable laboratory research—a career that might never have happened had she tried to work as a scientist outside the boundaries of a woman's world. At a time when most professions were male by force of implacable tradition, home economics was designed to give women their own careers, not in competition with men but as partners—partners, to be sure, who knew their place.

As it happened, Eleanor was introduced to home economics just six months after her infuriating experience at the 1924 Democratic National Convention, where women had been rudely shut out of decision making. At Cornell she found a small, enclosed world that operated on very different principles. Women made the rules, women set the tone, and women's contributions were honored at every level, whether they cooked a well-balanced dinner or taught advanced chemistry. And just as she had made her way into feminist activism guided by her captivating new friends, she was guided into home economics by Martha and Flora, who were longtime partners as well as colleagues. For the next fifteen years, she made sure to schedule a visit to Cornell during Farm and Home Week—an annual display of Cornell's work in agriculture and home economics—and no other engagement was permitted to override it. On the evening of February 15, 1933, Roosevelt narrowly escaped an assassination attempt in Miami; even so, Farm and Home Week was on Eleanor's schedule, and she was in Ithaca for breakfast the next morning. Despite her crammed calendar as First Lady, she sometimes managed to spend two full days at Cornell.

Pearl Buck, the American writer who grew up in China and won the Pulitzer Prize for her novel *The Good Earth,* was a graduate student at Cornell in 1926 when Eleanor made one of her visits. Buck was new to America and curious about this already celebrated woman, so she joined the committee assigned to meet Eleanor at the train and escort her through the day. "I can remember exactly how she looked," she wrote, which is understandable. It was seven in the morning, and Eleanor was wearing a long purple satin gown and sturdy brown oxfords. There was to be a reception at the end of the afternoon, and she had decided it would be most efficient to be fully dressed for it now, rather than make time to change clothes later. The shoes had been selected for comfort; she wore them all day and right through the evening. The committee took Eleanor to the home economics department first, where she made a speech, and later came a lunch—"invented," as Buck put it, by the home economists. "It seemed to be mostly raw cabbage," she wrote. "They were very proud of it because it cost only seven cents a person. My private opinion of it was that even seven cents was too expensive for it. It was an uneatable meal so far as I was concerned. Mrs. Roosevelt ate it with great gusto, however, and congratulated the head of the department on having achieved this meal."

Eleanor always had a hearty appetite for the food associated with the home economics movement. The meals at Cornell came from a laboratory-like kitchen and were designed to deliver proper nourishment at low cost—that was their entire beauty and function. Their simple, scientifically based efficiency made them a useful part of the state and later the federal effort to assist struggling families during the Depression. But these stark combinations of nutrients—creamed codfish, baked-bean soup, fried mush, chopped raw carrots—were aimed at appeasing hunger, not appetite. They certainly had no place on gracious tables such as Sara Roosevelt's. To Eleanor, this made them manna.

The food was utilitarian, not opulent; it was designed to help the poor, not impress the rich; it exuded the spirit of reformers like herself, not gastronomes like Sara. One weekend in 1932, when FDR was governor of New York, a couple of old friends came to visit them in the Governor's Mansion. They found Eleanor in splendid form, they said, apart from "her disdain for any interest in food!" The meals she offered were "very unattractive," and she had laughed outright at her mother-in-law when Sara began discussing various possible dishes for a dinner party. " 'As though,' said Eleanor, 'anyone now-a-days had time to spend twenty minutes planning what to eat!' " What she gained at Cornell was a usable, guilt-free perspective on food, one that classified it strictly as a management problem, to be handled with all the speed and intelligence a trained homemaker could bring to the task.

Cornell liberated her. Each time she visited, she saw in action an approach to homemaking that answered her worst insecurities. The messy, intractable difficulties in her life always had to do with home and family—the very realms in which women were supposed to excel, thanks to their God-given natures. For her, it hadn't worked out that way. She had lost her husband to another woman, she had handed over her children to nurses and governesses to raise, and now they were happier with their grandmother than they were with her. There was nothing to be proud of in her private record as a woman. Home economics couldn't transform her marriage or make her a different sort of mother, but it could package the traditional responsibilities of womanhood in a way that allowed her to achieve mastery. To remove domesticity from the realm of the emotions and place it among the sciences, to make it an activity for the brain rather than the heart—this was an ideal she could support with all her might. Being a wife and mother, according to home economics, wasn't a job managed by love, it was a job managed by serious, rational work; and if women learned to do it properly, the whole nation would benefit. Eleanor needed a way out of the corner her husband and family had left her in. At Cornell she found, for the first time in her life, a definition of femininity that made room for a woman like her.

FDR was inaugurated president for the first time on March 4, 1933, and less than three weeks later Eleanor brought the home economics movement directly into the White House. The idea was to stage a luncheon and feature one of Flora's low-cost Depression menus, with the press alerted beforehand to ensure maximum publicity. Family members and a few secretaries were summoned to the table, and Eleanor told reporters that the meal was a prototype of what she intended to serve for the next four years. It began with stuffed eggs, more typically a picnic dish but here transformed into a main course by being covered with tomato sauce and served hot. Five eggs were meant to serve six people, so each serving was modest, but it was accompanied by substantial side dishes of mashed potatoes and whole-wheat bread and butter. For dessert there was a watery prune pudding. According to *The New York Times,* the president was not at the table, but he was served the same meal on a tray in his office and said it was "good."

Good or grim, the meal was cheap—seven and a half cents per serving. All over the world, experienced home cooks were feeding their families at low cost by extracting every bit of flavor and nourishment out of the ingredients they had at hand, but Flora and her team were taking a different approach. They weren't looking for culinary economies based on taste and tradition; they were studying lists of nutrients and figuring out how to apportion them mathematically. In Eleanor's view, the lunch served every purpose a meal should serve. Nonetheless she assured the press that it would only be family members who ate Cornell meals on a regular basis. When the Roosevelts had guests, the kitchen would turn out more ample fare. As it happened, there were guests at every lunch and dinner she ate at the White House for the next twelve years, so her commitment was never put to the test.

Eleanor had never wanted to be First Lady. She hated the idea of surrendering her independence and pulling back from hands-on political work just to become a hostess. For the sake of the country she was glad FDR had been elected, but she knew exactly what First Ladies did: they got dressed up, they shook hands, and they made small talk, day after endless day. How could she submit to such a role? When FDR was nominated, she was the only person in the room who was stone-faced; and when he won, she wrote later, "The turmoil in my heart and mind was rather great that night, and the next few months were not to make any clearer what the road ahead would be." As she was organizing the household for the move to Washington, she made a tentative suggestion to FDR: Wasn't there "a real job" she could do in the White House? Perhaps answer some of his mail? "He looked at me quizzically and said he did not think that would do, that Missy, who had been handling his mail for a long time, would feel I was interfering. I knew he was right and that it would not work, but it was a last effort to keep in close touch and to feel that I had a real job to do." Eventually, of course, she created that job. She had seen how home economics operated: it was a woman's profession in a man's world. No lines were crossed, no fiefdoms challenged, but the women gave heart and soul to work they cared about. Now she, too, set out to find a professional place for herself, even while confined to FDR's sphere. She couldn't set policy, but she could travel, meet people, listen to them, investigate, pull myriad strings in Washington, make brilliant use of symbolic gestures, and give speeches that heartened the poor, the exploited, and the powerless. As Blanche Wiesen Cook put it, "Her vision shaped the best of his presidency"—an assessment that would have been supported overwhelmingly by the millions of Americans whose lives she touched, though Eleanor herself would have briskly turned away any such compliment.

Her first responsibility was one that FDR asked her to take on: he wanted her to manage the domestic side of the White House—a notion that must have reverberated in his mind for the next twelve years like a howl of triumph from Satan himself. Eleanor promptly set out to locate a first-rate housekeeper, someone who would plan and oversee the cooking, cleaning, laundry, and marketing for what was, in effect, a private hotel under public scrutiny. She thought she knew just the right person. Back in 1928, when FDR was running for governor of New York, Eleanor had become involved with the Hyde Park branch of the League of Women Voters and met a local woman who was also active in it: Henrietta Nesbitt, a homemaker with two grown sons and an unemployed husband. She was a strong supporter of FDR's and went to the same Episcopal church as Eleanor. And her family was hard up. Eleanor saw a way to help. She began hiring Mrs. Nesbitt to bake bread, pies, coffee cakes, and cookies for the constant entertaining that was going on at Hyde Park, and when the Roosevelts moved to Albany Mrs. Nesbitt kept right on baking for them, sending the orders upstate by train. Then FDR ran for president and won. Mrs. Nesbitt was delighted but also a little disappointed. The baking had been "a godsend," as she wrote in her memoir, *White House Diary*. Now it was coming to an end, and the Nesbitts, who had been forced to move in with their son and his family, were going to lose their only source of income. But shortly after Thanksgiving, Mrs. Roosevelt stopped by and said she was going to need a housekeeper in the White House. At the time she wrote her memoir, Mrs. Nesbitt was aware that her tenure in the White House was likely to be remembered as a national embarrassment—she had read all the bad press and heard all the complaints—and in her book she made a point of quoting Eleanor's job offer very precisely: "I don't want a professional housekeeper. I want someone I know. I want you, Mrs. Nesbitt."

It's not clear why Eleanor was so determined to hire an amateur for a job that called for supervising more than two dozen employees, maintaining sixty rooms and their furnishings, preparing meals for a guest list that often doubled or tripled on short notice, feeding sandwiches and sweets to a thousand or more at tea on any given day, and making sure family members and their innumerable overnight guests had everything they might require around the clock. Eleanor's contacts in Washington, not to mention her friends in home economics, could have given her the names of many candidates far more experienced than Mrs. Nesbitt. But Eleanor was comfortable with this Hyde Park woman, so loyal and accommodating, whose pies and cookies always arrived at the house when they were supposed to, and who very much needed the work. Why look elsewhere?

"Mrs. Nesbitt didn't know beans about running a White House," recalled Lillian Rogers Parks, who worked as a maid and seamstress for the Hoovers, the Roosevelts, the Trumans, and the Eisenhowers. Known backstairs as "Fluffy"—because

she was so very much the opposite—Mrs. Nesbitt had neither
the skills nor the temperament for the immense job she had
taken on, and she met the situation by becoming officious, over-
bearing, and peremptory. The staff loathed her. J. B. West, the
longtime White House usher, said the mansion began looking
"dingy, almost seedy" under her care, and the kitchen saw plate
after plate coming back with gray slices of meat and pallid vegetables barely touched. The president complained steadily about
the food, and by 1944 he was saying that the main reason he
wanted to win a fourth term was for the pleasure of firing Mrs.
Nesbitt. But to the end of Eleanor's life, she insisted she had
made a good hire. "Father never told me he wanted to get rid of
Mrs. Nesbitt," she claimed in a letter to her son James, who had
described in a memoir FDR's vehement feelings about the housekeeper. She added that FDR "often praised" Mrs. Nesbitt's
work—an assertion so blatantly untrue that nobody took it seriously except Mrs. Nesbitt, who made the same claim in her own
two books.

Yet Mrs. Nesbitt, the most reviled cook in presidential history, kept a careful record of the lunch and dinner menus she
had planned at the White House and gave them to the Library
of Congress with the rest of her papers. It's as if she wanted to
announce to all future detractors that contrary to her reputation
she had done a splendid job and fully deserved the faith that
Eleanor had in her. Hence we have a comprehensive picture of
what was served throughout FDR's administration—not just
the state dinners, which every administration publicized, but all
the other meals as well. They make it clear, in fact they make it
vivid, what everyone was so unhappy about.

Mrs. Nesbitt was under orders to practice strict economy,
first because of the Depression and later because of wartime ra-

tioning. Beyond this, her only culinary vision was the one she had developed as a small-town home cook who occasionally ate out in modest restaurants. Eleanor looked over the menus every morning, but she was even less adventuresome than Mrs. Nesbitt when it came to feeding people and rarely asked for changes. Apart from this daily conference with the First Lady, Mrs. Nesbitt insisted on absolute control in the kitchen. "Of course, Henrietta did not personally do the cooking, but she stood over the cooks, making sure that each dish was overcooked or undercooked or ruined one way or another," wrote Lillian Parks. Taste, texture, serving the food at the proper temperature, making sure each dish looked appetizing—these were niceties that did not concern the housekeeper. For dinner she typically offered simple preparations of beef, lamb, chicken, and fish, though by the time they arrived at the table they tended to be cold and dried out. She also deployed an occasional novelty of the sort that appeared in women's magazines under such names as "Seafood Surprise" and "Ham Hawaiian." Low-cost main dishes like sweetbreads, brains, and chicken livers appeared frequently, so frequently FDR took to complaining that he was never given anything else. But the greater cause for misery seems to have been lunch, which Mrs. Nesbitt saw as a fine occasion to save money. She built up a small repertoire of dishes based on leftovers and other inexpensive mixtures, and these turned up week after week as regularly as if they were on assignment. Sometimes these mixtures were stuffed into a green pepper, other times into a patty shell, but her favorite way to present them was the most straightforward—on toast. There were curried eggs on toast, mushrooms and oysters on toast, broiled kidneys on toast, braised kidneys on toast, lamb kidneys on toast, chipped beef on toast, and a dish called "Shrimp Wiggle," consisting of shrimp and canned peas heated in white sauce, on toast.

Another way to stretch just about any sort of food was to turn it into a creamed entrée or side dish, so day after day the Roosevelts and their company encountered creamed codfish, creamed finnan haddie, creamed mushrooms, creamed carrots, creamed clams, creamed beef, and creamed sweetbreads. Egg dishes also appeared with some persistence: she offered stuffed eggs and shirred eggs, and she featured "Eggs Benedictine" until 1938, when somebody finally corrected her. Sometimes the menus make it clear that she was at wits' end: we see her resorting to a dish she called "Stuffed Egg Salad" for two lunches in a row, and on another presumably frantic day it was sweet potatoes at both lunch and dinner. (She did vary them, adding marshmallows at lunch and pineapple at dinner.)

When it came to the salad course, Mrs. Nesbitt's interpretation of the possibilities came from a long, uniquely American tradition in which any combination of foods, however unlikely, could be designated a salad simply by serving them on a lettuce leaf. "We leaned on salads of every variety," she wrote in *The Presidential Cookbook,* her collection of White House recipes. "Mrs. Roosevelt was especially fond of salads. . . . And even the men, who seemed inclined to frown on vegetables in any form, showed a definite interest in greens when they were fixed in appetizing ways with a tangy dressing." How the men reacted to "Jellied Bouillon Salad" is not recorded. Other salads that appeared on the White House table, and these must have made quite an impression on foreign visitors unfamiliar with the tradition, included "Stuffed Prune Salad," "Ashville Salad" (canned tomato soup in a gelatin ring mold), and "Pear Salad," a hot-weather specialty featuring canned pears covered in cream cheese, mayonnaise, chives, and candied ginger. Mrs. Nesbitt said she sometimes colored the mayonnaise green.

Many of these dishes reflected the American eating habits of her time; others would have been extreme under any circumstances. Not many families began dinner with sticks of fresh pineapple that had been rolled in crushed peppermint candy. But on the whole, Mrs. Nesbitt was setting a familiar if dowdy table, a culinary standard that suited Eleanor very well. She was emphatic about promoting simple, mainstream cuisine as a Roosevelt administration virtue. "I am doing away with all the kickshaws—no hothouse grapes—nothing out of season," she told *The New York Times*. "I plan for good and well-cooked food and see that it is properly served, and that must be enough." And perhaps it would have been, if Mrs. Nesbitt had been able to bring the right instincts or training to her work. She had little of either to draw upon. The arrival of foreign visitors was especially challenging, though she liked to think of herself as rising to the occasion. "For Chinese people I'd always try for a bland menu," she explained in *White House Diary*. "Then for the Mexican dinner I'd have something hot, like Spanish sauce with the chicken." She was especially proud of the nondairy, vegetarian menu she was able to create for the ambassador from Abyssinia and his entourage, who were Coptic Christians, and she carefully kept it on file to reuse when she had to feed Hindus or Muslims. Those who couldn't eat the clam cocktail or the bluefish presumably filled up on the Mexican corn.

A few of the meals in Mrs. Nesbitt's collection are marked "Mrs. Hibben's menu," a reference to a rare dalliance with gourmandise that took place early in the first administration. After the election, Eleanor received a memo from Ernestine Evans, a former journalist and peripatetic literary agent who took an interest in food and thought it could play a useful role in the new White House. Why not showcase American cooking? Menus could include fine regional dishes—"cornbreads and gumbos and chowders"—authentically prepared with local ingredients. Just as the White House regularly supplied the press with the names of the guests at official dinners, it could also supply the menus; and a commitment to focus on America's culinary traditions would assure positive news coverage. Evans said she had the right person in mind to help make this happen: Sheila Hibben, author of *The National Cookbook* and "the best practical cook I know." Perhaps Hibben could work quietly behind the scenes in the White House kitchen for a few months, developing appropriate menus and recipes. "She should be used like a good architect," Evans mused. "She should go back and find out what Jefferson served, and be ready always with a great deal of lore, so that every dish has history as well as savor."

Sheila Hibben was a witty, cosmopolitan food writer who contributed regularly to *The New Yorker* and other chic magazines. In the introduction to *The National Cookbook*, she wrote that she had been inspired to start collecting regional American recipes the day she came across a picture in the Sunday paper of a bowl of soup topped with whipped cream—whipped cream, that is, in the shape of a Sealyham terrier. Off she went on a mission to rescue what was still excellent in American cooking, hoping the best recipes would act as a kind of seawall to protect fine regional cookery against crashing waves of the idiotic, the reductionist, and the dreary. A project that began with indignation, she added, ended in patriotism—"a special sort of patriotism, a real enthusiasm for the riches and traditions of America." Eleanor liked the idea of food that could teach history, and she invited Hibben to visit the White House kitchen and share her ideas and recipes with Mrs. Nesbitt. Alas, there seems to be no record of precisely what happened when Mrs. Nesbitt met this particular challenge to her authority, but in the end, victory went to the housekeeper.

Mrs. Nesbitt's most important adversary, however, wasn't in the kitchen; he was in the Oval Office. She and FDR were at odds from the start. "Father, who would have been an epicure if he had been given the opportunity, began grumbling about the meals served under Mrs. Nesbitt's supervision within a week of her reporting for duty," wrote his son Elliott in a memoir. "Restricted in his wheelchair from dining out except on ceremonial occasions, he was at the mercy of Mrs. Nesbitt's kitchen." FDR liked a decent fried egg in the morning; Mrs. Nesbitt's were invariably overcooked. He longed for a good cup of coffee; Mrs. Nesbitt's was bitter. (Finally she agreed to put a percolator on his tray in the morning, so he could brew his own.) His friends used to send the president gifts of quail, pheasant, and other game birds, which he loved; Mrs. Nesbitt served them dried out and ruined. Reminded that the president didn't like broccoli, she ordered the cook to make it anyway. When FDR asked that coffee be served to the guests he was entertaining in his office—they happened to be royalty—Mrs. Nesbitt sent up iced tea instead. She had no ill will; she was merely incompetent and inflexible, and she was always certain she knew best. Grace Tully, the president's longtime secretary, reported that when he was sick one day, she had asked him if there was anything he particularly wanted. He had a yen for "some of that big white asparagus that comes in cans," he said mournfully, but Mrs. Nesbitt had assured him they could not be found in Washington. (Tully located ten cans and had them delivered that afternoon.) Once, according to Lillian Parks, Eleanor remarked that she was constantly getting requests for White House recipes. "Laughing, FDR said she ought to send some of Henrietta Nesbitt's recipes for brains and sweetbreads—that would certainly dry up requests for recipes in a hurry."

When the president became truly irritated—for instance, after several days in a row of salt fish for breakfast and a similarly unrelieved stretch of liver and beans for lunch—Eleanor treated it blithely. "I had to do a little real housekeeping this morning because I discovered that my husband did not like the breakfasts and lunches that he had been getting!" she noted in "My Day." "It therefore behooves Mrs. Nesbitt and myself to scurry around and get some new ideas." They didn't scurry too hard, however, because Eleanor decided FDR was merely on edge—"in a tizzy," as she put it—owing to the pressures of office. That made sense to Mrs. Nesbitt. "When he said 'The vegetables are watery,' and 'I'm sick of liver and beans,' these were figures of speech," she explained in *White House Diary*.

FDR could have had Mrs. Nesbitt sent right back to Hyde Park the moment he tasted her coffee for the first time, but for all his exasperation, he never insisted that Eleanor change housekeepers. And Eleanor, famous though she was for her thoughtful hospitality, appears to have switched off that gene when it came to serving meals in the White House. The sight of guests toying miserably with their "Eggs Mexican"—rice topped with bananas and fried eggs—had no effect. Mrs. Nesbitt was still working at the White House when FDR died and Truman took over. Bess Truman finally fired her, in frustration, after asking Mrs. Nesbitt numerous times to stop serving brussels sprouts because the family hated them.

Why didn't Eleanor do the same? In part, she found it easy

to sidestep FDR's misery because they spent so little time with each other. She ate lunch, dinner, and often breakfast with her own guests, while FDR had meals in his study with his secretary Missy LeHand and often a few friends and advisers. His most sociable time of day was the cocktail hour, when he took charge of mixing the drinks and encouraged plenty of gossip, laughter, and flirtation. Eleanor couldn't bear this ritual, or indeed any manifestation of FDR's irrepressible appetite for all the good things in life, including women. It charmed his friends, and perhaps it had charmed his bride, but now it was only a source of pain. Often she skipped the cocktail hour, or came in late, or even tried to use it for work, which FDR considered unforgivable. "I remember one day when we were having cocktails," their daughter, Anna, told the biographer Bernard Asbell. "Mother . . . came in and sat down across the desk from Father. And she had a sheaf of papers this high and she said, 'Now, Franklin, I want to talk to you about this.' . . . I just remember, like lightning, that I thought, Oh, God, he's going to *blow*. And sure enough, he blew his top." FDR gave the papers a violent shove across the desk; and Eleanor stood up, expressionless, and walked to another part of the room, where she began talking to a guest. Anna told Asbell that she always suspected her father had encouraged Eleanor to travel so widely in part because he simply didn't want her around all the time.

She and FDR dined together on formal occasions, of course, and when their children and grandchildren showed up for a birthday or a holiday. And they made a point of honoring their longtime custom of Sunday-night suppers, with Eleanor at the chafing dish. Otherwise, as Lillian Parks wrote, "Eleanor and the President were like ships that passed in the night—exchanging signals but seldom stopping to visit." J. B. West said the staff had never seen Eleanor and FDR in a room without others present. "They had the most separate relationship I have ever seen between man and wife," he wrote. She never accompanied FDR to Shangri-La, the presidential retreat later named Camp David, which he cherished as a "secret paradise" far from the Oval Office. Nor did she share his fondness for Warm Springs, Georgia, the rehabilitation center he had established for polio patients, where he loved to swim in the therapeutic springwaters. Eleanor preferred Greenwich Village, where she kept an apartment all her life. They even built separate dream houses. Back in the 1920s Eleanor had established a private domain on the grounds at Hyde Park—a house called Val-Kill, two miles from the main house, which she owned with two of her closest women friends until she bought them out in 1938. Later FDR built his own private getaway on the estate, a cottage he treasured and hoped to retire to, about a mile and a half from Eleanor's.

So they were apart, as usual—Eleanor in Washington and FDR in Warm Springs—when he died of a cerebral hemorrhage on April 12, 1945. His aunt Laura Delano was in Georgia with him; so was his cousin Daisy Suckley, and so was Lucy Mercer, who hastily packed her bags and fled. Despite his long-ago promise, FDR had never given her up. When Eleanor arrived in Warm Springs that night, Laura Delano, long jealous of the president's famous and popular wife, spitefully told her that Lucy had been with FDR when he collapsed, that Lucy had been at Warm Springs for the last three days, and that Lucy had been visiting the White House for years during Eleanor's frequent absences. Listening to this, Eleanor was impassive; and she remained impassive during the long train ride back to Washington. Then, just before the funeral in the East Room of the White House, she said she wanted a few minutes with her husband and asked to have the casket opened. She took off her wedding ring and left it with him.

Most scholars of the Roosevelts have written only perfunctorily on the question of their culinary cold war, with the notable exceptions of Blanche Wiesen Cook and the culinary historian Barbara Haber. For Haber, whose essay "Home Cooking in the FDR White House" was the first extended analysis to take a close look at both the food and Mrs. Nesbitt, much can be explained by Eleanor's strong personal bond with the housekeeper. The fact that people raised a fuss about what they were having for lunch didn't strike Eleanor as any reason to fire a hardworking woman who was one of her most fervent allies, especially since Eleanor herself, in Haber's view, barely tasted what she ate. Cook, by contrast, zeroes in on the marriage. Eleanor had never gotten over the shock and grief of discovering FDR's infidelity. What's more, it was clear to her, as it was clear to everyone in their circle, that he had acquired something of a second wife in the person of Missy LeHand, his most important assistant. Missy was pretty, stylish, and indispensable. She lived in the White House, went in and out of FDR's bedroom in her nightgown, traveled with FDR, acted as hostess for the cocktail-hour gatherings, and understood him better than anyone else did. This was the sort of marriage that appealed to FDR. Eleanor pursued him with pleas for presidential action on her various causes; she was always serious and always on the job. Missy adored him and could make him laugh. Eleanor never tried to dislodge Missy from FDR's life, but three times a day the First Lady made sure that her husband received a large helping of pent-up anger. Cook calls Mrs. Nesbitt "ER's Revenge."

Both these readings move us closer to the heart of the issue, but we can get closer yet—indeed, we can solve this decades-long mystery—if we stop taking for granted Eleanor's legendary indifference to food. Yes, asceticism was a strong aspect of her personality, but what's striking about her culinary asceticism is that she practiced it chiefly in the context of being wife to FDR. Inside the White House, she was apathetic about what was on her plate. Outside, we get glimpses of a very different Eleanor.

Visiting Works Progress Administration projects in Seattle in 1938, for instance, she had lunch with her daughter and son-in-law and singled out the delicious crabs' legs for special mention in "My Day." "After all, when one travels, one should find out the food specialties," she wrote. In San Francisco on a speaking tour: "We went to a marvellous Chinese place for dinner & I think I ate too much!" she told her daughter. After FDR's death, Eleanor launched a fresh career as a writer, speaker, activist, political mentor, and international public conscience; and as she kept up an extraordinary public and private schedule of activities, she dropped appreciative notes on food into "My Day." On a trip to Beirut in 1952 she had a "delicious Arab dinner" and tried her best to convey a sense of the food—"The lamb had a wonderful kind of rice and almonds as a base. The salad was leaves of lettuce with a chopped-up arrangement the base of which was wholewheat"—before giving up, as helpless as any neophyte food writer. In Paris after the war she was never immune to what she was eating, especially at her favorite Left Bank restaurant, Les Porquerolles. "The French don't like you to hurry over a meal, but I had to consult Madame as to what we could order because we had less than an hour in which to enjoy her excellent cooking," she wrote after one visit. "She gave us a wonderful fish soup and then broiled langouste, which is about like our broiled lobster." In fact, she reacted to Paris just the way all the other Americans who turned up in France were reacting in those years—why is everything so delicious here? Why can't we do this at home? "There is one art practiced in this city that we do not treat with quite the same respect. That is the art of cooking and eating," she mused in her column on November 5, 1948. "I am quite sure that if we knew how to cook as well as the French do, we could serve an even more superlative variety of dishes than we do now. We certainly have the necessary ingredients." Two days earlier, Julia Child had arrived in France to begin her own adventure. Writing home, she would express her delight in the food far more eloquently, but the sentiment was the same.

It's not that Eleanor suddenly became obsessed with food or even knowledgeable about it. "She had no idea of cooking, none at all," declared Marguerite Entrup, who worked as Eleanor's cook from 1956 until Eleanor's death in 1962. And yet, as Entrup indicated about these post–White House years, whenever Eleanor ordered a menu for company she always wanted dishes that appealed to her own appetite—hearty, flavorful dishes she hoped everyone would like as much as she did. Any good hostess would do the same, of course—but Eleanor has gone down in history as a woman entirely aloof to the pleasures of food. Now, living on her own and greeted with rapture and respect by crowds around the world, she was eager to give everyone her own favorite dessert. "A pancake dessert," reported Entrup. "You make it large like a layer cake, and she had maple syrup which she used to bring from Vermont and maple sugar. What you had to do was put the maple sugar between, and then you poured the maple syrup over, and you served it warm." It never occurred to Eleanor, Entrup added, that many women were on diets and might not touch such a confection. "She wouldn't think," said Entrup. But Eleanor did think—she thought, for once, about what tasted good.

Eleanor was never a lyrical or evocative writer, but now and then she tried to be, and one such passage appears in a "My Day" column she wrote early in 1936. She had spent a weekend in the country, probably at Val-Kill, with some of her women friends; and in the column she described a long Sunday walk and then a quiet, lazy afternoon by the fire with books and knitting. The maid had gone home, so when suppertime came, she wrote, "We all became very busy housewives" and set to work in the kitchen. "My opportunities to satisfy a craving, natural to nearly all women, are rather rare," she explained; hence she did not try to turn herself into a cook that evening. But she wrote that she enjoyed making salads and setting a pretty table, and that was how she contributed to the meal—tossing the salad and putting out the pewter, the silver, and the blue-and-white china. "There is something healing and life giving in the mere atmosphere surrounding a country house," she concluded.

What was life-giving, in this simple party, was the presence of people she loved. This was the context that allowed her to share "a craving natural to nearly all women" and to handle food and homemaking with pleasure. At Cornell she had discovered that domesticity had a brain; here, in the beloved, safe home that was entirely hers, she was learning that it had a heart. Outside the confines of the White House, she experienced moments so abundant with love that she was inspired to feed people from her own hands. One of her most intimate friends was a former state trooper named Earl Miller, who had been her bodyguard when FDR was governor of New York. She and Earl became very close—some, including her son James, believed they were lovers—and although Earl had a number of women in his life, he and Eleanor remained devoted throughout the White House years and after. Once, in the mid-1930s, she and her ever-present secretary, Malvina ("Tommy") Thompson, spent ten days helping Earl settle into a new house near Albany. "I did the ironing . . . & made popovers which came out well & so feel very satisfied with myself," Eleanor wrote to a friend. Another day she reported—so shyly that she had to be self-effacing about it—"I've actually learned to get breakfast if no one eats anything." And a day later, almost wonderingly, "It's the first time I've ever learned to feel a tinge of confidence in a kitchen." On another visit she baked biscuits for Earl, and she made him an applesauce cake.

Clearly Eleanor had the ability to unleash her senses in the kitchen and at the table—but it wasn't going to happen inside the four walls of the White House. "On the whole, I think I lived those years very impersonally," she wrote in her second memoir, *This I Remember,* which was published four years after FDR's death. "It was almost as though I had erected someone outside myself who was the President's wife. I was lost somewhere deep down inside myself. That is the way I felt and worked until I left the White House." It was "the President's wife" who took charge of White House cuisine, and "the President's wife" who allowed Mrs. Nesbitt to strip the food of character and pound it into submission. But it was Eleanor, away from FDR and ensconced with the people she cherished, who discovered the delights of appetite; and it was Eleanor, "deep down inside myself," who learned what food could mean when love did the cooking.

Eva Braun

(1912–1945)

"How about a bottle of champagne for our farewell? And some sweets? I'm sure you haven't eaten in a long time."

—Eva Braun to Albert Speer, *Inside the Third Reich*

On April 23, 1945, Berlin was rubble and the streets were littered with corpses. Allied bombing had nearly ceased after hundreds of raids, but Soviet artillery fire was intense and the Red Army was starting to encircle the city. Cars, trucks, vans, and motorcycles poured out of Berlin, blocking traffic for miles. That morning Albert Speer, Adolf Hitler's favorite architect and his wartime minister of armaments, was trying to reach the city from Bad Wilsnack, some seventy miles away, but found he couldn't get anywhere near Berlin by car. He turned off and headed toward an airport in Mecklenburg, where he arranged to be flown the rest of the way, escorted by fighter planes. He wanted to say good-bye to Hitler.

The bunker where Hitler was hiding out had been built under the Reich Chancellery more than thirty feet belowground, a warren of rank little rooms wrapped in concrete under a roof some sixteen feet thick, with another six feet of earth atop the concrete. Speer arrived late in the afternoon and spent the next eight hours there as the Third Reich gasped and spluttered toward its end. Hitler was stooped and shaking, his eyes empty. He held a brief situation conference with the remnants of his entourage, but the battle reports from outside were too vague to give them anything to discuss. All he cared about by that time was keeping himself out of Soviet hands, lest the enemy make a public spectacle of his humiliation. He was determined to kill himself before that could happen. Around midnight he went to his bedroom to lie down, and Eva Braun, his longtime mistress, sent word that she would like to see Speer.

Nobody close to Speer, or at least none of the women, could understand how he had become such good friends with Eva. "I could never imagine what they found to talk about," recalled Annemarie Kempf, who worked for Speer throughout his years with Hitler. Speer was a man of education and culture; Eva was a charming lightweight who surrounded herself with pretty things and doted on her two Highland terriers. "She was of course very feminine," Speer told his biographer many years later. "A man's woman, incredibly undemanding for herself." Eva had been living in the bunker for nine days, in private quarters adjoining Hitler's, and was planning to die with him. Speer was struck by how untroubled she seemed, in contrast to the grim, nerve-racked state of everyone else in the bunker. She greeted Speer in full hostess mode.

> Eva Braun radiated an almost gay serenity. "How about a bottle of champagne for our farewell? And some sweets? I'm sure you haven't eaten in a long time." I was touched by her concern; she was the first person to think that I might be hungry after my many hours in the bunker. The orderly brought a bottle of Moët et Chandon, cake, and sweets.

They went on to discuss mutual friends, the skiing they both enjoyed, and their fondness for Munich, Eva's hometown. It was a celebration, an homage to gracious living, staged flawlessly in

Eva Braun with Hitler in the teahouse at Berchtesgaden, 1940.

the face of Eva's expected suicide and whatever awaited Speer at the hands of the Allies. More so than his farewell to Hitler, this interlude with Eva touched Speer deeply at the time and for the rest of his life. He described it with tenderness in his memoir, *Inside the Third Reich,* and returned to the subject years later talking with his biographer. "Oh that girl . . . ," he reflected. "She wished me luck and sent greetings to my wife. It was extraordinary. Don't *you* think it was extraordinary?" He saw nothing unsettling about toasting twelve years of terror, blood, and devastation with a bottle of plundered wine. And evidently, after his long stint underground without a bite to eat, he welcomed the cake.

If every life has a food story, every war has a thousand of them; and the one that has most powerfully defined the Third Reich is its saga of starvation. From the outset, Hitler was determined to avoid the drastic food shortages that swept Germany during World War I, making defeat seem inevitable to an exhausted and despairing population. Hence the Nazis waged war with the intent of forcing conquered nations to feed Germany, not only in the imagined future but immediately. As each nation fell and then struggled under occupation, its grains, fats, and meats were shipped off to Germany, ultimately amounting to nearly half of what the country consumed during the war. Meanwhile the invading army scooped up whatever could be bought or stolen from farms, shops, and restaurants, sending parcels of food back to their families and lugging more with them when they went home on leave. "The Führer repeatedly said, and I repeat after him, if anyone has to go hungry, it shall not be the Germans but other peoples," Hermann Göring announced in 1942. Local populations were left to fend for themselves in what remained of their shops and fields. Malnutrition and its attendant diseases were widespread in western Europe; famine killed thousands of Greeks; and across the Soviet Union and eastern Europe, civilians and prisoners of war were starved as a matter of policy. Within Germany, many of the handicapped and mentally ill—"useless mouths," as they were termed by the Nazis—were deliberately underfed until they wasted away. When rationing was introduced in 1939, it included a separate category for Jews, who were allowed to buy so little food that hunger tore away at many even before they were deported. Images of concentration camp prisoners, skeletal on an allotment of filthy soup and scraps of bread, have become the enduring symbols of that era.

But there were also people who ate very well in Nazi Germany, finding at the table all the convivial warmth that has long hallowed the act of dining. At those same concentration camps, for instance, food for staff and visitors was abundant. "I'm sitting down for lunch of lentil soup with bacon, omelette for dessert," wrote Friedrich Mennecke to his wife on his first day of work at Ravensbrück, the camp near Berlin that had been built especially for women. Mennecke, a food lover who kept his wife up to date on his meals when he was away from home, was a doctor; his job was to watch hundreds of naked prisoners walk by in procession, most of them Jews, prostitutes, the sick, and the mentally ill. Following this "examination," he filled out the forms that sent each to her death. "I feel wonderful," he told his wife one evening after a dinner featuring three different kinds of sausage. "Take more heartfelt kisslets from your lordling and embrace your faithful Fritz-Pa."

This image of plenty constitutes another Third Reich food story: eating and drinking with pleasure at the Nazi table. And it's where we find the food story peculiar to Eva Braun. Although she never joined the Nazi Party and paid scant attention to it until she fell in love with its rising star in 1929, she spent the 1930s and the war years sitting with Hitler and his entourage at countless lunches and dinners. In this setting the familiar domestic rituals of mealtime created a miraculous aura so true to itself and nothing else that Reich officials, their families, and their guests were able to dine at ease in their own charmed space. Food creates community, as we read again and again in culinary history and memoir, and when high-ranking Nazis gathered for a meal, they feasted on the rightness of their cause. Eva, whose place was always next to Hitler, was a mainstay of his domestic life, especially at the Berghof, the mountain retreat in Bavaria that was his favorite place on earth. Whatever Eva learned about Hitler, she kept to herself; whatever they discussed in private, she never reported; whatever she knew about the atrocities he was masterminding had no effect on her devotion. As any sort of influential player in the workings of Nazi Germany, she counted for little. But as a woman—a man's woman, as Speer noted fondly—she was able to generate a guilt-free zone in the heart of Hitlerdom that the squadrons killing children in his name had reason to envy. Passive, faithful, and decorative, Eva's version of femininity came naturally to her, and it functioned to keep her conscience well protected. She lived through the Third Reich encased in a sphere of make-believe morality, a comfortable bubble that held firm until the moment of her death. At the Berghof's well-laden dining table, where Hitler's cronies and their wives assembled regularly, she ate very little.

She took care to maintain a slim figure. Appearances were paramount.

In a three-part *New Yorker* profile that ran in 1936, the magazine's longtime European correspondent Janet Flanner confidently described Hitler as "celibate." Neither his friends nor his enemies, she wrote, could produce evidence of any love affairs, past or present. This was exactly how Hitler and his image makers wanted him to be perceived. Here was a leader who had given himself to the nation and now stood at its helm in solitary grandeur—no wife, no children, and certainly no smiling mistress twenty-three years his junior. For this reason Eva did not go out in public with Hitler, or greet his foreign visitors, or dine at his side on official occasions. When he received important guests at the Berghof, she had to stay upstairs in her private quarters. There was no danger of unwanted publicity in the German press, which had been stifled since the Nazi takeover in 1933. Abroad, however, occasional rumors slipped through the veil of propaganda. In November 1939, *Life* published several photographs of Hitler, including one with "Evi Braun," who was identified as a girlfriend but a platonic one. And a month later *The Saturday Evening Post*, relying on "sources inside Germany which we have always found dependable," reported that Hitler and "Evi" were secretly married. (Evi, according to the *Post*, was often seen in the Chancellery kitchen preparing salads, potato dumplings, and apple strudel.)

This notion of Hitler's secret hausfrau busily at work on potato dumplings tells us more about how the American press categorized women in the 1930s than about Eva herself, who probably never made a potato dumpling in her life and most certainly did not eat them. (As we'll see, she was a committed dieter.) Yet Eva's relationship with food did have something in common with the *Post*'s invented version of it. The magazine was trying to figure out how best to characterize this unlikely female as the leading lady of the Reich, and that was Eva's project as well. It wasn't easy: she had chosen a fantasy that demanded constant buttressing, and she, too, called on food—including champagne and sweets in the face of catastrophe—to help sustain it.

Fantasy was a great comfort to Eva, so much so that it's often difficult to glimpse her through the dreams of glory she assiduously piled up around herself—the glamorous wardrobe she assembled, the reels of home movies full of Bavarian merrymaking. She's not the only woman in this book whose life changed course after she fell in love, but she's the only one who made sure her life would never change course again. Nothing existed for her outside the context of her devotion to Hitler and the epic romance she constructed around the two of them. That's where we must look for her food story, and to a very great extent it will be Hitler's story, too. There was no Eva without him.

One of the photographs *Life* had obtained was a picture of Hitler, stern-faced in a trench coat, with the Bavarian Alps behind him. It had been taken by Eva herself. "Obviously not good photography," the caption noted, implying that only the picture's news value merited its placement on *Life*'s famous pages. Eva would have been irritated by such a dismissal. She had been an enthusiastic amateur photographer since she was thirteen; it was one of her few interests apart from sports and dancing. When she left school at seventeen, the first place she looked for work was a Munich photography studio called Photo Hoffmann, where Heinrich Hoffmann gave her a job as his general assistant. Hoffmann, an avid Nazi who had joined the party shortly after it was founded, was often busy with his most important client, a well-known but secretive politician who kept close control over his public image. In the studio Hoffmann referred to him as "Herr Wolf." According to Eva's mother, who told this story to an American interviewer in 1948, Eva was standing on a ladder one day, retrieving something from a high shelf, when Herr Wolf came into the studio. She took no notice of him until Hoffmann called her to come down from the ladder and run out to get beer and *Leberkäse*, a Bavarian sausage, for his guest. When she returned, she placed a mug of beer and the sausage in front of Herr Wolf, and the two of them glanced at each other over the food. The client was forty, with blue eyes and a scrubby mustache; Eva was a pretty teenager. She said politely, *"Guten Appetit."* They were the first words she ever spoke to Hitler. Then she blushed.

At the time Franziska Braun gave this account, three years after the war, the Brauns were in the midst of a court battle against the author of a salacious book purporting to be Eva's newly discovered diary. The court eventually ruled in their favor, finding that the author had plagiarized most of his text from the 1913 memoirs of a Viennese countess and invented the remainder. But the book was generating a great deal of lurid press coverage, and the Brauns were more bitterly sensitive than ever about the family's reputation. Meanwhile they had been tapped for questioning by Judge Michael Musmanno, who was leading an American investigation into Hitler's death and the possibility that he might still be alive. Dozens of Hitler's former associates were being interviewed, and a member of Musmanno's team had gone to see the Brauns at home, where they seemed to welcome the chance to . . . if not exactly right the record, then tilt it in a slightly more favorable direction. The interviewer described them as quite voluble, especially after the whiskey and wine that accompanied his visit. Franziska, who seemed eager to tell the story of Eva's initial encounter with Hitler, insisted that her version was the only accurate one of the many that had circulated. It came directly from a witness, she said, someone working for Hoffmann "who volunteered to testify in behalf of Eva if he were ever needed." Perhaps it was the blush that made this particular story so important to Eva's mother. Her daughter was the innocent here, not the temptress, and Hoffmann had thrown her directly in the path of the aptly named Herr Wolf.

"We come from a decent bourgeois family," Eva's father emphasized in the same interview. Fritz Braun said he had been a teacher in a Munich technical school, with no interest in Hitler or the Nazis—"I disliked politics and my wife did too"—when Eva suddenly began turning on the radio and listening to Hitler's speeches. "We thought it was just a flapper's admiration, the same as all women liked him and fell for him," Fritz said. Asked when he and Franziska had learned about the relationship, Fritz turned the question over to his wife.

"That was in 1933, shortly after the seizure of power," Franziska said. The Brauns had taken a day trip by car to Berchtesgaden, the charming Bavarian village that was a popular sightseeing destination; and on this occasion Franziska suggested they drive on up into the Alps to Obersalzberg, where the new chancellor had a house, for a look at the place everyone was talking about. "I was very much disappointed, for it was just a small house, nothing like later," she recalled. "All the people were standing in front, shouting 'We want to see our Fuehrer, we want to see our Fuehrer.' Well, I didn't want to see him, so I said we want to drive back." On the way back to Munich they made their usual stop for coffee at an inn called the Lambacher Hof, famous for its cakes and Bavarian atmosphere. "When we had got out of our car, a big car drove up [and] out jumps our daughter Eva," Franziska said. "I rubbed my eyes, I thought I had not seen right. I went up to her and said: 'Eva, you? What are you doing in this car?' And my husband came up too and said to her very strictly: 'Where have you come from, what does this mean?' She [said] very roughly and flippantly, 'I come from the Berghof.'" With that, she swept into the café and disappeared into a room reserved for Hitler.

Then another car drove up, and Hitler himself got out. "I suddenly knew why Eva had talked such a lot about the Fuehrer, why she always urged us to believe in him," said Franziska. She and Fritz were now desperate to leave, but an adjutant was summoning them—"The Braun parents, please"—and they understood they had no choice. They went inside the café. Hitler put Franziska in the seat next to him and kept up an amiable stream of chitchat about the cakes and the beauty of the scenery. Nobody mentioned his relationship with Eva, but when Hitler spoke to her using *"du"*—the intimate form of "you"—Franziska knew they were a couple. At the end of this excruciating social hour, Eva left with the entourage and didn't say good-bye. When she turned up at home later that night, her father demanded, "Is it true that you are the Fuehrer's mistress?" and she retorted, "What of it? If you don't like it I'll leave altogether."

But she couldn't leave home; she couldn't afford to. She made only a small salary at Hoffmann's. So the family went on together with its awkward secret, the parents mortified that she was anybody's mistress, let alone Hitler's. Eva had never been close to her older sister, Ilse, who worked for a Jewish doctor until 1937. But the younger sister, Gretl, who looked up to Eva, decided to become a follower of Hitler herself and began hovering at the radio, listening eagerly to his speeches.

Forgeries notwithstanding, Eva did keep diaries, and a few pages from one of them survives. Written during this period, it was obtained by the U.S. government after the war and is now in the National Archives. She started writing on her twenty-third birthday, February 6, 1935, and continued sporadically until May 28, when the last entry ends in the middle of a page. Unlike most of what we know about Eva, this is rare information that comes directly from her and opens a tiny but genuine window onto her mind and heart. What the handwritten pages reveal, disconcertingly, is not a young woman of twenty-three, but a lovelorn teenager, with all the narcissism and melodrama endemic to that age, as if she had stopped moving ahead in her life the moment she met Hitler and simply burrowed deeper and deeper into her obsession with him. Why, oh why didn't he come over on her birthday? And where was her present? Flowers didn't count; he should have given her a puppy or at least some nice jewelry. How could he stay away, on this of all days? A week and a half later he dropped by, and she was delirious—"I am so infinitely happy that he loves me so and pray that it will always be like this"—but a couple of weeks later he skipped a promised date and she was "mortally unhappy" again. She started wishing she were "seriously ill," for maybe he would pay attention to her if she were. "Why doesn't something happen to me? Why do I have to suffer like this?" That spring Hitler was setting up the German air force and building a submarine fleet, both initiatives in violation of the Treaty of Versailles, and in the fall he issued the Nuremberg Laws, which stripped German Jews of the rights of citizenship. Eva found such preoccupations bothersome and couldn't understand why they took up so much of his time. "Agreed that he's been busy with political problems but have not things eased off? And how about last year when he had lots of worries with Röhm and with Italy and still found time for me?" She might have been complaining about a boyfriend who spent too much time at soccer practice.

In May, Eva learned from Hoffmann's wife that Hitler could be interested in someone else—the six-foot British debutante Unity Valkyrie Mitford, who was living in Munich and was passionately devoted to him and to the Nazi Party. (Her middle name had been suggested by her grandfather, a friend of Wagner's.) "Her name is WALKURE and she looks it, including her legs," Eva wrote irritably. She didn't really believe Hitler had fallen for Mitford, but he had barely spoken a word to Eva in three months and she was in despair. On May 28 she sent him a "decisive" letter and vowed that if he didn't respond that evening, she would take an overdose of sleeping pills.

It would be her second attempt at suicide, both of them perhaps cries for help, certainly cries for attention. Three years earlier, in the autumn of 1932, Hitler was flying from city to city delivering as many speeches as he could cram into a day, whipping up support for the Nazis in preparation for the general elections to be held on November 6. Eva spent the time moping and wishing he would call. On the evening of November 1, when Hitler had just spoken in four different venues and was preparing for yet another big speech the next day, she took her father's wartime pistol and shot herself, aiming for the jugular or perhaps not, but at any rate missing it. Ilse found her and summoned help, Hitler hastily showed up with flowers, and Eva seems to have counted the event a success.

Now it was 1935 and they were three years deeper into their

relationship, but nothing of substance had changed. "The weather is gorgeous, and I, the mistress of Germany's and the world's greatest man, have to sit at home and look at it through the window." She settled on twenty pills rather than the thirty-five she had originally planned, and fell into a coma, but once again she survived thanks to another rescue on Ilse's part. This time the outcome was far more satisfactory: by the end of the year Hitler had installed her in a house of her own. At last she was independent, or at least no longer dependent on the parents who so deeply disapproved of her; and the teenage angst started to drop away. What's more, she now had mono-grammed linen, direct phone lines to Berlin and the Berghof, art on the walls (courtesy of German museums), a well-stocked wine cellar, and a maid. Gretl lived there with her, and nearby was the flat where "the world's greatest man" stayed when he was in Munich. Real life, or as close as she would ever come to it, had begun.

Much as she relished her Munich house, Eva's most important home was the Berghof, in effect her primary residence starting in the mid-1930s. Hitler could show up at almost any time, and when he did, he would settle in for as long as possible. Atop the mountain, his all-powerful private secretary, Martin Bormann, had organized the destruction of the idyllic village of Obersalzberg in order to create a sprawling Nazi headquarters complete with SS barracks, guardhouses, air-raid shelters, staff housing, guesthouses, a garage, and a hotel for visiting dignitaries, as well as a big house for the Führer. Eva's job was to live there and wait for him. The Berghof was the place where Eva could most easily don her favorite role: Hitler's beloved consort, the enchanting woman on his arm, the lady of the house. This fantasy didn't always run smoothly, since she had to be hustled out of sight whenever anybody arrived who wasn't supposed to know about her—she was furious when she wasn't allowed to meet the Duke and Duchess of Windsor—but it was a workable version of a shared domestic life, and she made the most of it.

All morning she looked forward to lunch, the main meal of the day and the high point of official social life at the Berghof. Hitler never saw anyone but aides and associates before that time, and guests invited to lunch often waited for hours while his meetings went on and on. Eva, who was known to change clothes up to seven times a day, was always beautifully dressed for this protracted meal. It was a chance for her to enjoy her status as hostess, if not precisely in public, then at least surrounded by company. Ten or twenty people were usually at the table, including Hitler's staff and other officials, sometimes their wives, and sometimes one or two of Eva's women friends, who visited regularly. Her parents, too, came to stay from time to time—they had grown accustomed to her situation and could see the advantages. Fritz had been advised to join the Nazi Party, which he did, and Eva brought her mother along on shopping trips to Italy. Her sister Gretl was such a frequent guest that she ended up marrying an SS general in a splashy Obersalzberg wedding. Even Ilse was allowed to visit, once she had quit her job in the Jewish doctor's office.

Albert Speer, who had a house and studio not far from the Berghof, attended countless meals there. In his second volume of memoirs, drafted in Spandau Prison while he was serving a twenty-year sentence for war crimes and crimes against humanity, he described the ritual gathering for drinks that typically preceded a summer lunch.

On the terrace we would stand around informally while the ladies stretched out on the wicker reclining chairs with cushions covered in red-and-white gingham. The ladies sunned themselves as if they were at some spa, for being tanned was the fashion. Liveried attendants, select SS men from Sepp Dietrich's Bodyguard Regiment, with perfect manners that seemed a shade too intimate, handed around drinks: champagne, vermouth and soda, or fruit juices. Sooner or later Hitler's valet would appear and report that the Führer would join us in ten minutes. . . . At the news of Hitler's imminent arrival, the buzz of conversation becomes more muted, the bursts of laughter cease. The women drop murmurs as they continue chatting about clothes and traveling. . . . Hitler appears in civilian dress, in a well-tailored suit that is somewhat too loud. His tie is not well chosen. Weeks ago Eva Braun several times proposed that she pick out suitable ties from his collection, but he ignored the offers. . . . His slight paunch gives his whole appearance a portly, comfortable cast.

Hitler greets each of the guests with friendly words and asks about everyone's children, personal plans, and circumstances. From the moment of his entrance the scene has changed. Everyone is tense, visibly trying to make a good impression. . . .

Another half-hour passes before we are asked to table. Hitler leads the way alone, Bormann following with Eva Braun.

Everyone had an assigned place at the long table. Eva always sat on Hitler's left, and the others looked for their names, written on the paper envelopes that held the napkins at each place. The china was Rosenthal, "a hand-painted flower pattern on a white background," wrote Traudl Junge in her memoir, *Until the Final Hour*. Junge, a secretary who went to work for Hitler in 1942 when she was twenty-two, never forgot the first lunch she had at the Berghof, in part because all morning she had been dreading the food. Hitler's vegetarian diet was notorious, and she was afraid the company would have to eat linseed mush along with him. To her relief, Hitler received a special tray with his meal on it, and the food that arrived for everyone else was comfortably recognizable. "Two orderlies brought large dishes of various salads for each side of the table and began serving down both sides from the middle. Two others asked what we would like to drink. The salad seemed to be a kind of starter, because everyone began eating it at once. But then the next course appeared too: braised beef marinated in vinegar and herbs, with creamed potatoes and young beans." This, of course, was sauerbraten, a traditional pot roast popular everywhere in Germany.

Speer's wife, Margarete, who was often invited with her husband, once wrote down her memories of the Berghof for her grandchildren and described an ambience so pleasant and easygoing it's possible to forget that this was a table full of Nazis, which perhaps was her intention. She called the food "nothing extravagant" but noted that it was always prepared well. "They never talked politics," she added. "They talked theater, opera, they liked talking about famous actors, singers." Once, according to Hitler's closest aide, Heinz Linge, an argument broke out at the table about the best way to make Bavarian meatballs. The Führer urged all the ladies to go right into the kitchen and prepare their own versions so that the men could compare them. Soon the table was laden with meatballs, some of them rolling about haphazardly; unfortunately Linge did not record the winner.

The group spent about an hour at the table and then set out

for a walk down through the meadows to a teahouse that had been built about twenty minutes from the main house, on a high bluff with a sweeping view across the valley toward Salzburg. Junge said the teahouse looked like a silo from the outside, but inside there was a large round room with marble walls and oversize windows looking out on the dazzling vista. Heavy armchairs were set around an enormous coffee table, and the guests were served coffee or tea. "Hitler himself would have apple-peel tea or sometimes caraway tea, never anything else," she wrote. "He ate freshly baked apple-cake with it and perhaps a couple of biscuits. The rest of us were given pastries bought in Berchtesgaden, and some of them could be stale and hard to chew." Junge rarely had a complaint about the way she was housed or fed, so the pastries on at least some afternoons must have been poor indeed. Meanwhile people were trying to converse, but it was difficult to keep a general discussion going except in voices loud enough to carry across the room, and once Hitler dropped off to sleep, as he usually did, nobody wanted to shout. When he woke up, the party was allowed to disperse. By then it was close to six p.m.

At the time Junge began participating in these all-afternoon lunches, wartime rationing had been in force for three years and the nation had been pursuing the goal of self-sufficiency in food for nearly a decade. When the Nazis seized power, they pushed industry and rearmament to the center of the economy, a shift of resources that demanded major reductions in spending on food imports. But foreign countries supplied a great deal of what appeared on the German table, both directly—coffee, bananas, oranges—and indirectly, such as the fodder that was essential for

Germany's meat and dairy industries. Meanwhile the emphasis on building up industry and the military meant that the rate of unemployment was dropping, leaving in its wake a more affluent population ready to spend money on these very foods. Throughout the 1930s, and especially after 1936, when Hitler announced the Four-Year Plan that would prepare Germany for war, the Nazis directed torrents of propaganda at homemakers in an effort to turn back the culinary tide and overhaul the nation's eating habits. The Nazi ideal was an all-German diet in the service of Aryan vigor, a regimen based on the whole grains, fruits, and vegetables that could be obtained locally. No foreign fruits, small portions of meat, little butter, no cream, ersatz coffee, and inventive ways with potato skins were among the principles of the patriotic kitchen. White bread, long preferred in Germany as elsewhere, was to be shunned in favor of rye and whole-grain loaves, for wheat was scarce and rye was plentiful. Hence *Vollkornbrot,* or wholemeal bread, a dark loaf heavy with bran, became an important icon of the Reich. Quark, a soft, fresh cheese made from curdled milk, had been known in Germany for centuries, but it was given a starring role and massive publicity as the spread that could take the place of butter. Perhaps the most ardently promoted emblem of culinary nationalism was *Eintopf-Sonntage,* or "stew Sundays," a custom instituted by the Nazis in 1933 and retained through the 1930s and the war years. On the first Sunday of the month, from October through March, dinner at home or in a restaurant was supposed to consist of a simple stew made from inexpensive, all-German ingredients. The money thus saved was to be donated to a fund for the unemployed, and party members called on their neighbors personally to collect the coins.

Hitler's kitchen dutifully observed *Eintopf-Sonntage*—Speer remarked that guests were notably fewer on those Sundays—but otherwise the household seems to have ignored many of the restrictions imposed on the rest of the country. When local residents swarmed across Obersalzberg after the war to explore what remained of the Berghof and other Nazi dwellings, they found underground bunkers stocked with massive supplies of sugar, tinned butter, coffee beans, champagne, cognac—enough to make it clear that Hitler and his circle were not skimping in wartime or any other time. And indeed, according to Junge's memoir and other accounts, meat (including the sauerbraten she never forgot) was served regularly, imported oranges were available, cakes and puddings were abundant despite the sugar and fats rations, and the breakfast table offered white bread, demonized though it was. (Junge noted that it was supposed to be reserved for guests with "delicate stomachs" who couldn't digest the *Vollkornbrot*.) A pat of butter appeared on every breakfast plate, and Junge made no mention of being served quark. Most luxurious of all, especially during the war, was a regular supply of fresh produce, available year-round. Bormann had set up what he intended to be a model farm, with cattle, pigs, an aviary, a cider mill, crops, and orchards. The idea was to demonstrate the most efficient methods of agriculture and animal husbandry, but despite his claims of being an expert agronomist, the farm produced very little. Heinz Linge remembered Hitler caustically remarking that the cost of producing a liter of milk on the farm was approximately twenty times what they would have paid to have it delivered from a local dairy. Even the orchard did so poorly that if they wanted to use the cider mill, they had to buy apples locally. But the greenhouses ran very well, and wherever Hitler happened to be dining—Berlin, Munich, or Obersalzberg—there was never a shortage of fresh flowers or vegetables. "Here on the Berghof in March the whole party was enjoying young cucumbers, radishes, mushrooms, tomatoes, and fresh green lettuce," Junge marveled.

Speer, whose father made a fortune as an architect and whose mother was fixated on every nuance of social status, had grown up in a richly furnished mansion run by a fleet of uniformed servants. He said the atmosphere at the Berghof reminded him of "the summer residence of a prosperous industrialist"—relaxed, that is, and far less formal than one would expect from the great and remote ruler of the Reich. His mother took a different view: as an occasional guest at the Berghof she found the place appalling. It was the errors of class that offended her. "How nouveau riche everything is there," she remarked. "Even the way the meals are served is impossible, the table decorations crude. Hitler was terribly nice. But such a parvenu world!" Maybe she was thinking of the containers of toothpicks on the table. Even Traudl Junge was a little surprised to see those.

Hitler had no wish to project an image of himself as someone who lived amid the trappings of the elite. He avoided showing off a luxury-laden table, and the food was largely unpretentious. He did want to be able to mingle comfortably with the rich, since their support was crucial to the Nazi Party, and early in his rise he made a point of learning the courtly manners he believed the role demanded. (Speer recalled that when Hitler met Elisabeth Förster-Nietzsche, the philosopher's sister, he greeted her using a highly ornate German he hoped would be suitable: "Most gracious and respected madam, what a pleasure to have the privilege of finding you in the best of health in your esteemed home.") But guests and staff who mention the meals in their memoirs typically recall dumplings, sausages, meatballs, roast pork, stews, and spaghetti—classic home cooking of the pre-Nazi era. There were no restaurant chefs at the Berghof: Hitler's half sister, Angela Raubal, did the cooking when he first moved there, but she got along badly with Eva and didn't last long once Hitler's mistress began spending more time in Obersalzberg. Later he installed husband-and-wife teams to run the household, and the wives customarily took charge of the food.

Arthur Kannenberg, who acted as majordomo at the Reich Chancellery and did the same at the Berghof when important guests were scheduled, was the only culinary professional on staff, apart from the special-diet cooks who prepared Hitler's vegetarian meals. Kannenberg had been a restaurateur: he understood formal entertaining and oversaw the waiters in Hitler's households, who had been recruited from the SS and trained in professional table service. He also made sure that the floral arrangements were properly lavish, however simple the menu might be—the staff was convinced, in fact, that the flowers cost more than the food. Once Kannenberg tried to liven up a dinner menu by introducing the Führer to caviar. Hitler loved it and downed it by the spoonful whenever it was served, until he found out how much it cost. Thereupon he banished it—not so much because of the expense, but because of the image. "The idea of a caviar-eating Leader was incompatible with Hitler's conception of himself," wrote Speer.

Hitler knew his eating habits would be talked about, along with everything else the public could glean about his personal life, and by the early 1930s an official version of his daily life had been established, casting him as a man of modest ways and simple tastes. Reporters from the foreign press who tapped their sources for human-interest stories about the Führer invariably "discovered" that he was a vegetarian who lived with monklike austerity. William L. Shirer, the CBS correspondent, said he learned from "my spies" that Hitler got up early and had a seven a.m. breakfast of rolls and marmalade with a glass of milk or juice. "He is of course a vegetarian, teetotaller, and non-smoker," Shirer reported. In truth Hitler never got up before noon, but the propaganda decreed otherwise.

Meanwhile the pro-Nazi journalists who supplied British and American publications with admiring profiles of Hitler throughout the 1930s were coming up with a range of flattering ways to describe his eating habits. Food struck them as an excellent rhetorical instrument for civilizing and humanizing a dictator. "Even in his meatless diet, Hitler is something of a gourmet," explained George Fitz-Gerald, who published widely under the pseudonym "Ignatius Phayre." "His Bavarian chef, Herr Kannenberg, contrives an imposing array of vegetarian dishes, savoury and rich, pleasing to the eye as well as to the palate, and all conforming to the dietic [*sic*] standards which Hitler exacts." This story appeared in the British magazine *Home & Gardens,* and Fitz-Gerald concocted a similar one for *Country Life,* in which he described how Hitler rose at dawn and headed out for a solitary ramble in the hills, breakfasting on a few tomato sandwiches that he brought with him. Another author, identified as "Hedwig Mauer Simpson," which was probably a pseudonym, wrote a piece in much the same spirit for *The New York Times Magazine*. No early morning tomato sandwiches here; instead she said that Hitler emerged from his bedroom around nine a.m. for a nutritious breakfast of oatmeal and prunes. "He is not indifferent to meals," she was eager to assure the *Times'* readers. "He likes well-cooked dishes; he can eat a gooseberry pie or a well-done pudding with relish, and he makes no secret of being fond of chocolate. He likes to see color on his table, and excellent tomatoes are supplied from near-by greenhouses, in which rows of ultra-violet lamps ripen fruit for his table. A fresh salad is served with almost every meal."

George Ward Price, the foreign correspondent for the *Daily Mail*, one of Britain's most enthusiastically pro-Hitler newspapers, attended a formal dinner party at the Chancellery in December 1934 that was clearly staged for propaganda purposes, though he was happy to take it at face value. Hitler was in evening dress, he emphasized, not Nazi uniform—in other words, here was a gentleman—and arrangements of "trailing pink begonias" decorated the table. "The menu, too, was of up-to-date simplicity. It consisted of a cup of thick white soup, fish, roast chicken and vegetables, and an ice, and was accompanied by white and red German wine." Mrs. Beeton herself could have catered this meal, and not a morsel of it would have looked unusual, much less threatening, to any reader living comfortably in England. David Lloyd George, the former British prime minister who called Hitler "the greatest German of the age" and likened *Mein Kampf* to the Magna Carta, had a different though equally stageworthy experience when he visited the Berghof in 1936. His party stayed for tea and was offered a meal so simple it was practically rustic—"slices of cold ham and halves of hard-boiled eggs," noted Thomas Jones, a former deputy secretary of the cabinet, who accompanied Lloyd George. "The Führer himself had what looked like Zwiebacks and petit beurre biscuits and butter and ate very little." Normally Hitler ate cakes with abandon at teatime, but on this occasion he apparently wanted the British to see him as humble and abstemious—again, a man whom nobody need fear.

While the Führer was indeed a vegetarian, he interpreted the term as loosely as most vegetarians have done for centuries. He loved the sausages of Munich, as his loyal photographer

Heinrich Hoffmann was well aware when he sent Eva out to fetch the *Leberkäse* that morning in 1929; and if he happened to eat at the party's guesthouse at the Berghof, he would order the liver dumplings. Not until around 1931 did he launch his vegetarian diet, partly because he hoped it would cure his chronic intestinal distress. He was what the nineteenth century would have called "dyspeptic"—perpetually assailed by digestive problems, real or imagined. Often he decided he was strong enough to take normal food, such as his favorite spaghetti or a few eggs and potatoes; other times he wanted gruel and crispbread, and sometimes it was a whole meal made up of potatoes, strawberries, and ice cream. He ate fast and he ate a lot. Franziska Braun said she was always surprised to see how much he put away—second helpings of everything, including the pudding he always had for dessert.

Nor was he a firm teetotaler, despite many reports that had him refusing alcohol in any form. He didn't drink often, but he had no objection to it on principle and avoided wine only because it was "sour." Once an associate saw him spooning sugar into a glass of fine Gewürztraminer and drinking it down happily. Hitler's addiction was to sweets: he had a perpetual, ferocious craving for cakes, pastries, and biscuits. Franziska Braun described him at tea one afternoon piling her own plate high with all his favorites, far more than she could eat, telling her how good each one was, and urging her to try it. Friedelind Wagner, the composer's granddaughter and a fervent anti-Nazi, remembered Hitler eating two pounds of pralines a day when he was visiting Bayreuth. While planning the invasion of Norway, his aide Heinz Linge wrote, he kept darting out of the conference room to gobble sweets in his study. Linge asked if he was hungry, but Hitler said no. "For me, sweets are the best food for the nerves," he explained. Even in the bunker, as the Russians approached and his own death loomed, he was stuffing himself with cake.

At the Berghof, the food on Hitler's personal tray came from a special-diet kitchen built alongside the main kitchen. He was intensely concerned about what he was served each day and often complained about his meals, fuming about how difficult it was to find a good vegetarian cook. When Ion Antonescu, the Romanian dictator, came to dinner in 1943, he said that he, too, had suffered from stomach problems until he hired a young Viennese woman named Marlene von Exner, who had been trained in dietetics. She had cured his ailments in three months. Hitler immediately hired von Exner and was delighted with the food, especially her soups and her fine Viennese desserts. Christa Schroeder, a secretary close to Hitler for twelve years, said he raved about von Exner's apple pies—"very thin pastry with thick layers of apple slices and if possible a small topping of whipped cream." A year or so later, however, a background check on the cook revealed the possibility of Jewish blood on her mother's side. Von Exner's family was actively pro-Nazi; nonetheless Hitler told her, regretfully, that he had to let her go because he couldn't bend the law against employing Jews without attracting criticism. He did instruct Bormann to issue documents that would aryanize her whole family, so they wouldn't run into this problem again. (After the war, von Exner was arrested and sent to an internment camp for a year. "The reason was that Frau von Exner had not poisoned the Fuehrer," Junge told an interviewer on Musmanno's team. "She answered, 'I was employed as cook and not as murderess.'") Von Exner's replacement in the diet kitchen was Constanze Manziarly, who came from the southern Tyrol and tilted her cooking toward what Junge called "the Italian way." Hitler liked her cooking very much, and Manziarly became one of his most faithful employees, making spaghetti for him on the day he died.

Eva refused to share Hitler's obsessions—she found his dietary regimen disgusting and said so—but she had her own complicated relationship with food, a combination of covetous delight and rigorous avoidance. She adored the special treats that came her way as the Führer's favorite, but nothing was more important to her than being able to show off a slender figure. The woman who starred in her daydreams as leading lady of the Reich was always picture-perfect, a term we can take literally in Eva's case, for as we'll see, she loved being on camera. So she ate with care, as lightly as possible from a menu often dense with pork and potatoes; and if her weight went up at all, she ate even less. Her cousin Gertrude, who visited Eva at the Berghof in 1944, keeping her company when nobody else was around, said she was always fixated on her figure and at mealtime wanted only salad and fruit. "She hated fat women and was very proud of being slim and dainty," wrote Traudl Junge. Hitler used to say he preferred women who looked like women, not boys, and once he told Junge she was too thin and should be eating more. "Eva Braun cast me a scornful glance, for compared to her I was the image of a buxom Bavarian rustic maiden."

At the same time, however, Eva never denied herself anything she really wanted, and when she was at home in Munich, Hitler made sure her kitchen was amply supplied. In 1942, as German soldiers plundered the Ukraine, he had special food parcels sent to Eva, with an extra stash of Ukrainian bacon since she was very fond of it. She liked to feel pampered. For the drive from Munich to Berchtesgaden, she always ordered her maid to pack a substantial snack—sandwiches, coffee or tea, some chicken—though she was rarely hungry and the food often went uneaten.

She resisted sweets, she resisted fatty foods, but like everyone else she knew, Eva drank champagne. Heinz Linge, Hitler's aide, used to see her sitting with Hitler in his study at night, wearing a dressing gown, having champagne while he drank tea. She and her cousin Gertrude drank champagne every night when the two of them were alone at the Berghof; and when the house was full of company, as it usually was, champagne appeared regularly. Guests were offered a glass before lunch and dinner, and again at the evening's entertainment, typically a movie or two, unless Hitler felt like listening to a recording of one of his favorite operettas. (He loved *The Merry Widow*.) When he and Eva finally retired to their private quarters, to everyone's relief, the group relaxed into conviviality and more champagne was poured. It was the social fuel of the Reich.

Many Germans, to be sure, used the term "champagne" to indicate any sort of sparkling wine, from locally produced *Sekt* to the finest French vintages. Often, in fact, people seem to have used *"Sekt"* and "champagne" interchangeably—the original sin in the French wine industry, which has long insisted that only sparkling wines from the Champagne region deserve the honored name of "Champagne," always capitalized. But casual drinkers in other countries have typically ignored this distinction. In the original German-language version of the incident quoted at the start of this chapter, for instance, Eva greeted Speer in the bunker with an offer of *"Sekt."* What arrived was a bottle of Moët & Chandon, as she surely knew it would. Hence it's not always easy to determine precisely what was in the glass when the term "*Sekt*," "champagne," or "sparkling wine" turns up in a diary or memoir. But judging from the context as well as the nature of those doing the drinking, it's usually possible to make a good guess; and some recollections were indeed specific. Writing in his diary in Spandau Prison, Speer remembered quite clearly that Göring had appropriated vast quantities of vintage Roederer, while Hitler's household "had to make do with Moët et Chandon."

Few of the Nazi officials swarming the Reich after 1933 had grown up drinking champagne of any sort, but with their political legitimacy they suddenly had access to high society and all its glamour. (Hitler's professed antielitism did not filter down very far into the ranks.) Bella Fromm, the anti-Nazi journalist who became Berlin's first society columnist in 1928 and covered the diplomatic scene for the next ten years, watched with disgust as the city's most resplendent homes opened their doors to the new elite. "Torrents of champagne bubbled down their greedy throats," she wrote in her diary after a reception attended by numerous high-booted Nazis. At the time, they had been in power only ten months, and a longtime diplomat standing next to her observed that an abundant supply of champagne was, in fact, the main attraction of the evening. "Most of the new gang did not know before January, 1933, that things like champagne, caviar, and the like would ever be within their reach," he commented as the guests pounded up the marble stairway to the bar. "They knew them only from window displays in expensive shops." Fromm had Jewish ancestry, but thanks to numerous useful connections she was able to keep working until 1938, when friends arranged an American visa for her. Meanwhile she went everywhere, met everyone, including Hitler (who kissed her hand, to her horror), and took notes on all of it, including the grotesque birthday party Göring threw for himself at the Berlin State Opera, in 1937—"cleared of seats for the occasion," she noted. "Dinner started with mountains of caviar. Champagne ran in a continual gushing stream all night long. The lavishness was on a scale almost bordering on insanity."

Three years later the Nazis took over France, and champagne became the celebratory leitmotif of the occupation. When the first German soldiers arrived in Paris on June 14, 1940, it was dawn and nothing was open, but by lunchtime they were sitting in cafés ordering champagne. "It's like a liquid symbol of their conquest of Gay Paree," wrote Janet Flanner in *The New Yorker*. "They demand and expect champagne wherever they go. As one peasant said, '*Ces cochons*, they come into my cottage and ask me for champagne—I, who have never given myself anything better than a bottle of *mousseux*, even for my son's first Communion.'" In the province of Champagne, which was located in the northern two-thirds of France that came under direct military occupation, soldiers looted homes and cellars freely all summer until more organized forms of plunder could be put into place. By autumn Germany was demanding regular shipments of champagne, up to two million bottles a month, to be paid for at the low prices guaranteed by manipulating exchange rates. The Nazis also soaked up most of the other wine being produced, as well as all the wine held in reserve. Harry Flannery, the CBS reporter who replaced Shirer in Berlin, was on Wilhelmstrasse one day in 1941 when he saw "huge trucks, filled to the top with cases of French wines . . . being unloaded in front of the Propaganda Ministry." Soon afterward he found he was drinking that very wine, served with ample quantities of roast beef, at a banquet staged by the head of the Nazi press office. The French themselves were permitted to buy only two liters a week, and the wine ration, like that for tobacco, was restricted to men. Concurrently the Nazis were making sure that France was stripped of nearly everything else it produced. Up to three-quarters of the nation's cattle, pigs, vegetables, fruits, grains, and cheese were shipped to Germany during the war, forcing the French to make do with ersatz coffee, ersatz beer, bean soups, and the rutabagas they were accustomed to giving their live-stock. Loading the famous cider apples of Normandy and Brit-tany onto trains bound for Germany, French farmers managed to scrawl a bitter joke on the outside of the car—"For Ribbentrop, ersatz champagne." (Nazi foreign minister Joachim von Ribben-trop had married into a *Sekt*-producing family and considered himself a distinguished oenophile.)

All over Paris, the shops emptied. "The Germans who are there have money in their pockets for the first time in twenty-two years and can buy French luxuries the like of which some of the younger Germans have never laid eyes on since they were born," wrote Janet Flanner. Official policy permitted, in fact en-couraged, members of the army to mail generous gifts to their families and to stuff their bags and pockets with as much as they could carry when they went home on leave. For many Ger-mans, this sudden abundance of silk stockings, watches, jewelry, furs, and perfume, as well as coffee, tinned butter, cognac, and other foods, made the war years quite a bit more livable, at least on a sporadic basis. Others sold the booty on the black market or traded packages of expensive lingerie for a little fresh fruit. But for those with ready cash, it was easy to buy wine. "Every little bureaucrat in the capital could produce at dinner a fine, fat bottle of the best French champagne," wrote Howard K. Smith, who reported from Berlin until the end of 1941.

Other memoirs of wartime Berlin make it clear that while food supplies were erratic and often skimpy, champagne was everywhere. Marie Vassiltchikov, working at the Reich Broadcasting Corporation and then at the Foreign Ministry, ate yogurt and porridge for dinner on many days. But when she had friends over, they brought champagne. There was wine on the table for a birthday party even when the only food she could offer was fried potatoes and bread. At a guesthouse south of Berlin, while she and her family were waiting for their rooms, they ate tuna sandwiches she had "wisely" packed for the trip, "washed down with a jeroboam of champagne." On Easter Sunday 1944, she decided to try to eat out in Berlin with friends. "After a fist fight with some brute who burst into the telephone booth and tried to push me out, I rang up Loremarie," she wrote. With their friend Tony they went to the Hotel Eden, which had been heavily bombed, and used the service entrance "as the front is still non-existent." To her delight they were able to have an excellent lunch—"radishes with butter and delicious venison schnitzels (unrationed)"—and plenty to drink. "We first had cocktails, then several wines, then champagne, topping it off with a bottle of Tony's brandy." Another young woman who spent the war years in Berlin, Marianne Feuersenger, worked for the Reich's military historian and later published *Mein Kriegstagebuch* (*My War Diary*). In late 1943, she wrote, she began commuting to nearby Potsdam after a bombing raid destroyed their office. When she arrived on the first day she found only "empty rooms" and "empty tables"—and her boss, welcoming everyone with a bottle of Veuve Clicquot. Then he realized they had no proper champagne glasses and was so disappointed he lost his temper. At that point one of her colleagues remarked that perhaps they would all look back someday and remember how good they had it, drinking champagne from water glasses.

Among the highest-ranking Nazis, sumptuous living had been the rule since 1933, and wartime conditions made no difference. The leaders, wrote Speer, "all needed big houses, hunting lodges, estates and palaces, many servants, a rich table, and a select wine cellar." Joseph Goebbels, as head of propaganda, had been trying for years to promote an image of the Nazi leadership as men of modest living standards and forbade the publication of photographs showing them relaxing at tables amid the remains of splendid feasts. But few of these men were interested in restraint, and decrees issued by Hitler in 1942 and 1943 urging more seemly behavior on the part of the leadership had no effect. Hitler himself took more care, once ordering the window shades lowered in his private train after it pulled into a station alongside a freight train packed with hungry, wretched soldiers from the front lines. He didn't want them to see inside his dining car and glimpse the china, the silver, the flowers, and the abundant food. In December 1942, when some 280,000 men of the German Sixth Army were surrounded in Stalingrad under desperate conditions, he refused to allow surrender, but in a flourish of solidarity he announced that there would be no more champagne or cognac served at his eastern front headquarters. A few weeks later the wine was flowing again, and it was still flowing when the Sixth Army surrendered in February, after 165,000 men had been killed, frozen, or starved to death.

Champagne was the world's reigning symbol of high-class gaiety, and nothing that was under way in Germany or the nations in its grip was going to break the bubbles. For Eva, who was looking forward to starring in a movie about herself when the war was over—Hitler had promised—life itself was tanta-mount to a glass of champagne. She luxuriated in her perfumes and silver brushes, her handmade Italian shoes, the fresh flow-ers in her room every day, the scores of dresses and evening gowns in her closet. Still, people who were interviewed about her after the war regularly described her as sweet and nice. "She had a very natural and pleasant manner, while her charm and graceful figure enchanted us all," reported Heinz Linge. (Her mother remarked that Eva could be "rather strict," but only when she had to instruct the maids.) This pleasant de-meanor came easily to her—she had an extraordinarily cosseted existence—but what's striking is that it seems to have been in-destructible. Even during the long, sometimes lonely days at the Berghof, she found plenty to occupy her attention thanks to the two motivating passions of her life. The first, of course, was her devotion to Hitler. And the second, which took up far more time, was an unwavering dedication to her figure.

She dressed it, she photographed it, she displayed it, and she took care to maintain it by persistent dieting and frequent exercise. Eva was determined not to become one of the curva-ceous Bavarian damsels that Hitler half-jokingly praised in her presence, though she enjoyed going about in the traditional costume—puffed sleeves, vest, dirndl, long white stockings, and apron. But that was only one of her numerous outfits. Changing her clothes as frequently as possible in honor of a social schedule that was often imaginary, she kept track of her wardrobe by means of a meticulously detailed filing system. "She opened a file on every single dress, every coat, noting where it was bought, what the price was and including a sketch of the garment as well as a comment on shoes, purse, jewelry that were worn with it," wrote Henrietta von Schirach, daughter of Heinrich Hoffmann and wife of the Nazi official in charge of Vienna. One of Eva's favorite ways to give herself a treat was to dress up in something chic and pose for a formal portrait photograph, which she would present to Hitler. She spent so much money on clothes that before she killed herself she asked her sister to destroy the bills from the dressmaker, lest they be made public and give her a bad reputation.

This rigorous attention to self-presentation tells us, even more explicitly than the diary does, how she met the psychic demands of the life she had chosen. She did it by keeping her gaze fixed on the surface of things. In this respect she was lucky that her education had been skimpy and her imagination fueled chiefly by popular culture. All she brought with her when she moved into Hitler's orbit was a fondness for fashion and movies. She would have loved to be included in his official social life, but only because she longed to show herself off to the world beautifully gowned and on Hitler's arm. The rest of his job didn't interest her, and she had no trouble maintaining a cocoon around herself, bland and incurious, that resisted any challenges to her equanimity. She didn't read newspapers or listen to the radio; and if people began discussing politics in her presence, she shushed them by putting a finger across her lips.

Eva's focus on appearances was also literal: she owned a Rolleiflex and a movie camera and used them regularly. Dozens of her photograph albums survived the war, as did eight reels of her home movies. Clearly other people were behind the camera at times, since she herself was often included in the picture; hence the imagery offers a look both at her world and at the way she preferred to live in it. She was enraptured by her own social life: again and again we see the leading Nazis and their wives gathered on the terrace at the Berghof, with a uniformed waiter bringing in the apple cake. Hitler greets people with stiff courtesy; clusters of men confer over documents; children run about with delight or sit obediently in a grown-up's embrace, having their pictures taken. There are picnics, weddings, elaborate tea parties for children. And everywhere, it seems, there's Eva, charmingly dressed and always performing. She's intent on making us see what a good time she's having. She cuddles a dog, then a rabbit. In a stylish dress with a dotted skirt and tightly fitted contrasting bodice, she sits in a chair, leaning eagerly toward the camera, and smiles. She stretches out on the wall of the terrace in a bathing suit, enjoying the chance to bask in the sun and the camera's attention. On a secluded shore of the Königssee, the picturesque lake that was a short drive from the Berghof, she's again in a bathing suit and displays a backbend, or stands precariously on one leg while lifting the other as high as she can, or dangles from a tree branch, trying to hoist herself over. She and Speer's wife, both in Bavarian dresses, gather wildflowers in a field. In loose pants and a fitted jacket, she goes ice-skating and briefly holds an arabesque. Occasionally her women friends get together by themselves—one day they're in Eva's sitting room, drinking champagne, and on another day they're drinking wine on a pretty patio in the Mosel wine district. And of course, there are many photos of Hitler. He was at the Berghof in most of them, but she included one that captured him in a reverent moment at the Reichstag. He was standing with his arm out in the Nazi salute, eyes cast upward as the national anthem played—a scene she found so affecting that she annotated it with a caption: *"Deutschland, Deutschland, Über Alles, Über Alles in der Welt!"*

Eva didn't pay much attention to the threat of war, apart from its potential to complicate her romantic life. Her response to the Anschluss—Germany's takeover of Austria—was to arrange a quick trip to Vienna to surprise Hitler on the day of his triumphant speech at the Heldenplatz. Surprising him turned out to be a bad idea; he was furious at this unexpected arrival of a woman he wanted kept out of sight, even though she had carefully checked into a different hotel. Otherwise, however, Eva's indifference to world events and political issues suited him perfectly. He believed women should be kept as far as possible from such matters, and throughout the war he forbade any talk of deportations, killing campaigns, and other atrocities when women were present.

Eva was generally quite good at representing the sweet and sunny side of life, but as the war went on she worried more and more—not about Germany or herself, but about Hitler. She was frantic when she received word of the Stauffenberg plot, an attempt to assassinate Hitler by smuggling a bomb into a conference room at his East Prussian headquarters. He survived but sent Eva his blood-soaked uniform as a sign that providence had protected him. "I shan't go on living if anything happens to you," she vowed. Obersalzberg wasn't bombed until the very end of the war; nonetheless there were many nights when she and the other women living there were rushed into the air-raid shelter under the Berghof living room as Allied planes flew overhead. All the women were under similar orders to avoid discussing sensitive topics, but the prohibition was nerve-racking. "Everything is kept secret from me," Eva once complained. "I have no idea what's going on." During the autumn of 1944 she wrote her will; she also visited Hitler in Berlin and did a little shopping there—she wanted a new dress. She spent that Christmas in Munich with her family, where she saw firsthand the almost total destruction of the city. Yet a month later, when her sister Ilse called Hitler a fiend who was destroying Germany,

Eva was outraged and told Ilse she deserved to be shot like a traitor. The demands of the fantasy Eva had been nurturing for all these years were becoming excruciating to fulfill, but she kept at it. In March 1945, she left the Berghof to join Hitler at the Reich Chancellery, knowing she would probably die there.

They moved into the bunker on April 15, when the Chancellery had become unlivable. The Russians were some fifty miles away, advancing with thousands of tanks, guns, and mortars; the bombardment began the next day, and on April 18 they broke through the forces defending Berlin, which were mostly made up of terrified young boys in makeshift uniforms. Speer offered many times to help Eva get on a flight out of Berlin. The Allies had already divided the country into four zones of occupation, and he had moved his own family to Holstein, an area that would fall to the British, trusting that they would treat Nazi wives and children decently. Berlin, on the other hand, would fall to the Russians, a prospect that terrified every woman in the city. But he had to make his offers to Eva discreetly, because Hitler was treating such preparations for defeat as treason. In any event, Eva refused all suggestions that she seek safety.

The bunker had been amply supplied with food, wine, cognac, and champagne, and during the last weeks, desperate celebrations broke out. Hitler turned fifty-six on April 20, and at midnight on the eve of his birthday he sat silently in his study as Göring, von Ribbentrop, Speer, and a few others, including the secretaries, offered champagne toasts in his honor. Eva was wearing a new dress purchased especially for the party—"silvery blue brocade," recalled Traudl Junge—and gave him a present, yet another photograph of herself, this one in a silver frame. A few nights later there was another impromptu party. A kitchen maid married a driver from the fleet of official cars, and Heinz

Linge gave them a reception complete with champagne, cognac, and an absentminded greeting from their Führer. ("Children, I wish you the very best.")

By this time the bunker was emptying, as officials and staff scrambled to get onto planes headed for safer zones. Among those who remained were the four people closest to Hitler—his secretaries, Traudl Junge and Gerda Christian; his cook, Constanze Manziarly; and Eva. He ate only with them, as if the meals served within a female fortress would protect him as long as he needed protection. The talk was primarily about death. Under the incessant clamor of bombardment and artillery fire, with the Russians nearing them hour by hour, they discussed whether to shoot themselves or take poison. Hitler had handed out cyanide capsules, but he personally advised shooting, as death would be quick and sure. Eva didn't like that idea; she had it in mind to choose the cyanide. As she remarked to the others, "I want to be a beautiful corpse."

Eva had been writing her last letters as the dreary days passed, and although she never complained or resisted her fate— on the contrary, she displayed to everyone a calm willingness to die—the cataclysmic end of the Third Reich struck her as some kind of mysterious punishment for unknown offenses. "I cannot understand how it has all come to pass but it is impossible to continue believing in God!" she exclaimed to her best friend, Herta Schneider. Speer, who made his farewell visit to Eva a few days after she wrote this letter, heard a similar lament. "Why do so many more people have to be killed?" she asked him wonderingly. "And it's all for nothing." There seems no possibility that she was concerned for anyone except her friends and family, yet Speer, ever admiring, decided this made her "the only person in the bunker capable of humane considerations." One more letter survives, written to her sister Gretl. In this, probably Eva's final written communication before death, she urged Gretl to destroy all the correspondence stored in the house in Munich, explained how she wanted her jewelry to be distributed, and said she should give away the tinned food, tobacco, and chocolate stashed in Munich and at the Berghof. "Unfortunately my diamond watch is being repaired—I will give you the address at the end of this letter. With any luck you should still be able to get it back." The address was added in a postscript.

The last time Eva heard the pop of a champagne cork and the fizz of the bubbles was on her wedding day. Sometime around two in the morning on April 29, wearing a navy-blue dress with sequins and a pair of black heels from Ferragamo, she married Hitler in a brief ceremony conducted by a Berlin city councillor who had been hastily called to the bunker. There was a quiet reception afterward. From then on, people tried to remember to call her "Frau Hitler."

Many historians, journalists, and survivors have reconstructed the final hours in the bunker, often in minute-by-minute detail, but there is remarkably little documentation of the last meal served there. We do know that it took place on April 30, that it was a late lunch, and that it was over quickly. Hitler most probably had a dish of spaghetti with tomato sauce; some accounts add a salad. Eva ate nothing, and it's possible she wasn't even at the table. The next time she appeared, she had washed and styled her hair and was wearing, according to Junge, "the Fuhrer's favourite dress, the black one with the roses at the neckline." She and Hitler stood in the corridor outside his quarters and said good-bye to the few people remaining in the bunker. When it was Junge's turn, Eva hugged her. "Please do try to get out. You may yet make your way through. And give

Bavaria my love." A few minutes later, curled up on a sofa in Hitler's sitting room, she bit into a cyanide capsule while Hitler shot himself, and they both died instantly. Toward the end of the afternoon Manziarly, sobbing, set about preparing dinner. She had been ordered to maintain the facade of a normal schedule so that the deaths would remain secret as long as possible. Hitler had been frantic lest the Russians use his body to flaunt their triumph and instructed his adjutants to burn both bodies right away. Junge recalled that the cook made fried eggs and creamed potatoes for this faux supper. Nobody ate.

Evdokia Domina had been at work in the fields in eastern Ukraine when the Nazis swooped down, grabbed her, and shipped her to Ravensbrück, the women's concentration camp. It was December 1942, and her family didn't even know she had been taken until she failed to return home that afternoon. A Siemens factory had been built a mile from the entrance to Ravensbrück, and the camp was supplying slave labor to manufacture electrical parts for planes and weapons. Every morning prisoners staggered through the snow to the factory and set to work, hunger raging. They trudged back to the camp for lunch—watery soup and a few potatoes—but often the guards chased them back to the factory, screaming at them, before they could swallow anything. Later Evdokia was transferred to a subcamp at Genthin, and she was there during the last days of April 1945, when the guards fled the approaching Allied forces and left the women suddenly free. "We just thought to head east," she said. "We walked into deserted houses and found the bedrooms with beds to sleep in. And it was so nice with these sheets and quilts. We ate the food and never washed the plates, just took another one."

They were hungry, they were starving, they ate everything they could find, but when she told this story to a historian many decades later, what she marveled at were the plates they left unwashed. Perhaps she enjoyed that memory of how a feminine reflex simply stopped operating, and nobody missed it. Or perhaps it was easier for her to talk about dirty dishes than about snatching up a feast in the wake of so much death. But the truth is, you never just eat. No matter how hungry you are, it's never just food. Evdokia Domina's food story, which culminated at the very time the inhabitants of Hitler's bunker were frantically making their way through bottle after bottle of champagne, was about the harsh cost of surviving. Eva's food story was about how often, and how easily, she died.

Barbara Pym
(1913–1980)

Tonight she set before us a pale macaroni cheese and a dish of boiled po-
tatoes, and I noticed a blancmange or "shape," also of an indeterminate
colour, in a glass dish on the sideboard. Not enough salt, or perhaps no
salt, I thought, as I ate the macaroni. And not really enough cheese.

—Excellent Women

Like generations of food lovers before her, Julia Child came away from her first trip to Britain convinced that there really was no hope for such a nation. It was the spring of 1949, and she and her husband, Paul, had come over from Paris to tour the north of England. "[We] stopped at a beautiful Tudor Inn, which was truly oldey woldey and charming," she recalled several years later in a jovial letter to her friend Avis DeVoto. "Dinner, and we had boiled chicken with the hair still on partially covered with a real honest to goodness English white sauce. I had always heard of it, but thought it was just a lot of French chauvinism. But this was really it, flour and water with hardly any salt, not even made with the chicken bouillon." The fact that rationing was still on, that hotels and restaurants had taken a dive during the war, that many hadn't recovered—none of this entered into her appraisal. By the time she was looking back on that meal it was 1953, and she had returned to England many times, always staying with friends who served delicious meals. No matter. These particular friends loved France and French food, she pointed out. So as far as Julia was concerned, they didn't really count as British, at least when they cooked.

Julia's attitude toward British food—that it was inedible, that it had little relevant history apart from being inedible, and that a more sensible population would simply take its meals in France—had been locked into place for a long time, and no respectable gourmand would have contradicted her. Even Rosa Lewis, unusual in her day for freely criticizing French cooks as well as British, made sure that her menus were written in French no matter what was on the plate. After all, her clients were perfectly aware of the difference between "Soup" and "*Soupe,*" even when the former was "Clear Turtle" and the latter was "*Tortue Claire.*" By 1928, when classic French cuisine had been priced out of most British homes and restaurants, critics such as the food and wine writer Morton Shand were castigating "faded lettuce . . . bottled sauces . . . and flaccid, malodourous cabbage," and four years later a story in the *Manchester Guardian* about a movement to promote the best in British cooking was headed, defiantly, "Our Cooking Not Stodgy." Elizabeth David, who spent the late 1940s working on what would become a landmark of culinary literature, *A Book of Mediterranean Food,* once remarked that it was almost the first British cookbook to appear after the war. "It was a time really when they didn't have cookery articles," she pointed out. "Why should they? They didn't have food."

But they did have food, often excellent food, and one of the reasons we know about it is Barbara Pym, whose fiction sprang directly from the life around her. Barbara was an observer by nature; her eyes and ears were on permanent alert. What inspired her was the world she knew, and that world was England. Her novels have suffered from an odd reputation over the years: widely praised, they're nevertheless often summed up as depicting drab spinsters pouring tea for the clergy while life dwindles

Barbara Pym at her typewriter, 1979.

quietly away. Nothing could be less accurate. Yes, there's tea, there's clergy, and there are spinsters, but the women are radiant with personality, the clergy are subjected to gentle, persistent ridicule, and the tea plays so many symbolic roles that another writer would have had to create a whole slew of walk-on characters to say what Barbara says with a cup. She loved Englishness. She loved Englishness in all its manifestations, and she took particular pleasure in what the English ate.

Barbara was not a food writer, but she saw the world as if she were—as if every piece of cake or even just the crumbs on the plate offered the most enticing clues imaginable to time, place, class, and character. The novels she published from the 1950s through the 1970s are full of food; and in the little notebooks that she carried everywhere she used to jot down her daily sightings of food, sometimes the moment they occurred. "Soup, jelly and bread and butter—*That's* not much of a meal for a man— I think as I sit [in] the Kardomah." To read her novels, especially in concert with her diaries, is to discover a revisionist history of midcentury British cooking. She didn't set out to overturn any long-cherished assumptions about the horrors of British food, but character after character, meal after meal, that's exactly what happens.

In 1949, for instance, the very year that Julia Child encountered a ghoulish boiled chicken with the hair still on, Barbara had just completed the final draft of her first novel, *Some Tame Gazelle*, and sent it off to a publisher. Boiled chicken with white sauce shows up early and often in that book. In fact, it's the centerpiece of the novel's first extended scene, in which two middle-aged sisters, Belinda and Harriet, are entertaining a curate newly arrived at their village church. Here's the dish as Barbara Pym saw and tasted it:

In the dining-room Harriet sat at one end of the table and Belinda at the other, with the curate in the middle. Harriet carved the boiled chicken smothered in white sauce very capably. She gave the curate all the best white meat.

Were all new curates everywhere always given boiled chicken when they came to supper for the first time? Belinda wondered. It was certainly an established ritual at their house and it seemed somehow right for a new curate. The coldness, the whiteness, the muffling with sauce, perhaps even the sharpness added by the slices of lemon, there was something appropriate here, even if Belinda could not see exactly what it was.

Same year, same dish, but an entirely different—and tempting—version of a prototypical British company meal. It's true that Barbara wrote the first draft of *Some Tame Gazelle* in the mid-1930s, and the book reflects that period, not the postwar era. But according to Morton Shand, the food was already disastrous in 1928; and according to Julia, it was just as disastrous in the early 1950s. In other words, the reputation of British food stands on its own, independent of real time. It has to be bad, because bad is its identity.

And yet, it's not bad in *Some Tame Gazelle,* where Belinda and Harriet live well and pay a great deal of attention to what they eat. Harriet likes her roast beef rare; Belinda makes ravioli by hand; the scones at tea are fresh and hot. The boiled chicken on their table would not have borne any resemblance to the miserable dish Julia described. More likely they offered the curate something along the lines of "Boiled Chicken with Special Sauce," from a 1935 cookbook by Helen Simpson. It's not inconceivable that Barbara would have known this cookbook. Simpson was a prolific, reasonably successful novelist living in London in the 1930s; she also wrote occasionally about food, and her cookbook, *The Cold Table,* was published by Jonathan Cape, the house that would publish most of Barbara's work, including *Some Tame Gazelle.* Simpson's chicken isn't boiled at all, despite its name; it's carefully simmered with onion, parsley, and carrots. The "special sauce" is a white sauce made with flour, butter, cream, mace, and lemon peel, then stiffened with gelatin and spread on the chicken. Cold, white, tasting of lemon just a bit— Belinda's description evokes this very dish.

There is terrible food, too, in *Some Tame Gazelle.* Invited to dine in a household where nobody much cares about cooking, Belinda politely tries to ignore the cigarette ash that falls into a pot of baked beans. Dinner at the archdeacon's home isn't much better: his wife serves dry rissoles, "stringy cabbage," tinned soup, and instant coffee. What's revelatory, from the standpoint of culinary history, is that the terrible food in this book is noteworthy rather than inevitable. Barbara took it for granted that a comfortable English life would have fine, fragrant cooking in it. Here, in her very first novel, she was already deep into a radical retelling of the state of the British table.

As soon as her books began appearing in 1950, Barbara won a small circle of devoted readers who pounced on each new publication with joy. But in the critical establishment that mattered in postwar Britain, her work received little attention—so little that after six books the publishing industry lost interest in her modest sales and dropped her. From 1963 to 1977 she received nothing but rejection letters. Then an unexpected critical coronation prompted a splendid rush of fame, and she spent the last few years of her life grateful and jubilant.

But it's easy to see why she occupied such a relatively obscure niche for so long. Barbara specialized in a minor-key world located well back from fiction's cutting edge, with a gentle stream of irony running quietly below the surface. Her mild-mannered narrators are often found musing on their favorite lines from Anglican hymns or making Ovaltine at moments of late night crisis. When Barbara sets a scene in a bedroom, there's generally a book of Victorian poetry nearby and a nice cup of tea. ("Life's problems are often eased by hot milky drinks.") Yet these are women who can skewer a narcissistic male with wit so deft he barely notices, and their hilarious, finely tuned perceptions light up every page. Her admirers regularly evoke Jane Austen, and she shares territory with Anthony Trollope as well; but she was up against a postwar literary canon that didn't have a lot of patience with Ovaltine. Critics seemed embarrassed to praise her work even when they loved it. Reviewing Barbara's second novel, John Betjeman said many people would surely find it "tame," what with all the church bazaars and the boiled eggs. He added, almost apologetically, "To me it is a perfect book."

Barbara's sudden fame after 1977—the new publishing contracts, the interviews, the fresh attention to her work—is always termed the "rediscovery" of Barbara Pym. But I'm not sure that's the right word. Maybe "redefinition" would be more accurate. What really happened is that the postwar literary canon was forced to wriggle around a bit in order to make room for a writer who plainly had no assigned seat. Barbara's readers, the longtime fans and the new ones, never had any trouble appreciating the savvy sensibility of her churchgoing heroines, even if they were distinctly unglamorous and rarely turned their attention to sex. But some critics simply didn't know what to make of all these women in their shabby cardigans, helping out at jumble sales and poring over *Crockford's Clerical Directory*. Did characters like these belong in the ranks of great contemporary fiction? Margaret

Drabble, Edna O'Brien—that's what groundbreaking women's writing was supposed to look like. Barbara's work was nothing like theirs, and yet it was undeniably powerful. Many reviewers came to the only viable conclusion: surely the books were as heartbreaking as they were comic, the women best understood as brave but barren females in an England stripped of empire. How else to account for the genuine dignity of Barbara's world, not to mention the excellence of the prose? Such terms as "tragic" and "tragi-comic" began turning up in discussions of Barbara's work. Critics detected "neglect, desolation and loneliness" in the stream of consciousness moving through each book, as if the tone of wry, gentle amusement so fundamental in Barbara's voice were simply not there. John Updike, writing about Barbara after her books began appearing in the United States in 1979, admired them greatly—for their "wanly Christian world," for the sense of "atomic aloneness in a crowded world," for the "extremely meagre social fabric Miss Pym weaves for her characters."

Barbara was mystified when people talked about the unhappy lives of the women she invented. One reason she loved them was for the pleasure they took in all aspects of the ordinary. She herself went through life that way, with an unlimited capacity to be fascinated by whatever passed in front of her. She also had a healthy respect for the marriage plot and took care to create male soul mates for most of her heroines, though critics committed to the doomed-spinster interpretation rarely took note of the suitors who were waiting in the wings. But perhaps the most overlooked theme of her novels—the motif that tells us again and again at top volume that these are women with a passion for life—is the delight they take in food. Intensely curious herself about what people were eating, whether they were characters in books or real people sitting across the table from her, Barbara was always disappointed when novels and memoirs left out the culinary details. Hence she made a point of embedding them in her own fiction. Bad food, good food, other people's food, the food on their own tables: Barbara's narrators are captivated by all of it. How could so many discerning critics miss this glorious proclamation of faith? Perhaps it was because Barbara was neither a gastronome nor a sensualist, which meant that whatever she said about eating tended to slip quietly off the page.

11 March 1938: "I went to lunch with Julian in Balliol. We had fish, duck and green peas, fresh peaches and cream. Sherry, Niersteiner, and port."

Barbara was a culinary historian's dream. She started keeping diaries soon after she arrived at Oxford as a student in 1931 and continued writing in them for the rest of her life, mentioning food all the while. At first she simply tossed in an occasional reference to what she ate—"the loveliest cocktail I've had—a sidecar very iced"; an eighteen-pound turkey at a family Christmas dinner; "huge toast sandwiches" at Selfridges; lunch with a new beau ("We had eggs with cream on the top, chicken, and chocolate mousse"). Later she realized that the life around her was always going to be her favorite source of inspiration, so she made a point of paying more consistent attention to food, and sometimes she used the same diaries to jot down a shopping list or a recipe. All her personal and professional papers went to the Bodleian Library at Oxford; hence it's now possible to track the eating habits of middle-class, midcentury England filtered through the life and times of a lively, very funny writer who happened to be addicted to the practice of spying and eavesdropping on everyone within reach. It's a splendid archive and thoroughly rewarding for a culinary-minded researcher who's more accustomed to turning page after fragile page of somebody's diary and finding only "After dinner, we decided to . . ." or "He stopped by for lunch, and then . . ." or, most irritating of all, "Breakfast didn't take long." The more unremarkable the food, the more likely it was to have gone unremarked. Not so with Barbara.

At Oxford, however, she had a number of competing preoccupations, chief among them men. She was eighteen when she arrived in 1931, tall and high-spirited, with an eager smile, and she spent her academic years as well as the decade following in a flurry of love affairs—some brief, some extended, all absorbing, many unrequited, and a few imaginary. As an undergraduate she also fell deeply in love with English literature, and this was a relationship that lasted the rest of her life. "Our greater English poets," as Belinda refers to them in *Some Tame Gazelle*, would always occupy the very center of Barbara's heart. After Oxford she went home to Shropshire with a degree in English, a vague ambition to write, and a feverish devotion to a literary scholar named Henry Harvey, who had shaken her off and moved to Finland to teach. There seemed no way to free herself from this *amour fou*; even pursuing other men didn't help. That summer her father brought home a secondhand typewriter, and, using the two-finger system she would retain for decades, she started to dream up *Some Tame Gazelle*. The title came from Thomas Haynes Bayly, one of our distinctly lesser poets of the early nineteenth century:

> Some tame gazelle, or some gentle dove:
> Something to love, oh, something to love!

The first draft of the novel, which remains with her papers at the Bodleian, is an awkward mess of bad writing and chaotic plotting—not surprising, perhaps, since the project was essentially therapeutic, meant to help her gain some distance from Henry and her hopeless passion. She set the novel in a classic English village and made all the characters heavily caricatured versions of her Oxford friends. Henry became a pompous, self-absorbed archdeacon, and she herself played the role of Belinda, a dreamy-eyed spinster who has been pining for the archdeacon ever since their long-ago Oxford days. Her friends, who of course recognized themselves, greatly enjoyed reading the manuscript; for the rest of us it comes across as an endless, tedious in-joke. When she had no success finding a publisher, she put the manuscript away; but she continued to work on stories and novels until 1941, when single women her age had to register for war work.

During the war, which she spent in the Censorship Office and later in the Women's Royal Naval Service, Barbara had one more spectacularly doomed love affair, this time with a journalist who was in the process of getting divorced from one of her best friends. As far as he was concerned, the affair was a fling, but Barbara took it more seriously. She seems to have believed, or persuaded herself, that he would propose once his divorce was final; but by the time he was free, it was obvious that he had lost interest. Yet even during the time she was most obsessed with him, Barbara wrote very little in her diary about marriage per se. She was far more likely to record "snatched kisses," or poignant farewells over a glass of sherry, than she was to set down any blissful reveries about weddings. Much as she relished her social life with men, she never made a sustained effort to find a lifelong partner among them. One or two swains proposed; she refused them. It was as if she knew, back when she was creating Belinda in her own image, that this poetry-loving English-woman was far happier remaining single than she would have been if she had married the man of her dreams.

After the war she set up a home in London with her sister, Hilary, and took a job as an editor at the International African Institute, which published scholarly monographs and a journal of anthropology. The institute would inspire some of the most hilarious moments in her novels, but she was working there chiefly to pay the bills; and once she was settled in the flat, she turned her attention to what mattered most. She wanted to write, and she wanted to call herself a writer, and she wanted to feel as though "writer" were her proper and permanent identity. There was nothing for her in the term "wife." She still had one more painful love ahead of her—a man so much younger than she was, and so plainly homosexual, that she probably knew even at the time that his role in her life was to reappear in some future novel. (Sure enough, he became James in *The Sweet Dove Died*.) Meanwhile, as she told a friend, "There is so much that I want to write now, that I hardly know where to begin." So she began at the beginning. She pulled out the unsuccessful draft of *Some Tame Gazelle* and determined to get it right.

One of her early readers had been Robert Liddell, an Oxford friend who was teaching English at the University of Cairo and had already published his own first novel. Liddell was enthusiastic about the draft, but he could see numerous problems and sent her pages of questions and suggestions. With his help, Barbara did an extraordinary job of self-editing: she sharpened the characters, simplified the plot, slashed away every scrap of extraneous prose, and allowed her natural sense of irony to reach its level. Most important, she swept out the in-joke sensibility and placed the novel in a real-world setting that was wide-open to readers who had never heard of Henry Harvey or, for that matter, Barbara. The real world was going to be the key to her literary kingdom—she could see that now, and all her instincts confirmed it. "More household detail," she instructed herself as she did the rewrite. "Knitting patterns . . . doing the altar flowers . . . Jam." She underlined the word "Jam" and added, "Victoria plum 1907 with mould on the top." She had found her center of balance.

Some Tame Gazelle was published in 1950 and won a number of warm reviews—Barbara was placed in the very good company of Mrs. Gaskell and Angela Thirkell, as well as Jane Austen and Anthony Trollope—and while she was reading them she was already deep into her next book. This time her imagination was focused, right from the start, on what she could see. Years earlier she had noted in her diary that she didn't really like having lunch at the Lyons Corner Houses, since they were so big, "but the food isn't bad and one can observe life from there." Now she felt justified in treating her intense, habitual gaze on the world as professional practice. Writers carried notebooks and used them religiously; she would, too. One day in 1948 she sat down in a department store cafeteria, looked about her, and took out a small, spiral-bound notebook. "Two women at my table in D. H. Evans Help Yourself," she wrote. "Talking about somebody who has died. Hushed voices." That little notebook would be the first of eighty-two that she accumulated over the next three decades, each a torrent of scribbles. "What riches!" she used to crow after a particularly fruitful viewing session in a park or restaurant.

This middle-aged lady is sitting in Lyons reading the Church Times and eating Scrambled Egg Beano. Her fluty voice.

The back view of a man ordering drinks, while you stand or sit nonchalantly.

In the hotel—two women are talking at lunch of how to relieve the vicar's burdens.

Later (in Lyons) . . . He used to get whale meat and boil it all up. Of course there were dog hairs everywhere. I'm sure that if anything happened to Madge he'd get another dog.

It's not always clear in these notes whether she was recording her actual observations of the moment or whether she was trying out phrases and ideas for possible later use. Scenarios, characters, incidents, experiments with wording—she filled page after page but often didn't bother to say how an item originated. (She was puzzled by this herself at times. Going over one of her notebooks later, she scribbled next to a scrap of conversation, "What is this and where did I get it?") Reading through the notebooks today, we feel as though we're tracking Barbara from novel to novel, following the footprints she left behind as she wandered across the landscape she would turn into fiction. She copied down signs posted in the vestry of a church, newspaper headlines, plaques on historic buildings, bits from letters she received at work ("Dear Colleague—are you interested in the origin of the word 'zebra'?"). One day she noticed a headline in the *Daily Mirror:* SECRET LOVE OF VANISHED VICAR. She could almost sing the words—the meter was exactly that of a hymn tune. She made a note of it. Another day she was in the Kardomah, a lunch spot she favored in part for its excellent viewing opportunities, when she overheard a bit of gossip about a man who had gone on a trip to Madeira—"and he didn't like it *at all,* but then he isn't very enthusiastic about anything except bird-watching." She wrote it down. It was all fuel, it all made the engines run. Once she tried describing her method to an audience in Barnes, the suburb where she and Hilary lived in the 1950s. "Often it is just a single reference or idea that fires the imagination," she told the group. "I have a collection of newspaper cuttings on a variety of subjects—A stuffed crocodile found on a beach . . . a woman who annoyed her neighbours by playing the harp and banging on a tin tray . . . a woman who fell in love with a clergyman she saw on television and proposed marriage to—those are just a few that have taken my fancy, but what *use* they will ever be I can't possibly imagine." Yet everything was useful; everything had a niche in that abundantly stocked museum she carried about in her notebooks like a personal Victoria and Albert.

Her favorite place to watch human behavior was a restaurant, for there she could sit quietly in the background while people interacted with food. Each glimpse of the intimate relationship between the person and the plate cried out to her. Cafeterias, tea shops, cafés, pubs, dining cars, a park at noon—anywhere people were eating was fertile ground. To be in the presence of food—appetizing, appalling, it hardly mattered—was to start creating. "Hazel and I lunched at the Golden Egg," she wrote in 1964. "Oh, the horror. . . . The cold stuffiness, claustrophic placing of tables, garish lighting and mass produced food in steel dishes. And the dreary young people—the egg-shaped menu. But perhaps one could get something out of it. The setting for a breaking off, or some terrible news, or an unwanted declaration of love. . . ." It's no wonder that *Excellent Women,* her best-loved novel and the one fans and critics inevitably conjure when they're trying to describe the world of Barbara Pym, took shape in her mind around images of food. She was at work on the book, which would become her second published novel, on that same day in 1948 when she was sitting in the D. H. Evans Help Yourself with her first notebook.

"Food—a fresh salad dressed with oil and salt, gruyere cheese and greengages—crusty bread," she wrote. Then she changed "salad" to "lettuce." Thanks to this visible editing, we can guess that she was thinking in terms of the new novel. The rewrite was an improvement: "salad" was too fussy for this particular image. With "lettuce" she arrived at a classic little meal, put together from a few simple but perfect ingredients and ideally served outdoors, perhaps on a sunny French hillside. When *Excellent Women* was published in 1952, this lunch appeared in almost the exact form Barbara had originally imagined; the only thing she altered was the cheese, from "gruyere" to "Camembert." The lettuce, the cheese, the crusty loaf—she had spied a character emerging from these materials, and she wanted to keep them intact.

Barbara wrote *Excellent Women* in the first person and placed the rest of the novel close to home. She and Hilary were living in Pimlico, in a flat overlooking St. Gabriel's church in Warwick Square, and she put her narrator in a similar flat right in the same neighborhood. A modest spinster in a drab skirt and cardigan, Mildred helps out with the church jumble sale and works part-time for an organization that assists "impoverished gentlewomen." There is nothing chic or worldly about her: she is the daughter of a vicar and carries a biography of Cardinal Newman in a string bag to read on the bus to work. But one day she has occasion to make an impromptu lunch for the man who lives in the flat downstairs, who's become an entrancing new friend. His wife has just left him, and although Mildred can see that Rocky is too handsome and sophisticated for a mousy spinster like herself, they get along extremely well and she has surprised herself by developing an exciting little crush on him.

I washed a lettuce and dressed it with a little of my hoarded olive oil and some salt. I also had a Camembert cheese, a fresh loaf and a bowl of greengages for dessert. It seemed an idyllic sort of meal that ought to have been eaten in the open air, with a bottle of wine and what is known as "good" conversation. I thought it unlikely that I should be able to provide either the conversation or the wine, but I remembered that I had a bottle of brandy which I kept, according to old-fashioned custom, for "emergencies" and I decided to bring it in with the coffee.

Apart from the missing wine, nothing could be in better taste than this iconic repast, expertly prepared from the ingredients at hand. And nothing could be less British, at least according to popular perceptions then and now of the nation's postwar eating habits. "How one learns to dread the season for salads in England," Elizabeth David wrote in *Summer Cooking,* which appeared three years after *Excellent Women.* "What becomes of the hearts of the lettuces? . . . What is the object of spending so much money on cucumbers, tomatoes, and lettuces because of their valuable vitamins, and then drowning them in vinegar and chemical salad dressings?" She went on to give three "absolutely essential rules" for salad making: very fresh lettuce, the barest possible trace of vinegar, and the dressing added at the last minute. Each rule, of course, had been anticipated by Mildred. David had been an authoritative voice on aspirational culinary standards for middle-class British food lovers ever since publishing *A Book of Mediterranean Food* in 1950. Her sun-drenched recipes, laced with wine and garlic, were far indeed from the boiled mutton and mashed turnips long associated with English dinnertime, not to mention the corned-beef curries and "Spaghetti

Americaine" that had been making their way across the land since the 1930s. Yet Barbara had scribbled "Food—a fresh salad" in her notebook a full two years before the now legendary birth of *Mediterranean Food*. As a writer who breathed the air of real life and couldn't survive in any other medium, Barbara used the food she knew to tell the stories she knew. If she decided that Mildred, dowdy and unprepossessing and very, very British, was thinking this way about salads in the late 1940s, then there's reason to believe that it was not a startling way to think about salads.

To be sure, Barbara was hardly implying that droopy salads had disappeared from the British table. They didn't even disappear from *Excellent Women*. Later in the novel, Rocky moves away and a dejected Mildred watches his furniture depart in a van. "I went upstairs to my flat to eat a melancholy lunch. A dried-up scrap of cheese, a few lettuce leaves for which I could not be bothered to make any dressing, a tomato and a piece of bread-and-butter. . . ." Hopeless love, always a cherished emotional state with Barbara, had flourished in the company of a man and a fine salad; but Rocky's absence is simply depressing, and Mildred's lunch follows suit.

Mildred's olive oil is "hoarded" because Barbara started writing *Excellent Women* in 1948, when postwar rationing was still in effect. Elsewhere in the novel, fresh eggs are scarce, "curried whale" appears on a Lyons menu, and the food Mildred is able to obtain for her plain meals at home is often, she admits, uninteresting—a chop, a bit of fish, a few tins. But on the whole there's little emphasis on privation in Mildred's life: she eats well in Soho restaurants, and at the end of the novel, during a cozy evening at the fireside of the man she will probably marry, they share "a very nice bird" and a bottle of red wine. Only when

Barbara wants to make a point about spinsterhood does Mildred deliberately prepare a meager meal for herself, as she did at lunchtime after Rocky's departure. Yet these solitary meals have different nuances, depending on what Barbara intends them to convey. When the vicar becomes engaged to a new parishioner, for instance, everyone assumes that the news will be a devastating blow to Mildred. She is single, he is eligible, the two are friends—surely she must have been hoping to marry him. In truth she has no romantic interest in him at all, but the next time she shows up at church, she can't seem to make anyone believe that she isn't heartbroken. "After the service I went home and cooked my fish. Cod seemed a suitable dish for a rejected one and I ate it humbly without any kind of sauce or relish." Here Mildred's perception of herself is tinged so delicately with irony that Barbara doesn't even put words to it, letting her heroine reflect on the plainness of the fish with a smile that's kept out of sight. Like the sorry remnants of salad that bring an end to Mildred's fantasy about Rocky, this unadorned fish is also "a *woman's* meal," but it's one that doesn't depress Mildred in the slightest. It's impossible to miss the amusement in her voice.

"Why is it that *men* find my books so sad?" Barbara wondered once. "Women don't particularly." But she was wrong: critics of both sexes have regarded her heroines as exemplars of loneliness and sterility, and Mildred has been a particular target of pity. In his introduction to the 2006 Penguin edition of *Excellent Women*, A. N. Wilson underscores what he sees as the "quite extraordinary deadness and flatness of Mildred's life," and he calls attention to the food to press his point. Wine, he suggests by way of an example, "is regarded as an extraordinary luxury, and it is warmed up in front of gas fires." But even though Mildred doesn't drink wine every day, several other characters do. In fact, wine flows as readily through Barbara's work as it did through her life. And yes, in *Excellent Women* it's warmed up in front of gas fires—Barbara made sure of that. She thought men who made a fetish of the proprieties of serving wine were silly, and among her earliest notes for the novel we find "Man fussing about wine—chilled etc." This image helped to supply her with the character named William, a stuffy friend of Mildred's who prides himself on his expertise in wine and once orders a bottle of Nuits-Saint-Georges while pompously warning her that not every bottle under that label was as good as it should be. (" 'It might,' he said seriously, 'be an *ordinaire*. Always remember that.' ")

It's true that Mildred herself never claims to be anything but "mousy and rather plain"—the day she nervously buys a new lipstick called "Hawaiian Fire" she's almost too embarrassed to say the name aloud in front of the clerk. But we begin to suspect what lies under her nondescript exterior just a few pages into the novel, when Barbara sends her out to a dinner party. Barbara loved writing dinner party scenes, for they allowed her to put home cooking right up front where everyone could interact with it. Not that Mildred or anybody else at the table would have called this event a "dinner party"—it's a plain family supper at the vicarage, and Mildred, who has dined there often, knows just what to expect.

I sat down at the table without any very high hopes, for both Julian and Winifred, as is often the way with good, unworldly people, hardly noticed what they ate or drank, so that a meal with them was a doubtful pleasure. Mrs. Jubb, who might have been quite a good cook with any encouragement, must have lost heart long ago. Tonight she set before us a pale macaroni cheese and a dish of boiled potatoes, and I noticed a blancmange or "shape," also of an indeterminate colour, in a glass dish on the sideboard.

Not enough salt, or perhaps *no* salt, I thought, as I ate the macaroni. And not really enough cheese.

A. N. Wilson singles out this meal as a study in drabness, which it surely is. But notice how Mildred experiences the food. It is clear that she has a palate and that she can size up the defects in what she's eating. She understands that life holds much better versions of macaroni cheese than the pale blob in front of her. There's an implication, at least if we read between the lines, that she makes an excellent macaroni cheese herself. (Maybe hers is like the one Evelyn Board included in her 1952 cookbook, *The Right Way to His Heart*, which begins: "This uncompromisingly English dish is one of our great national stand-bys, and very good it is, too." Board's directions are to prepare a "rich cheese sauce, not forgetting to stir in a spoonful of French mustard," then mix it with the cooked macaroni and top everything with grated cheese, bread crumbs, and melted butter—"far better than dotting it with little bits." Bake until "sizzling and golden.") Later in the novel we find that Mildred keeps a Chinese cookbook by the bedside to read when she can't fall asleep. And by the time she starts washing the lettuce and sprinkling olive oil over it for lunch with Rocky, we can see that here is a spinster very capable of meeting the world on pleasurable terms. Bland macaroni may be dinner, but it's not her doom.

Mildred was the only one of Barbara's heroines who had to put up with rationing, both at home and in restaurants. The women in all her other books were free to eat as they chose, and most of them cook well and easily. In fact, they seem quite unaware that they're turning out meals of a quality that was supposed to be unheard-of in postwar England. Catherine, for instance, the bohemian writer in *Less Than Angels*, is an expert cook whose hands "sometimes smelled of garlic." She can throw together a risotto at short notice and always has a bottle of inexpensive wine on hand. Making *bœuf à la mode* one day: "Oh, what joy to get a real calf's foot from the butcher, she thought, and not to have to cheat by putting in gelatine." Then there's Dulcie in *No Fond Return of Love*. She likes bottled mayonnaise and has been known to drink orange squash with supper, but she also puts up the fruit from her garden every year, makes her own marmalade, roasts lamb "to perfection" with sprigs of rosemary, and for company sets out a roast duckling and a bottle of Clos Vougeot 1952. Leonora, in *The Sweet Dove Died*, is older than most Pym heroines, a fragile figure touched with pathos. But she, too, is an accomplished cook—chicken tarragon, chocolate mousse, roast beef, and Yorkshire pudding, all beautifully prepared and served. Even in *Quartet in Autumn*, where most of the food reflects the narrow, often lonely circumstances of the four main characters, there's a woman trying to woo the local vicar with *poulet niçoise*. She serves it with a good Orvieto.

Of course, there was never a shortage in England, or in Pym's fiction, of some of the world's worst cooking. Elizabeth David once described staying in a household where the same Sunday dinner appeared every week: overboiled potatoes, overboiled sprouts, overboiled cabbage, and overdone meat. She managed to slip a glass of wine into the gravy one week, but her hostess was so distressed that the experiment didn't happen again. Barbara ran into dreary cooking like this on innumerable occasions over the years, and she had no intention of ignoring it when she wrote. In houses, flats, cottages, and bed-sitters throughout the books, we find characters opening tins, making Nescafé, putting out a store-bought cake for tea, and heating up frozen peas—"like *Americans*," Ianthe reflects guiltily in *An Unsuitable Attachment*. In *No Fond Return of Love*, Dulcie visits an aunt and uncle whose cook, Mrs. Sedge, sends up a dish known as "boiled baby"— "mince with tomato sauce spread over the top"—to be followed by semolina pudding. "Mrs. Sedge, who had come to England twenty years ago from Vienna, had apparently retained little knowledge of her country's cuisine, if she had ever possessed it; Dulcie was always surprised at the thoroughness with which she had acquired all the worst traits of English cooking."

But if there's a culinary moral in these books, it's that good food can be found anywhere. Certainly it's not reserved for the sort of people who consider themselves gourmets. Barbara didn't feel she had to send a heroine to France and sit her down at a café table with a glass of wine just to prove she was capable of enjoying life's riches. Where we find a Pym heroine is at home, in comfortable shoes, turning the pages of a nineteenth-century housekeeping manual while she has some decent cheese and a couple of tomatoes from the garden. This is a good life, Barbara is saying; this is luxury; this is genuine contentment.

Barbara herself had a relaxed and wide-ranging appetite that was open to just about everything. "How would she eat when alone?" Barbara wondered while she was working on the character of Dulcie in *No Fond Return of Love*. "Half a lobster and a glass of chablis at Scotts—or baked beans on toast and Coca Cola in the Kenbar cafe at Barkers." She left out the question marks when she made this note, perhaps because both choices appealed to her, and not just for their literary qualities. Barbara's meals and snacks ranged up, down, and across most of the possibilities at hand for a middle-class woman living within easy reach of London or Oxford. One day it was a poached egg at the Kardomah, another day there was nothing available except "a dry sausage roll" in a train station; she had a "delicious creamy cake tasting of walnuts" at the Wimpole Buttery, and she had a memorably all-brown lunch at Lyons ("Macaroni Bolognaise with a brownness of meat in the middle, browny soup and coffee, dark brown chocolate trifle"). With a friend at an Italian restaurant she had "Tio Pepe, ravioli, salad, sweets, coffee"; more opulently she dined at Simpson's, famous for "gorgeous roast beef . . . and here a woman is given as much as a man." Lunches with publishers always took place at London's better restaurants, and when Macmillan accepted *Quartet in Autumn* she was taken to Terrazza Est on Chancery Lane. "We had much congenial talk and ate smoked salmon, bits of veal in a buttery sauce, straw potatoes and courgettes (for me) and profiteroles. JW [James Wright, her editor] and I had some white wine," she wrote. "All the other diners in the room seemed to be men."

At home she seems to have cooked quite simply, according to the shopping lists and a few menus she wrote down. Most often she cooked from scratch: "I am writing this rather hurriedly before lunch with an Irish Stew bubbling on the cooker and a blackberry and apple tart for afters (made with free apples from neighbours and blackberries from 'Nature's supermarket'!)." But she showed no aversion to frozen "fish fingers"; and although she bought mayonnaise, she considered giving "Miracle Whip??" a try at least once. Margarine shows up on her list, a classic economy purchase; and so does olive oil, a classic good-cooking purchase. Brown sugar, white sugar, and self-rising flour signal the baking she liked to do—recipes for Victoria sandwich cake and a date loaf turn up—and the numerous bottles she brought home attest to a fair amount of convivial drinking, including vermouth, sherry, "Vin rouge," and "Coke, Beaujolais."

For a short time in 1956, Barbara kept a record of what she cooked for company. The notes are abbreviated, she just jotted down the three courses and the initials of the guests (except for "Hazel," perhaps her good friend and later biographer Hazel Holt), but these brief menus offer a glimpse of how she liked to entertain. For the most part she chose honorable dishes from the best-tablecloth tradition of British cookery, including potted shrimps, "veal escalopes," salmon timbales, and lamb chops, with summer pudding and "Strawberries & Cream" among the desserts (as well as something called "Coffee marshmallow," which sounds more ominous). On her occasional travels in France, Italy, and Greece she always enjoyed the food, and there's a recipe for "Pesto Alle Genovese" in a late notebook. But what she really liked were the flavors of home. In 1977 she had the chance to entertain the poet Philip Larkin, a longtime friend and strong supporter of her work whom she rarely got to see, and afterward described what she and Hilary had served. "We ate kipper paté then veal done in a casserole with peppers and tomatoes—pommes Anna and celery—cheese (he didn't eat any Brie and we thought that perhaps he only likes plain food?) then summer pudding." Nothing in this meal would have been out of place in the menus she had recorded twenty years earlier. It was her favorite festive cookery.

Around the same time as the Larkin lunch, Barbara happened to write down a week's worth of more pedestrian menus, the dinners she and Hilary shared on ordinary nights at home. Most of these, like the earlier company menus, were so timeless they could have been drawn from pretty much any week in her life. She omitted Sunday's main meal, but a glance at the rest of the week suggests roast lamb.

> Sunday—eggs and bacon
> Monday cold lamb & salads
> Tuesday sausages & apple rings
> Wednesday Curried lamb & rice
> Thursday Gourmet fish fingers w/peas
> Friday Macaroni cheese w/peas
> Saturday Peppers stuffed mince-rice

"Gourmet" fish fingers probably referred to the name of a recipe she found in a magazine—it was not a word she used except while rolling her eyes—and the curried lamb was surely more English than Indian, though she did buy basmati rice. (Two years later, Hilary returned from a trip to India with an assortment of spices, and Barbara assured a friend that "our Indian cooking has taken on a subtler more authentic flavour.")

Perhaps the most vivid aspect of these menus, especially cold-lamb week but also the more elevated cooking she did for guests, is a certain quality of the eternal. How many plates of bacon and eggs were set on the supper table, at Barbara's house and across England? How many apple rings? Barbara once remarked on what she called "all those Sundays after Trinity"—summer's uneventful church services, week after week of them, with nothing on the horizon but a speck in the distance that was All Saints' Day. She didn't mind saying she was bored, sometimes, in church; but she was never bored by the food in her life. Nor did she ever show signs of outgrowing her usual preferences, with the possible exception of livening up the spices in the curries. Food captures our aspirations as well as our appetites, and

Barbara was deeply content with what she knew best. If she was ever startled by the hodgepodge of class and cultural implications that sprang from her shopping lists—avocados, Marmite, "Tin fruit Garlic Vino," beetroot, "Steak, etc."—she never said so.

One of the best fictional meals Barbara ever prepared—best by today's standards, at any rate—takes place in *Jane and Prudence*, and it's served in a restaurant on the day that Prudence must mend a broken heart. A young woman working in London at a vague editorial job, Prudence has just learned that her current swain has become engaged to someone else, and although she didn't like him all that well, she is giving the end of the romance a full dose of sweet sadness. Normally she spends her lunch hour at nondescript cafés, but on this day she takes herself out to an expensive restaurant.

> Here, she knew she could get the kind of food she deserved, for she must be more than usually kind to herself to-day. A dry Martini and then a little smoked salmon; she felt she could manage that. . . .
>
> "And what would you like to follow, madam?" asked the waitress. "I can recommend the chicken."
>
> "Well," Prudence hesitated, "perhaps just a slice of the breast, and a very few vegetables." No sweet, of course, unless there was some fresh fruit, a really ripe yellow-fleshed peach, perhaps? And afterwards, the blackest of black coffee.

Barbara put this meal on paper sometime between 1950, when she started working on *Jane and Prudence*, and 1953, when it was published. Few people today reminisce lovingly about restaurant meals in London in the early 1950s. Yet here is a lunch so simple and apparently seasonal that it could have been designed by Alice Waters, mastermind of California cuisine and the food revolution. (Depending, of course, on how the side dishes were prepared, but considering how fussy Prudence is about the peach, it seems unlikely that she will put up with soggy vegetables.) Not every delicious meal in Barbara's books leaps directly to our own time the way this one does, but she began sending her characters to fine restaurants as early as *Excellent Women*, and they continued to eat out very well for the next thirty years. Most often, of course, we see her characters sitting in Lyons or in an overcrowded cafeteria that serves sausages and steamed puddings—the sorts of places where Barbara herself sat at lunchtime, eavesdropping. But her characters also go to little French and Italian restaurants in Soho, where lunch might start with a Tio Pepe and there's always a bottle of wine. The high end shows up, too: Wilmet, in *A Glass of Blessings*, has a memorable lunch at Simpson's, "where great joints were wheeled up to the table for one's choice and approval," and Leonora, in *The Sweet Dove Died*, has a post-opera supper at which she forgoes the Parma ham in favor of the avocado with shrimp. Dulcie, in *No Fond Return of Love*, whose zeal for people-watching matches Pym's, spies on the guests in a hotel dining room one evening and can practically taste the scrumptious-looking turbot they're being served.

Was Barbara delusional on the subject of postwar British restaurants? Julia Child would have said so, vehemently; but Raymond Postgate might have taken Barbara's side, at least in the early 1950s. Postgate was a left-wing journalist and gastronome who was so irritated by the sorry state of British restaurants that he once proposed organizing a Society for the

Prevention of Cruelty to Food. Instead he founded the Good Food Club, a kind of consumers' crusade aimed at raising the standards of public dining across Britain. Anyone could participate, simply by sending in a report on a restaurant he or she had visited recently. All visits were supposed to be anonymous; all meals had to be paid for; and contributors had to sign a statement saying they were not financially involved in the restaurant. Postgate edited the reports himself, and the first issue of *The Good Food Guide* appeared in 1951. It's still being published today.

Looking through the reports that piled up in his office after he announced the project, Postgate was startled at the amount of praiseworthy food he was encountering. "The first picture that anyone has of British cooking, outside the home, is of dullness and incompetence," he wrote in the 1951 *Good Food Guide*. "But this list makes it clear that there are literally hundreds of places of which [this picture] is totally untrue." Fine cooks, painstaking proprietors, and notable dishes existed across the land, he added, though of course "this is not France and cannot be." Since the point was to call attention to excellent eating places, not criticize bad ones, every report was positive in tone; but contributors were very clear about their personal standards. "*Real* cream" was often singled out, as well as "*real* coffee" and "real mayonnaise (hand made)." A traveler stopping at the Dixon Arms Hotel in Cheshire praised the "duckling which really is duckling and not an ancient drake," and another who ate at the Greyhound, in Penrith, reported "home-cured mild sweet bacon, farmyard fresh eggs, and real thick cream on the porridge, with a bowl of fine sugar. . . . Own herd of Jersey cows for milk and cream; own poultry." Many contributors welcomed "good, plain English cooking" when it was done properly, as at the Rope and Anchor in Lancashire: "For once in a blue moon, the vegetables were beautifully cooked, too—you could turn the plate upside-down and no waterfall would descend on the table-cloth."

Restaurants offering foreign food—it was not yet called "ethnic"—abounded in London, and contributors loved being able to praise the authenticity of their favorite dishes. Caletta's was "the best place for ravioli in all London," and upstairs at York Minster could be found "the authentic, best *cuisine bourgeoise:* for an hour or so you are back in a small Paris restaurant, for a cost of about 5/6. Specialties: Navarin printaniere, Pied de porc, Tete de veau." In Soho, many Pym-type restaurants were noted, including the Blue Windmill ("Food rich, substantial and cheap; escalopes, steak and chips") and Au Savarin, "an excellent little restaurant kept by an Alexandrian cook. Greek and other Mediterranean cooking." All across town, moreover, restaurant-goers were tasting Burmese curries, iced cherry soup, a Danish "smor-rebrod," "Pekinese chicken noodle soup," Tyrolean beef with dumplings, "Arroz alla Valenciana," and "Apfel strudel in generous portions." It was less than a decade after the war, but according to these food lovers, the restaurant scene in London was lively and enticing, and it continued to flourish, judging from the reports that came in throughout the 1950s and '60s.

Yet even Postgate found it hard to shake the preconceptions that had prompted the *Guide* in the first place. Preparing the introduction to the 1963 edition, he took a look at the original *Guide* published twelve years earlier and decided that less than half the hotel restaurants praised in that volume would have qualified for the current one. "They were only tolerable then because there was nothing better," he declared. Most had earned their place in the first *Guide* merely because they produced food that was at a somewhat higher level than the usual "overcooked meat in tiny portions, sodden vegetables, and saccharined or tinned fruit with packet custard," he asserted. And with that, he dismissed all those dinners that had delighted his first contributors—"roast woodcock with herbs and white wine," "splendidly cooked chateaubriand with little vegetables," "first-class French chef," "delicious jugged hare, lovely light pastry, and an abundance of home-cured bacon."

Maybe, despite the praise, all those 1951 meals really had been mediocre. But I'm inclined to trust Postgate's original impression—"unexpectedly high quality"—rather than the reverse nostalgia he was practicing in 1963. Styles change, tastes change, and he himself may have wondered how he ever could have enjoyed the earlier food, once he had tasted the more adventurous cooking that came later. Not to mention the fact that by 1963 the write-ups were becoming more intimidating. "First-class French chef" used to be high praise; now reviewers were casually mentioning that "only French butter is used for cooking." No self-respecting gastronome was going to look back on the 1950s with anything except pity.

Barbara had been publishing steadily—six novels in thirteen years—when her longtime publisher, Jonathan Cape, abruptly rejected the seventh. Wren Howard, cofounder of the company, wrote the letter she received in March 1963: "Several of us have now read, not without pleasure and interest, the typescript of your novel *An Unsuitable Attachment*, and have discussed it at considerable length, but have unanimously reached the sad conclusion that in present conditions we could not sell a sufficient number of copies to cover costs, let alone make any profit." He added that it was "distasteful" to him to have to tell her this, in view of their friendly relationship over the years. And that was it—he didn't encourage her to revise the manuscript, and he expressed no interest in seeing any future manuscripts. He was ejecting her from Jonathan Cape.

Similar letters had been going out to other Cape authors, ever since a wunderkind named Tom Maschler had been made editorial director three years earlier at the age of twenty-six. When he arrived, Maschler told an interviewer years later, the company "was really run down." He wanted the house to jettison its sleepy past, liven up the list, and start making money. "For my first seven years at Cape I was in sole charge of all book acquisitions," Maschler wrote in a memoir. "Except for new books from Cape authors of the past (and there were very few of those), every book we published was brought in by me." By the time the manuscript for *An Unsuitable Attachment* showed up on his desk, he was working with Joseph Heller, John Fowles, Ian Fleming, Thomas Pynchon, and John Lennon. A novel about a spinster who reads Tennyson and falls in love with a librarian would not have kept him avidly turning pages. Barbara's books tended to sell around thirty-three hundred to six thousand copies each— enough to allow Cape to break even, but far from the kind of sales figures that would have impressed Maschler. Just as important, the modesty and good manners of her writing were wholly out of place on the provocative list he was rapidly assembling.

Barbara was shocked and angry, but she had heard about the ax that was falling at Cape and realized it was no longer a good home for her work. "I have got a new typewriter and propose to improve the novel a little before trying it on some other publishers," she wrote to Bob Smith, a friend teaching at the University of Lagos in Nigeria. "I don't think the book is much worse than my others, just not to present-day taste." By the end of the summer, however, *An Unsuitable Attachment* had been turned down by three more publishers. She continued sending it out; then she wrote another book and sent that out, too; but nobody wanted to risk investing in "mild novels by Barbara Pym," as she termed them in frustration. Often the rejection letters were full of praise—"so well written, subtle, witty and all that jazz," she reported to Smith, "but of course 'not a commercial proposition.'" The reader at Barrie & Jenkins remarked, "I am bound to admit that I enjoyed it," while turning down the manuscript. Macmillan admired her "perfection of taste," and Hodder & Stoughton said her work was "in perfect taste"; the publisher Peter Davies said she was "accomplished" and a "minor tour de force," but in the end they all agreed with Constable, who told her "it was 'virtually impossible' to publish my kind of book nowadays." "They are all like SHEEP!" she raged.

Barbara had never parsed her reviews very closely. If she had, the sight of the publishing world suddenly backing away from her work might not have come as such a surprise. There were always a few critics who went into raptures, especially about *No Fond Return of Love*, which *Tatler* described as "a delicious book, refreshing as mint tea, funny and sad, bitchy and tender-hearted"—a review Barbara appreciated, though it's impossible to locate a single sentence she ever wrote that qualifies as "bitchy." But as we've seen, most reviewers couldn't bring themselves to rave over work so seemingly slight, or female characters who just couldn't take seriously the various passions associated with men. A short review of *Less Than Angels*, appearing in the *Times Literary Supplement* in 1955, may have settled her fate: she was praised for being "amusing" despite the limitations of "a small canvas and a neat, feminine talent."

She spent fourteen years of ignominy the same way she spent

the previous thirteen years of success: she kept on writing. Some days she was hopeful, other days distressed, often she was bewildered, but she never stopped scribbling in her notebook or working at the typewriter. "My new novel is beginning to flow, for what that's worth, and ideas come crowding into BP's bounding heart and teeming brain (isn't that in a hymn?)," she wrote to Smith in 1964, still early in the rejection years. Three years later she was more pessimistic—"I have finished the draft of another novel, but doubt if it will ever see print"—but she was determined to keep going. She knew her work attracted the term "cosy," apparently the worst possible category to fall into, and wondered if she could get around that tendency. "I am trying not to write so much about the clergy which/who seem to be totally unacceptable now, and to find other subjects within my limited range. But I suppose one can't really alter the *way* one writes or the things one notices." Of course she couldn't help it; she was addicted. "Lunch at the Royal Commonwealth Society with Bob," she jotted down one day in 1968. "Why aren't more of these elderly ladies wearing *canvas* shoes? I wonder. And in the restaurant all those clergymen helping themselves from the cold table, it seems endlessly." Then she pulled herself back. "But you mustn't notice things like *that* if you're going to be a novelist in 1968–9 and the 70s," she scolded herself. "The posters on Oxford Station advertising confidential pregnancy tests would be more suitable."

But she couldn't stop. Three priests got into a car on Good Friday, while she watched and wondered: "Is there a rather good fish pie in the oven—or salmon steaks cooking gently foil wrapped. Or are they really austere?" At lunch in a cafeteria: "I think, why, those women sitting round one are like lunatics in some colour supplement photograph of bad conditions in a mental home. Twitching or slumping or bending low over the food like an animal at a dish (especially if eating *spaghetti*)." She read Kingsley Amis, she read Margaret Drabble—writers who never seemed compelled to zero in on the fateful implications of a steamed pudding, writers blissfully in step with the desires of publishers and editors. "What is wrong with being obsessed with trivia?" she wailed in her notebook. "Some have criticized my novel *The Sweet Dove* for this. What are the minds of my critics filled with. What *nobler* and more worthwhile things."

Barbara worked hard to come to terms with failure, and in the notebooks of the long fourteen years we can see her trying to rub the concept into her consciousness. Over and over she set down careful reminders that she was no longer a published writer, no longer the proud claimant to an identity she had donned back in 1948. " 'Notebook of an unsuccessful novelist' might be a good thing to do," she wrote, as if prodding herself to accept defeat. "I have so much material." She was "a failing novelist," she wrote, as well as a four-time failure at her driving test. She was "an unpublished novelist," she was "Miss Pym (a failure)."

The article that would rescue her life's work, restore the only identity she ever wanted, and allow her to die in peace ran in the *Times Literary Supplement* on January 21, 1977. In honor of its seventy-fifth anniversary, the *TLS* had asked forty-two well-known figures from the literary, scholarly, and artistic worlds to nominate the most overrated and underrated writers or books of the past seventy-five years. The contributors plainly enjoyed themselves on this mission, especially when it came to the over-rateds. In this irresistible category a few names came up several times—André Malraux and E. M. Forster won two nominations each, and Malraux would have merited a third had not Hugh Trevor-Roper called him a "charlatan" and thrown him out of the running entirely. David Hockney and Bob Dylan both cited the Bible as the most overrated work, though Dylan also cited it as the most underrated. (A. J. P. Taylor, too, felt the Bible was seriously underrated, but only the King James version.) For his "overrated" selection, Eric Hobsbawm rounded up "almost any contemporary United States novelist who gets into college syllabuses," and Rebecca West singled out *Anna Karenina*. ("Young girls in love for the first time in their lives do not go to their first ball in a state of lust which would have done credit to the heartier class of hussar.") But it was the underrateds that sparked the most publicity: only one living writer was named twice in this category, and it was Barbara Pym. She had been nominated by Philip Larkin, her friend and admirer of many years, and the biographer Lord David Cecil.

She didn't know a thing about it until two friends called that night, but the next day the news was reported in *The Times* of London—"my name appeared on the front page," she said wonderingly. Even so, she was wary about celebrating too soon. If the article didn't prompt any attention from publishers, she still had to count herself a failure, *TLS* accolades or not. Then the friendly letters from Tom Maschler started rolling in. Perhaps, he hinted, they would reprint some of her backlist . . . and he was curious about what had happened to the manuscript he had seen (and rejected) the previous summer. This was *Quartet in Autumn*, which she had sent to Macmillan shortly after the *TLS* article appeared. Macmillan quickly accepted the book, so when she wrote back to Maschler she had the pleasure of informing him that he had lost out. "Hilary and I invented a Maschler pudding—a kind of milk jelly," she told Larkin.

Macmillan also asked to take another look at *The Sweet Dove Died*, which they had turned down earlier. Now they snapped it up. Reporters from *The Times* and the *Guardian* came to interview her, which was exciting, though when the articles appeared she was taken aback. "I sometimes think that if you put them all together you would gain a rather curious impression of me," she told the audience at a talk she gave a year later. "A tall, gawky woman who wants to go to South America on the Concorde and who reads Ovid and Vergil—a formidable combination, but only the gawky part is true, and even that was rather a surprise to me." Cape did go ahead and reissue her older books, the BBC made a TV film called *Tea with Miss Pym*, in which she somewhat awkwardly entertained Lord David Cecil in her garden while trying to keep the cat out of the cream jug, and in October 1977 she learned that *Quartet in Autumn* had been short-listed for the Booker Prize. Paul Scott won that year for *Staying On*, but even reaching the short list was impressive enough to be emblazoned on book jackets. *The New Yorker* asked her for a short story (she was thrilled, and "Across Crowded Room" was published in July 1979); she was made a fellow of the Royal Society of Literature; and *The Sweet Dove Died*, which had been turned down by ten publishers, became a best seller. There could not have been a more gratifying rebirth into the profession she treasured. Once again she was, as she wrote joyfully in her notebook, "Miss Pym the novelist."

As an observer of British foodways, Barbara might have been hailed as an early practitioner of culinary fiction—that is, if she hadn't been so incapable of taking serious gastronomy seriously. It was impossible for her to pour streams of lavish prose over a meal, and she was far more interested in what the food was saying than in what she herself could say about the food. She did read *The Good Food Guide* on occasion (it appears on a reading list she kept in 1970), and once, inviting a friend to lunch, she offered to take him to a restaurant she had found in the *Guide*—namely, her own home. "(*Finstock*. Barn Cottage Restaurant. Small cramped dining room; cat too much in evidence; carafe wine warming on storage heater; service willing but inefficient.)" In truth the whole idea of the *Guide* struck her as nonsensical, which made it just right for a novel, so when she started planning the characters for what would become her last book, *A Few Green Leaves*, she decided to include someone who reviewed restaurants for a living. Hilary brought home a copy of the *Guide*, and Barbara spent some happy moments with it, imagining a slew of restaurant critiques by one of the "awful good food guide people." Ultimately she created Adam Prince, a fussy, self-important food critic whose very name assures us that he is first among men. Traveling from meal to meal, "tasting, sampling, criticizing," Adam lives in fear that he has been served tinned soup or frozen vegetables and might unwittingly praise them. "That celery, cleverly disguised in a rich sauce, *had* it come out of a tin? The mayonnaise with the first course served in an attractive Portuguese pottery bowl, was it *really* home-made?"

Perhaps if Barbara had been able to work up similar indignation on the subject of tinned soups and bottled mayonnaise, she would have established better credentials among food-minded readers. But she loved her gastronomic era just as it was, a time when frozen fish fingers and Chablis were invited into the same kitchen. Elizabeth David and Raymond Postgate were also living in that era, but they greatly preferred the good food to the bad and were hoping to liberate Britain from the latter. Barbara was different. As far as she was concerned, British cooking was not defined by awfulness; awfulness was simply one of its many entrancing facets. What she prized in life were its contradictions. To be alive and eating in the culinary mélange of postwar Britain was to have a splendid seat at the banquet.

There's a lovely passage capturing this sensibility in *The Sweet Dove Died,* when Leonora, painfully in love with a younger, homosexual man named James, is touring Keats's house in Hampstead with James and his lover. The only other visitor is a middle-aged woman in a raincoat and plastic boots carrying a shopping bag full of books; and Leonora, who is one of Barbara's many fine home cooks, glimpses atop the books a frozen dinner in its bright packaging. "Leonora could see the artistically delineated slices of beef with dark brown gravy, a little round Yorkshire pudding, two mounds of mashed potato and brilliantly green peas. Her first feeling was her usual one of contempt for anybody who could live in this way, then, perhaps because growing unhappiness had made her more sensitive, she saw the woman going home to a cosy solitude, her dinner heated up in twenty-five minutes with no bother of preparation, books to read while she ate it, and the memory of a visit to Keats's house to cherish. And now she caught a glimpse of her face, plain but radiant, as she looked up from one of the glass cases that held the touching relics. There were tears on her cheeks."

Barbara, who put something of herself into all her heroines and occasionally wrote herself directly onto the page, turns up here as both Leonora and the plain-faced visitor. Her own ardent, rueful crush on a young gay man was transferred directly to Leonora; and in the raincoat-clad visitor, moved to tears at Keats's house, we see the Oxford graduate whose heart was always open to our greater English poets. It's the food that sparks the connection—fine cooking and a frozen dinner, caught for an instant in the same frame. Barbara's world was there.

Early in 1979, Barbara went into an Oxford hospital for a series of tests that revealed an unspecified malignancy. She had been treated for breast cancer back in 1971 and felt confident after the surgery that the disease was vanquished. Now she learned it was not. She started a course of radiation, and although her condition worsened in the course of the year, she managed to finish *A Few Green Leaves* and send it to Macmillan. She even started planning a new novel—two young women, college, World War II. By November it was difficult to write, but when she was admitted to the hospital that month she kept her notebook with her—just in case there was something to notice, one more jewel dropped in her path by a benevolent deity, to be gathered up and saved in a scribble. Happily, there was indeed one more, and it became part of the final entry in her literary notebooks. "I've just eaten a kind of supper—vegetable soup, baked beans and sausage!" And, noticing that the ward housed both men and women, she added a couple of lines from one of our greater English poets, John Donne—"Difference of sex no more we knew / Than our guardian angels do." She died on January 11, 1980, right after breakfast. Virginia Woolf said that death was the one experience she would never describe; for Barbara, it was that last tray of porridge and tea.

Helen Gurley Brown
(1922–2012)

If we're home for dinner—perhaps around 8:00 P.M.—I cook for David, bring his simple little repast on a tray, don't eat with him but have something satisfying before going to bed around midnight. Are we weird or something . . . separate dining times and separate menus? Lean Cuisine meatballs and spaghetti, chocolate milkshake made with Optifast for hubby. . . . If my weight's okay, dinner for me might be muesli with chopped prunes, dried apricot, six unsalted almonds, dusting of Equal, and a cup of whole milk. Delicious! If weight-fighting, it's back to tuna salad with one slice seven-grain toast and half a tablespoon of diet margarine. Dessert every night is that whole package of sugar-free diet Jell-O in one dish just for me—one envelope couldn't possibly serve four as directions suggest—with a dollop of peach, lemon, strawberry or whatever Dannon light yogurt on top. Fifty cals—heaven!

—*I'm Wild Again*

Helen Gurley Brown wrote her life story many times; in fact, she seldom wrote anything else. Of the ten books she published between 1962 and 2004, eight were autobiographical, including *The Writer's Rules*, a highly personal guide to turning out "positive prose." She also kept herself on display in the pages of *Cosmopolitan*, the magazine she edited for thirty-two years, not only via the editor's column that appeared every month, but throughout the rest of the issue. No matter who wrote an article or what it was about, nothing went to press until every paragraph glittered with her personality, her convictions, and her writing style. The enormous archive of her papers at Smith College contains drafts of more such personal writing—some two hundred pages of an autobiography, for instance, typed and revised in 1962–1963 but never finished, and a similar project that she began three decades later and also left incomplete. "Never did write a *real* biography," she scribbled on the latter manuscript before packing it up with her other papers. The word "biography" jumps out here. Was she always writing about somebody else, as she typed her life story again and again? It's as if she knew she hadn't said it yet, or said it right, or reached the center. Helen may not have read T. S. Eliot—she said her favorite poet was Rod McKuen—but her archive sits at Smith, boxes and boxes of it, like a plaintive homage to Prufrock: "And how should I begin?"

What she liked about her life story was its fairy-tale quality, though she always made it clear that she herself had never relied on a fairy godmother or, worse yet, settled down for a hundred-year nap expecting to still look good when the prince arrived. *Sex and the Single Girl,* published in 1962, became the template for all the versions of her story that would follow: she had been a young woman with nothing special about her by way of looks or money; she worked hard for many years to support herself while learning to become chic and alluring; and finally she walked off with the prize—a perfect husband. "David is a motion picture producer, forty-four, brainy, charming and sexy. . . . And *I* got him! We have two Mercedes-Benzes, one hundred acres of virgin forest near San Francisco, a Mediterranean house overlooking the Pacific, a full-time maid and a good life." Unlike the Brothers Grimm, she put this happy ending on the first page of the book. Then she filled the rest of it with practical guidance, covering everything from how to take care of woolens (sponge

Helen Gurley Brown promoting her second book,
Sex and the Office, *1964.*

the spots, never dry-clean) to whether or not it's a good idea to husband-hunt at an AA meeting (doubtful, except in Beverly Hills). *Sex and the Single Girl* sold more than 150,000 copies in hardcover and more than a million in paperback; it was published in twenty-eight countries and translated into sixteen languages. Small wonder she wrote it again and again, and although none of her other books was as successful as the first, she didn't need the sales. What she needed was to keep writing the book. And to keep telling the story, which she did in countless articles and interviews for nearly half a century—delivering anecdotes from her seventeen secretarial jobs, explaining the exercise schedule she maintained every morning of her life, discussing the pros and cons of having sex with somebody else's husband, reflecting on what it was like to work and travel and socialize the way Helen Gurley Brown worked and traveled and socialized. "There's nothing left inside Helen," her husband remarked. "It all comes out."

Throughout the years of this persistent telling and retelling, however, one aspect of Helen's life eluded her capture, and that was her food story. She talked and wrote about food all the time, but never with the sure-footedness that characterized her leaps and twirls across every other subject. Sometimes she said eating was a pleasure, one of the three best things in life (the other two were sex and breathing). Sometimes she said she enjoyed starving herself, gorging only on vitamin pills. In one interview she declared that she made a lot of pasta—"I like it with a light cream sauce with mushrooms, peas and ham." In other interviews she said her favorite meal was tuna salad. "Eating is sexy," she announced in a *Cosmopolitan* story that appeared in the second issue she edited. Years later she told a reporter, "If I eat I feel guilty. And I'd rather feel hungry." At various times she described herself as a poor cook, a "struggling" cook, "a pretty good cook," and an expert cook who made a hot breakfast and a full dinner for David throughout their marriage. Once she described her routine at the end of the day: she went straight into the kitchen after work and started cooking, she said, without even stopping to pull off her high heels. Even her editorial instincts, in general so perfectly tuned she was able to reinvent an entire genre of journalism in her own image, went awry when she took on food. A brunch menu in *Sex and the Single Girl* could have run in *Woman's Day* ten years earlier: "Lots of canned sausages piping hot; canned peach halves with grated orange peel, brown sugar, cinnamon and a maraschino cherry on top, baked half an hour; really *good* coffeecake from the bakery, heated . . ."

But if we follow her culinary paper trail through the archive, zigzagging from hot-fudge sundaes to protein powder to homemade fish cakes, we start to see that even in a maze of contradictions, Helen always knew how to find her way home. All she had to do was focus on dieting. It was as if a pile of celery sticks constituted one ruby slipper and a small portion of broiled fish the other. As soon as she fixed her attention on the challenge of eating as little as possible, she was in a safe space. "Skinny to me is sacred," she proclaimed—an affirmation of faith that bordered on the ecstatic. When she prepared the sugar-free Jell-O she describes in the excerpt at the top of this chapter, she liked to mix the powdered gelatin with only one cup of water instead of four, so that the dense, rubbery results would deliver the strongest possible hit of chemical sweetening. "Heaven!"

For Helen, dieting was a mission that went well beyond weight loss. It was a crusade against every enemy she had ever imagined lurking in her future, from poverty to spinsterhood to a pitiable old age. Fat—measured by a tiny increase in the num-

ber on the scale, a tiny change in the fit of a skirt—was the enemy that stood in for all the rest. Yet the skinnier she was, the
more persistently she proclaimed her passion for food, whether
she happened to be analyzing cottage cheese as a delicious staple
of her diet or black-bottom pie as a delicious temptation to be
shunned. Maybe she was always hungry. Or maybe her real passion was for the act of eating, a ritual she carried out with the
care and precision that the faithful bring to the telling of the
rosary. "Heaven!" she called that heap of rubbery Jell-O. Food and
comfort, food and safety, food and emotional support—it's the
oldest relationship there is, and since when did it arrive only in
the form of a good chocolate mousse? Every time Helen took a
spoon, or possibly she needed a knife and fork, but at any rate,
when she came back to her favorite Jell-O night after night, she
was tasting perfect calm and sweet security.

Helen, who was slim and not at all worried about her weight,
nevertheless started dieting during the summer of 1959, when
she was thirty-seven and engaged to David Brown. She had been
planning to marry him since the night they were fixed up at a
dinner party, and after their yearlong affair he had reluctantly
surrendered to her ultimatum and agreed to become engaged.
In her published writing, she treats this chase lightly; but the
unpublished version exposes an awkward underside. "He makes
me feel like a nothing," she complained in an undated manuscript filed at Smith with her other papers. The first Christmas
they were together, he gave her a string of "beautiful pearls"
before going off to New York to spend the holiday with his family. When she took them to be appraised so that she could have
them insured, she found the necklace was worthless: he had

spent $44.46 including tax. She was astonished and furious. She had seen the way David spent money, he was lavish with it, never stinting when there was a chance to be generous toward friends or family. The maître d' at Romanoff's, his favorite restaurant, had gotten a check for $50 as a Christmas tip. Meanwhile Helen, a self-described miser who was normally just as stingy at Christmas as she was the rest of the year, had gone ahead and bought David an expensive pair of cuff links and a box of cigars. In hysterics over his gift, she called her psychiatrist for the first time in two years.

But she didn't break up with David over the pearls. She didn't even confront him. She tucked the insult out of sight and resumed her campaign, because she desperately wanted to marry him. David was rich, smart, and presentable, a studio executive with a glamorous Hollywood life; and Helen, as she admitted outright in one of her unpublished memoirs, had been planning to marry money ever since she was a little girl. By the time she met David she had been in Los Angeles for more than twenty years, focusing her zest and a very sharp mind on earning, saving, and strategizing. The long-term goal was a good marriage— good in the sense of both love and finances—but she was also committed to having an enjoyable career and a great social life. Her widowed mother and an older sister confined to a wheelchair were back home in Little Rock, and Helen had put herself through business college before starting out to make a living as a secretary. Every scrap of the polish and charm she brought to a dinner party she had acquired on her own. Now she was doing well as a copywriter in one of the big advertising agencies—so well she had just bought a Mercedes-Benz 190 SL and paid cash for it, an achievement she still recalled with pride decades later— and she firmly believed that she deserved David Brown. But David was resisting. It was nearly a year before he was willing to give her his home phone number; until then she had to call his answering service. Even after he agreed to marry her, he didn't want to set a date. She spent the summer of 1959 making wedding plans and canceling them five times over because he kept backing out. With each disappointment she grew more frantic and depressed.

That summer Helen's job took her to Long Beach, California, where the Miss Universe pageant was about to take place. In preparation for the telecast, which would feature interviews with the contestants, she was supposed to meet with them and collect information about their families, their hobbies, and their goals in life. She spent two weeks with these women, most of them in their late teens and early twenties and all of them stunning. Helen had always been pretty and popular, there had been plenty of men in her life; but even so, she had never been forced to compete for attention with eighty of the prettiest young women in the world. Not that she had to go up against them onstage, of course, but she did have to follow them around and ask them questions, and the women were constantly surrounded by mobs of admirers and autograph seekers. To her dismay, she found that she had become invisible—too old and too ordinary looking. "People would walk right through me clawing to get at the girls," she wrote in *Sex and the Single Girl*. Meanwhile, she still didn't know where she stood with David. Would he marry her, or would she end up a lonely, rejected old maid? She drove home more demoralized than ever. On the way she stopped at a store she had heard people rave about for years—Lindberg Nutrition.

Gladys Lindberg was one of the most influential health food authorities in Los Angeles, a city long known as the health food capital of the nation. She and her husband, Walter, had opened Lindberg Nutrition in 1949, stocking it with vitamins, liver powder, soy flour, and all the other products associated with medicinal eating. Her "Serenity Cocktail," mixed by the pint in a blender, was famous across Hollywood and beyond: pineapple chunks, soybean oil, calcium lactate, vanilla, fresh milk, powdered milk, and brewer's yeast. "Have half mid-morning, half mid-afternoon," Helen instructed when she published the recipe in *Sex and the Single Girl*. Her description of that first visit to Lindberg Nutrition had all the elements of a conversion narrative in which a lost soul discovers the source of truth. Gladys, she wrote, was perpetually surrounded by devotees—"like Gandhi"—but on that first visit she asked Helen to stick out her tongue and quickly made a diagnosis of acute fatigue and vitamin deficiency. Helen, who had walked into the store miserable, was so grateful to hear kind words of advice that she burst into tears. Then she bought everything Gladys encouraged her to buy and drove home dazzled with a new philosophy of how to eat.

Her goal at first wasn't weight loss—she wasn't fat and never had been—she simply wanted to feel better. The soy-flour pancakes, the glasses of milk, the heavy doses of vitamins were all meant to boost her physical and emotional health; and she swore they worked. They certainly gave her the energy to keep prodding David toward a wedding date as he twisted and squirmed. On September 25, to her immense relief, he finally showed up at City Hall, and a brief ceremony took place. Helen had arranged a small reception at the Hotel Bel-Air, followed by a dinner with friends—nothing elaborate, since she was so afraid of having to cancel at the last minute. It all went smoothly. Then David sprang one last defensive move. It was symbolic at that point, but it gave a nasty flourish to his surrender. After dinner he took everyone to see his favorite stripper, Candy Barr, at the Largo on

Sunset Strip. Helen didn't complain, then or ever. "Candy is a damned fine stripper and I thought it a perfectly fine place to spend our wedding night," she wrote. She was always gracious in victory.

More important, she had a new source of inner strength, and she would draw on it for the rest of her life. She was dieting. "Suffice it to say I used to spend half my life in doctors' offices, which is very expensive on a secretary's salary, and I don't anymore," she wrote in *Sex and the Single Girl.* And she did live until ninety, crediting her nutritional philosophy all the way. But better health was only part of the reason she changed her approach to eating. Helen was nearing forty as she wrote *Sex and the Single Girl,* and she dreaded what she saw coming: she was about to lose her personal claim on the title "girl." There was nothing about the designation "woman" that commanded respect in the 1950s; popular terminology wouldn't start shifting for another couple of decades. Girls had the glow and the sex appeal, whereas women were dumpy and forgettable. Helen was determined to fight. "Whatever your age you can stay cute and petite and sexually attractive," she told an interviewer years later, and it was the core belief of her life. No, she couldn't control the calendar. But she could control her appearance. She could look young no matter how many years piled up.

Later on, plastic surgery would become an important lifeline, but Helen's first and most enduring commitment was to the bathroom scale. Be thin forever, she advised readers; be thin at any price. "If you are already mounds of pounds overweight, you must *Do Something* or you can't hope to be blissfully single," she explained in *Sex and the Single Girl.* "The few men who insist they like girls plump are usually the ones who prefer cleaning rifles or exchanging jokes in the locker room to flirtation." Normally

Helen encouraged women not to rule out any male over twenty-one without at the very least scrutinizing him with an open mind, but she did maintain a category of bad bets that included "the weirdies, the creepies, the dullies, the snobs, the hopelessly neurotics and mamas' darlings," and with them she filed all men who were capable of loving a fat woman. Happiness while being overweight was impossible, she decreed, a cruel fantasy. Any woman living in peace with an imperfect body, any woman who couldn't be bothered to pare away every unjustifiable scrap of flesh, was plummeting to a lonely, sexless old age. "The fact is, you vote for or against being slender," she told a reporter. "You vote for or against a sex life as you get older. . . . It's a straight decision you make in your forties." Helen made it a little earlier, the moment she noticed that her forties were barreling toward her. The nutritional principles she learned from Gladys Lindberg—eat mostly protein and ingest dozens of pills per day—remained the mainstays of her diet, but the rationale shifted from health to weight. "We health nuts are never fat!" she crowed in *Sex and the Single Girl*. "The foods that make you sexy, exuberant, full of the *joie de vivre* are also the ones that keep you slender." Her fortieth birthday came along right on schedule, but she faced it in full battle dress, including wig and makeup. She had David safely in her keeping now, and she had a credo—"I diet every day of my life." She would never let go of man or motto.

Not long after they were married, she and David spent an evening with friends that was so perfect, so "particularly happy," that she treasured the memory for years. They invited people to a private screening in a projection room at the studio, and afterward the group went on to a party given by her advertising colleagues in honor of the newlyweds. There, surrounded by everyone important to her, she proudly showed off her movieland husband. All evening, the champagne flowed and David was at his most charismatic. Recalling that night years later, she wrote of the joy she felt as a radiant image kept racing through her mind: "I'm a *wife*," she told herself over and over. "I'm a *wife*."

Marrying David was an achievement she celebrated for the rest of her life. No version of her story appeared without David at the center of it, a living amulet that she couldn't help touching constantly for luck. Every time she mentioned him, in print or in public, she garlanded his name with flattery, praising his brilliance, his good looks, his incomparable sex appeal, and his Hollywood successes. The daily routine of their married life, their luxurious travels, and their occasional squabbles appeared regularly in her books and magazine columns; and she gave him lavish credit for inspiring *Sex and the Single Girl* and guiding her through the remake of *Cosmopolitan*. Without him, she knew, she would never have been "Helen Gurley Brown," a name that would resonate with sex and pizzazz around the world by the end of the twentieth century. But there was another, more fundamental reason why Helen placed her husband at the center of her existence. Simply put, he had married her. When she called him "MY WHITE KNIGHT" in an unpublished memoir, she meant it. What made the Single Girl such an enormously satisfying persona for her was that she wasn't, in fact, single. She wasn't dependent upon herself to generate an aura of desirable femininity. She wasn't a nothing who got cheap pearls for Christmas or a lonely spinster envious of other, luckier women. She was the wife of a glamorous husband, an identity so important to her that she made it the heartbeat of her entire career.

"I am not your truly liberated woman," Helen claimed in *New York* magazine, in an article dated August 31, 1970. Five days earlier, tens of thousands of women had marched down Fifth

Avenue in the biggest demonstration for women's rights in half a century, and thousands more had marched and rallied in some ninety cities across the country. It was the first nationwide outburst of the feminist movement, and in its honor *New York* magazine had approached eleven famous couples "to see how lib is affecting their lives together." The article opened with Helen and David Brown, and the first thing Helen did was play down her professional ambitions. "I probably became a real hot-shot career lady by being married to David," she offered. (This was five years after she had presided over a turnaround at *Cosmopolitan* so speedy and comprehensive, it made publishing history.) "My job just isn't nearly as high-powered as David's," she added. "He's a tycoon." David protested that her job was just as important as his—"possibly more important"—and Helen acknowledged that they both operated in the world at a very high level. But she backed away from even the slightest hint that she considered herself David's equal in the marriage, and she was adamant about how she defined her role. "When I go home, I'm a wife," she declared, "and I do all the cooking."

To be a wife was to cook. Not to eat—that was a different matter entirely—but to cook. As we've seen, Helen's remarks on the subject of herself and cooking typically flew in all directions; but when she was talking or writing about David, she most often placed herself squarely at the stove. During their courtship, she said, she cooked for him all the time. And as soon as they were married, she fired his longtime housekeeper, whose cooking was terrible, and hired a better one. On the weekends, when the new housekeeper was off, Helen took over the kitchen herself. In later years, even if she was dining on vitamin pills, she continued making "regular" food at night for David, or else she personally heated up the Lean Cuisine she prescribed for him when she was watching his weight. "She's most pleased when she's cooking dinner for me," he confided once, in a story about their "private life." Most strikingly (and this became a running motif in her accounts of married life), she always cooked his breakfast. And it wasn't just toast and coffee. He liked Welsh rarebit, eggs Benedict, roast-beef hash, and codfish cakes; and she cooked them from scratch, morning after morning, until she started worrying about his health and switched him to hot or cold cereal. "I take good care of David," she said firmly.

If Helen could have chosen a national anthem for women, it would have been the 1958 Rodgers and Hammerstein song "I Enjoy Being a Girl," which had an opening line worthy of being inscribed on her stationery: "I'm a girl, and by me that's only great!" Absent a song by way of introduction, she made a point of projecting girlish charm, and she worked it expertly. A reporter from *Life* magazine described what it was like to meet her: "When she receives a male visitor in her office, she will smile bashfully, float away from her desk to a couch, curl up her legs, wrap her arms around a pillow, raise her eyebrows and begin talking in a soft, very intimate voice about how small and tiny she is and how she uses a padded bra and Pan-Cake Makeup and wears a wig and false eyelashes."

Helen was devoted to this particular version of herself, and year after year she played the role with determination. "I'm the geisha girl," she used to say. Sometimes she even cast herself as a submissive little wife who turned over her paycheck to hubby— an image considerably at odds with her strong belief in financial independence for women. Indeed, it was an image at odds with her own marital history. As a bride she had been eager to jump into the family finances, and as soon as David opened the books to her, she scanned them disapprovingly and introduced a few economies. In the course of the 1960s, however, she pulled back from the job of family accountant, or at least she changed the tone of her public utterances. By 1976, she was telling the press that she could write herself a check anytime she wanted, but she much preferred having David give her an allowance. "Money is sexy," she told a reporter, and snuggled up to her husband as she said so.

Money was sexy, but asserting control over her own earnings, at least in public, was not. "Sexy" may well have been the most important adjective in Helen's vocabulary; she used the term in every possible context from pedicures to stock portfolios, always to bestow an impression of perfect desirability. But the qualities that made a woman sexy were overwhelmingly identified with her being, as Helen put it, "a geisha." Helen believed in equality between the sexes, but she wanted it to operate silently in the background, like good air-conditioning. Out front she liked to see the natural order of things—girls who were cute and appealing and men who were powerful. She was the rare feminist, possibly the only feminist, with an unabashed commitment to male supremacy.

The persona eventually identified with "Helen Gurley Brown" began to take shape about a year after David and Helen got married, when Helen's career in advertising suddenly swerved off course. Without notice, her boss informed her that she was making more money than any other female copywriter; consequently he had decided to cut her salary in half. David urged her to quit at once, but Helen accepted the pay cut. Justifying this decision in the autobiography she drafted years later, she explained that she didn't really need the money and that she would not have been able to find another good copywriting job. After all, she pointed out, the number of women copywriters and the number of decent jobs available lined up just about evenly. Neither of these points makes much sense: needy or not, Helen kept a death grip on every dollar in her possession, and to relinquish a huge chunk of her potential earnings would have been agonizing. What's more, she was climbing steadily higher in her profession, albeit on the female side of it. She didn't have to bow to this extraordinary insult: she was employable. Yet she bowed, and the reason can be gleaned from her description of what happened when she heard the bad news. Helen was personally, not professionally, devastated; all she could utter in response was, "Don't you like me anymore?"

She didn't ask him about the quality of her work, she asked him about herself: was she suddenly unlovable? Not pretty enough, not young enough, not skinny enough? Something had gone badly wrong, and she panicked. Of course she would stay in the job. Of course she would work as hard as ever. As for the loss of income, she soothed herself by stealing stamps and carbon paper and smuggling them out of the office.

But she also began to wonder what else she could be doing, and one day she asked David, who had left the movie business temporarily and was working in publishing, if he had any ideas for a book she could write. He said yes, he had just outlined an idea and sent it to an editor in New York—maybe it would suit Helen. The book would be about single girls and how they arranged their sex lives—what they wore, how they set up their apartments, how they learned to talk and flirt. "I said, 'That's my *book*! Get it back!'" The two of them went to work, Helen drafting quantities of material and David editing—"ruthlessly," she said later. "We had bloody battles, none of which I ever won." David insisted on rewrite after rewrite, especially when they were working on the chapter about how to conduct an affair. Helen had to revise it three times. Later on she regularly gave him credit for the book's success, phrasing her own role in strangely passive terms: "In other words, though he only wrote a few lines of it, David was able to produce a hit out of me."

What he produced "out of me" was a character, a literary construction that would personify the author of *Sex and the Single Girl* and, soon, everything else surrounding Helen's name. The lifeblood of "Helen Gurley Brown" was always going to be her zeal for sex, hence the special attention David gave to the chapter on having an affair. But judging from an early draft of the book in the Smith archive, another chapter that needed a heavy edit was the one about food. The "Helen" that was under construction had to be able to pull off delightful meals and parties with the same airy self-confidence she brought to the bedroom, the office, the department store, and the hairdresser. For the real Helen, however, this aspect of her narrator was difficult to package. She had no trouble using her own experience as the basis for the nutrition chapter, for she was comfortable with the image of herself as a dieter. But despite the years she spent making breakfast and dinner for David, she was never comfortable with any single image of herself as a home cook. Hence the pileup of conflicting claims that marked her discussion of the subject over the years. Getting the meals on the table was one thing; writing about them was quite a different challenge. To type the words that would characterize her relationship with food, the most intimate and nerve-racking relationship of her life, seemed impossible. Helen didn't trust herself around food; what sort of role model could she possibly be for a culinary "Helen"?

The food world offered little help with this problem. It was the early 1960s, and the best-known names in home cooking—

Fannie Farmer, Betty Crocker, Irma Rombauer, Dione Lucas—projected a warm and cozy domestic image that was the opposite of what she and David were after. Julia Child hadn't started her television career yet, and in any event a character like Child wouldn't have suited the book's purposes, which called for someone young, chic, and seductive. Nigella Lawson would have been a good prototype; unfortunately, she was still a baby. So Helen cast about in popular culture for a stand-in she could place at the stove.

The first one she came up with was a dimwit. "I can't cook and I know it," the draft begins, and continues with a litany of embarrassing flops—tough garlic bread, limp bacon, burned butter, clumpy eggs. Trying to make a cheese fondue, this particular "Helen" reports, she ended with a single impenetrable mass of coagulated cheese. She says she made frosting from a box of mix so old it had gone rancid, and she served fruit cup in scooped-out grapefruit skins left over from a previous party but perfectly clean since she had washed them in soap and water. As for cookbooks, they only created more problems; and to prove this point she quotes from Escoffier, adding her own despairing comments in parentheses. "(They assume I *have* a soup tureen.)"

We can't know whether Helen had *I Love Lucy* specifically in mind when she created this frantic female, but in the course of the 1950s Lucille Ball had become the most famous haphazard wife on television, throwing herself into one project after another with high hopes that invariably ended up in pratfalls. It's easy to see Lucy as the cook in Helen's imagined kitchen, especially washing the grapefruit shells. In one or two places, we can also hear Helen channeling Peg Bracken, whose hilarious *I Hate to Cook Book* came out in 1960 and became an instant best seller, beloved for its heartfelt commitment to getting food on the table with the least possible creativity. Helen was choosing well, but she wasn't accomplished enough to lift what she needed from these two experts and reframe it in a distinctive voice of her own, especially in the fraught realm of cooking.

In the end she settled on a "Helen" whose years as a kitchen klutz are safely behind her. The disasters—"failing with the never-fail hollandaise a few times and all that"—are mentioned only briefly, and although the inane reference to Escoffier remains, it's succinct. Most important, she sums herself up as "a pretty good cook," which allows her to sound relaxed and confident as she gives advice on how to stage cocktail parties, picnics, brunches, and "fabulous little dinners." But there's a kind of shield between the cook and the food, a studied air of lighthearted sophistication that Helen sprays over the text like perfume. Put "Rumanian gypsy music" on the record player at your cocktail party, she suggests, and wear "a ruffled frock" to the picnic, "as Emma Bovary might have done." And don't forget, you'll want to have the makings of a "hearty little breakfast" on hand at all times, since you don't always know the night before that you're going to have a guest in the morning. ("But there he is . . . *ravenous!*") Whenever she zeroes in for a closer look at the food, however, the whole edifice collapses. Suddenly Emma Bovary is serving quick 'n' easy vichyssoise made from frozen potato soup mixed with half-and-half. To start off a seductive candlelight dinner at home, "Rosa Rita frozen cocktail tacos are delicious." As for that unexpected morning guest, he'll sit down to a glass of tomato-clam juice and an omelet filled with canned mushrooms, canned pimentos, American cheese, and chopped onions. "Or use canned tomatoes instead of *all* of these."

Later in the chapter Helen sets out more formal menus, with many of the high-end touches popular in that era—lobster tails,

French sauces, a cinnamon stick in every cup of coffee. She acknowledges that she "borrowed heavily" from sources including *Joy of Cooking* and *The Gourmet Cookbook,* and she certainly did: some of the recipes were copied almost word for word. But she was thinking about how to show off, not how to cook and still less how to eat. Her menus are arrayed as if for a food-styling session, with no need to apply a sense of taste. One dinner features fresh artichokes; another has a "Marinated Vegetable Platter" in which everything is canned. Fresh garlic appears, then disappears in favor of garlic powder. The chocolate soufflé is a classic version, complete with vanilla bean; it's accompanied by a "Foamy Vanilla Sauce" made from a package of instant pudding. Helen didn't mind. She never imagined herself tasting any of it, so the disarray was invisible to her. But she had just done the equivalent of sending "Helen" to a party wearing a cocktail dress and bedroom slippers.

It's fair to assume that very few readers of *Sex and the Single Girl* were bothered by its culinary incoherence: the book took off with such a roar that even Helen was taken aback. Her publisher, Bernard Geis, was well-known for masterminding torrents of publicity, and her book tour expanded into months of press interviews, speaking engagements, radio shows, and television appearances. David became her business manager and publicist, as well as chief adviser and most fervent supporter. At his urging she signed a contract with Geis for a second book, as well as an option for a third. She and David started to envision a media empire built around Helen's now famous persona. And as David worked his innumerable connections in Hollywood and New York, the two of them brainstormed.

What about Broadway? The hit musical *How to Succeed in Business Without Really Trying* had been running for more than a year—perhaps Helen's advice to single girls on getting ahead could be seen as a kind of female counterpart. She signed on with the theatrical agent Lucy Kroll, where she joined Martha Graham and Carl Sandburg on a distinguished client list. Kroll loved the book and thought it definitely had the makings of a musical, but Warner Brothers had already purchased the film rights, so the stage rights would not be available for the next several years. Reluctantly, they all shelved the project.

Television? Surely there was a sitcom in the story of young Helen's perils and exploits as a career girl. She and David wrote a synopsis for a series called *The Single Girl* about a young woman working in an advertising agency and sent it off to ABC. The company mailed it back with a discouraging letter. Building a series around a female lead was too risky, the Browns were advised, and the advertising business was a poor fit as a background since most people didn't understand it. (Mary Tyler Moore and later *Mad Men* would prove that the Browns were ahead of their time on both counts.) They had no better luck with another of their sitcom ideas, this one for a show called *Normal Like Me,* set in a psychologist's office. The heroine would be the receptionist, a young woman—like Helen—who manages to help all sorts of patients solve their problems. One week the patient might be a man fearful of women; naturally the receptionist can guide him to a cure. Another episode might focus on a woman who can't seem to lose weight. As Helen saw it, this would be a madcap episode, yet it would have universal appeal, since with the receptionist's help the woman would lose twenty pounds. "It's a chance for everybody to live through his own dieting experiences again," she wrote confidently.

Perhaps a talk show? Helen drafted a proposal for a program called *Frankly Female,* which she would cohost alongside a man—

"to say some of the things out loud that women have heretofore only said to themselves!" She also saw possibilities in a series of programs aimed at helping people relax. She herself was anxious and hard-driving by nature; and she was always terrified that a restaurant or hostess would serve her real coffee instead of Sanka—a mistake guaranteed to keep her awake and jumpy for hours. Hence she was certain that a show she titled *The Unwind Up,* to be led by a skilled hypnotist, would have wide appeal. She envisioned thirty minutes of "soothing, soporific talk," interrupted every ten minutes with a round of actual hypnosis that would put the audience to sleep. She didn't address the question of how sponsors would react to viewers dropping off en masse, possibly missing a commercial; it's likely that David was not involved in this proposal.

Her life, her feminine perspective, her therapy—all these struck Helen as excellent possibilities for TV shows, and so did her preocccupation with food. *Cook's on the Fire* was a proposal for a daytime game show aimed at women, and Helen appears to have given this a good deal of thought: she described it in detail and added a list of possible sponsors. An emcee would pose increasingly difficult questions about food, cooking, nutrition, menu planning, and table setting, and each contestant would collect prizes for her correct answers. The set would be outfitted with a spice rack, cooking equipment, stove, and raw and cooked foods, all to be used in the course of the game; Helen wrote out six pages of sample culinary challenges. Which of these foods has the most protein per four-ounce serving? Which of these six greens is not suitable for a salad? You are going to see dancers performing five dances from five different countries— after each dance, go to the table and choose the food from that country. (Tacos, for instance, would be the correct choice in response to a Mexican hat dance.)

Far-fetched though they were as TV shows, these proposals reveal something of how Helen's mind worked whenever she had a creative project in front of her, be it a book or a TV script or a magazine. She was reluctant to think beyond her own instincts. Nothing else interested her, and the huge success of *Sex and the Single Girl* seemed proof that her body, her emotions, her mind, and her psyche constituted the single most valuable trove of research material she would ever possess. David felt the same way, and ultimately the two of them came up with a well-defined project for realizing more of the profits they could practically see hovering around Helen's very being. They would produce a monthly magazine wholly identified with Helen: she would be the editor, and it would be aimed directly at the readers who were making *Sex and the Single Girl* a phenomenon of postwar popular culture. A tentative title for the magazine was *Femme,* but more important was the subtitle: "For the Woman on Her Own." Just about anything could catapult women into this category: they could be single, divorced, or widowed; they could be "separated and otherwise neglected wives"; they could even be married—"the Betty Friedan set."

Helen, whose voice is apparent in much of the proposal, was emphatic about where *Femme* would be positioned among the competition. No lunch box suggestions, no laundry dilemmas, no tips on renovating the attic. Instead, *Femme* would take up problems that were far more pertinent to . . . well, Helen. She proposed stories on the difficulty of achieving a perfectly flat stomach, for instance, and on the "fight against aging." She herself would write a column called "The Men in Your Life," answering readers' questions about their relationships. And she had it in mind to run a true story by an author she identified as "Anonymous" about how an older woman successfully fought off hordes of younger competitors and won "a superbly eligible man." She also wanted the magazine to become identified with literary journalism: *Femme* would be "New Yorker size," with paper quality the equivalent of *Playboy*'s. Nobody, she insisted, would ever mistake *Femme* for a typical women's magazine.

Perhaps that's why nobody wanted to publish it. David shopped it around without success. Then, early in 1965, he took it to Hearst, the publishing conglomerate and owner of *Cosmopolitan*, where David himself had been an editor back in the 1940s. *Cosmopolitan* was nearly eighty years old and had once enjoyed an impressive reputation as a home for high-quality political writing and important fiction. After World War II, it began running more stories on fashion, marriage, and other female-friendly topics, but it never acquired a distinctive profile as a women's magazine. By the 1960s its efforts to define itself had become largely incoherent—"Great Stars and Their Illnesses," "Four Lousy Husbands Explain Why," "Neglected Magic in Every Woman's Voice." Advertising revenues and circulation figures were dropping, and Richard Deems, president of Hearst magazines, had lost faith in the current editor. Deems wasn't interested in starting a new magazine, but he was very interested in Helen's potential as an editor and the possibility of reaching an untapped market of female readers. He offered her *Cosmopolitan*, a two-year contract subject to renewal, and a great deal of freedom.

Apart from the research and imagination she put into planning *Femme*, Helen knew nothing about magazines; David said later he didn't think he'd ever seen her read one. She was appropriately nervous about taking on the equivalent of a gut renovation in a world where she could barely recognize a hammer. But she had written *Sex and the Single Girl*—an achievement that was already her personal touchstone, a constant reminder that, yes, she was at one with the female zeitgeist. She started at Hearst in March 1965, and her first issue was on the newsstands in July, perched alongside the other women's magazines like an audacious stranger making herself at home in a startled neighborhood. The model on the cover evoked neither a mom nor a career girl; instead, she looked a lot like Emma Bovary at that picnic. Thick blond hair fell almost to her shoulders, and she wore a low-cut, ruffled pinafore. Her eyes were heavily made up, and she gazed out with a cool, blank stare, holding her pale pink lips slightly open. Next to her, heralding the stories inside, were the suggestive cover lines that would become one of the most famous features of the magazine. "The new pill that promises to make women more responsive" was the most prominent, and right under it came "World's Greatest Lover—What it was like to be wooed by him!" Helen was intent on reaching the only reader who counted—namely, herself. "I always knew exactly what I wanted," she told a media industry publication fifteen years later. "My motivation for changing the magazine was to make it the kind of magazine I could produce. It didn't matter what readers said or what advertisers said. I only knew how to do one thing." By November the magazine's sagging circulation had jumped to a million copies per issue, advertising was up by 50 percent, and she was a legend in her brand-new profession for pulling off what *Life* called "one of the fastest and most remarkable successes in the history of publishing."

One of Helen's earliest and most definitive acts at *Cosmopolitan* was to seize control of the writing. Unlike most editors in

chief, she was not willing to leave the details of sentence struc-
ture, vocabulary, and punctuation to staff members lower on the
masthead. Every night she took home a pile of manuscripts and
rewrote them until story after story rang with her own distinctive intonation, the one she had first floated in *Sex and the Single
Girl*. Not until her second year at the magazine did she relax her
personal grip on the prose and assemble a list of writing rules—
sixteen pages' worth, along with eight pages of clichés to avoid—
and distribute them to her staff with instructions to wield them
on every article that came in. Most of these rules were unsurpris-
ing ("Every new paragraph must have some connection with the
paragraph before"), but some were extreme. Helen wanted prose
that had been stripped to its essentials, and she deleted every
word she judged useless, including "the," "an," and "a" if they appeared more than twice per sentence. Then, once the paragraph
had been reduced to bare scaffolding, she added the accessories—
chiefly ellipses, exclamation points, and italics. The voice that
emerged became her trademark. "You and I are such old friends—
ten years together now—that I have this odd desire to *tell* you
about myself!" she wrote in a 1975 editor's column. "I rise at 8:00
A.M., fix David's breakfast if he's in town, exercise for an hour and
ten minutes (*nothing* interferes . . . I've only missed two days in
eight years), dress, do my hair, makeup, arrive at the office at
11:00. Once there I usually stay—lunch, unless I have a business
date, comes *with* me in a brown paper bag."

Not everybody found this kind of prose as attractive as she
did. "If Mrs. Brown never italicizes another word or uses another exclamation point, she'll still have used both devices more
than one woman should in a lifetime," commented a critic at the
Miami News, reviewing *Sex and the Single Girl*. Nora Ephron, who
wrote for *Cosmopolitan* a few times early in her career, said it

drove her crazy to see every story bombarded with "italics, exclamation points, upbeat endings, and baby simpleness." But Helen cherished the way she sounded in print: she used this voice in all her books, and she was proud of imposing a literary style on *Cosmopolitan* that made it, she declared, the equal of any magazine in the country, including *The New Yorker*. "I would say the writing in *Cosmopolitan* is 60 to 70 percent of our success," she told an industry publication. "It's non-boring writing . . . and even if it happens to be about how not to have jitters on your first date, it is just as carefully crafted as a book about Henry Kissinger's White House years." True, books about Henry Kissinger rarely included terms like "pippy-poo" and "depthy," which were two of Helen's favorites, but she never apologized. As she told an interviewer from *Playboy*, "Let's just say I've made a thing out of writing very girlishly."

Cosmopolitan was famous for sex, not food; nonetheless Helen ran stories about cooking and eating in every issue. She ran dieting stories, too, including a monthly column called "Dieter's Notebook." But she was eager to attract food and liquor advertising, which meant she had to offer her readers regular, vicarious experiences with delicious meals. The other important categories in *Cosmopolitan* were men, beauty, work, and love, and Helen had no trouble whittling these topics into stories that slipped easily into each month's editorial package. But she flailed for years trying to figure out how best to package a food-and-recipes story.

As we've seen, she bushwhacked her way across this terrain when she was trying to figure out the right culinary approach for *Sex and the Single Girl*, but the challenge of a monthly magazine was more daunting. Her own experience, which typically guided her like a miner's lamp whenever she dreamed up a story or edited one, wouldn't have been wide-ranging or pliable enough to be useful even if she trusted it. "Cooking *is* part of wooing when you have a live one, and I can't count the dinners I cooked old David Brown," she had written in *Sex and the Single Girl*, and the image of herself as a wife who cooked was one that she brandished often throughout her career. Yet she felt most comfortable with this image when she was keeping it as far away as possible from any actual food. She liked reciting David's breakfast menus, but that was as close as she was willing to get. When she chatted in interviews about making dinner for him, she rarely spoke in specific terms: she mentioned "regular food" or, later in life, the kinds of frozen meals she kept on hand. It's possible, of course, that she never did cook, despite her various claims otherwise. But somebody had to get the meals together when she and David didn't go out, and Helen hated the idea of paying anyone else to cook. As a confirmed skinflint, she was certain that anyone she hired would just sit around the kitchen all day downing filet mignon at Helen's expense. What jumps out from these dinner references and much of her other personal food writing is a deep reluctance to give life to a specific dish by naming it—unless the context was a diet. Only when she was writing under that rubric did she feel safe enough in the presence of a plate of food to discuss it. She wrote often about the desserts she adored, for instance, but chiefly when the surrounding prose made it clear that she had no intention of eating them. Then she was able to name each item—a frozen lemon mousse, a slice of black forest cake, a pint of ice cream—and castigate it like a righteous Puritan. Any morsel that wasn't low-calorie was "sinful," "naughty," "gobble gobble gobble," "*heavy* sinning," or "a cruel but devastating lover."

Just once, in an unpublished autobiography she began drafting in the early 1960s, did she try to put meals onto the page as if they constituted a normal, nonthreatening aspect of her daily life. She was writing about her newlywed years, depicting herself as a young wife happily cooking for David and doing a much better job of it than his inept housekeeper. Here, in the very specific context of youthful wedded bliss, she was able to insert occasional references to what they ate, including lamb chops, avocados stuffed with orange ice, lima-bean casserole, "Poulet Negresco," Caesar salad, and raspberry Jell-O mold. Some of these dishes are implausible: "Poulet Negresco," which she described as roast chicken basted with honey, was in fact a chicken-and-pasta casserole. But even if one or more of these bouts of culinary activity were imaginary, they constituted—like Marianne Moore's definition of poetry—imaginary cooking with real food in it. Helen named all the dishes, and she placed them front and center in a self-portrait that showed her consuming normal meals. Not dieting, not bingeing—just eating.

It never happened again. She put the manuscript away, and from then on she indulged in mentions of mouthwatering food or drink only when she was advising readers how to avoid it. At parties, for instance: "I have dumped champagne (which I adore) into other people's glasses when they weren't looking or, in a real emergency, into a split-leaf philodendron, wrapped eclairs in a hanky and put them in my purse, *once* in an emergency, sequestered one behind the cushion of an upholstered chair—in a napkin of course," she wrote, the sentences sounding a little hiccupy because of the writing rules. "To get myself to abstain I help other people fill and refill their plates, have passed a hundred thousand brownies with whipped cream in my time without having *any*. . . ." Real food would always be enemy territory; she would never feel safe near it.

Her first decision on *Cosmopolitan*'s food coverage was the best she ever made: she ran monthly excerpts from Mimi Sheraton's *The Seducer's Cookbook*, published two years earlier. Sheraton, the knowledgeable and sophisticated food writer who would go on to become the first female restaurant critic at *The New York Times*, took as her cheerful premise that the best way to get someone into the bedroom was to start in the kitchen. The text was good-natured and a little risqué—she included gastronomic guidelines for extramarital affairs as well as courting couples—and it's easy to see why Helen loved the idea of defining the magazine's culinary outlook this way. It's also easy to see why the recipes struck her as just right for a women's magazine that aimed to establish its own niche. Sheraton wasn't writing about convenience or lunch boxes; she was writing about taste, enjoyment, the whole sensual experience of a fine meal. Her recipes ranged widely, from strawberries in white wine to filet of beef *en croûte*, but even the simplest menus radiated a sense of gustatory pleasure that was highly unusual in mass-market food journalism aimed at women.

After this very smart move, however, Helen lost her nerve. Apparently she wanted to offer readers a range of cooking styles, but she couldn't seem to come up with a catchy approach that would cover all the possibilities. She published dinner party classics such as poached salmon, *blanquette de veau,* and chicken with wine and cream, all simple versions made from scratch; and she published a vaguely Italian menu for a "Passionate Antipasto Party," culminating in a dessert called "Lime Chiffon Capitoline" (lime gelatin mixed with whipped cream and topped with canned chocolate syrup). Frozen eggrolls and frozen crêpes suzette showed up; so did "Lobster Fra Diavolo," and so did "hearty open-faced steak Tartare sandwiches," recommended for Saturday afternoon after a baseball game. "Over coffee, join him in smoking a tiny-tip cigar fresh from your refrigerator! That's one man you'll see again." A decade earlier, popular magazines had started to run food stories set up as photo essays, showing how the rich and/or famous entertained at home. Helen never missed a chance to put celebrities in the magazine, so she adopted the idea and produced her own culinary photo essays, featuring starlets who loved giving dinner parties. Dyan Cannon could be seen making quiche lorraine, and Barbara Ferris was pictured pounding away at minute steaks for steak Diane.

Was she editing for a daring cook or a conservative cook? A skilled cook or a befuddled cook? She could never decide. In one issue she published the highly regarded wine writer Robert Misch, in another she made a pitch for organic produce because she admired Adelle Davis. Meanwhile she ran a recipe for "Exotic East Indian Meat Loaf" with ground beef, curry powder, garlic powder, and instant onion. Going over the "easy feast" menu scheduled for a Christmas issue, Helen advised the food editor to add detailed instructions on how, precisely, to baste the Cornish hens with melted butter. But if there were any novice cooks willing to tackle the recipes for a Japanese dinner ("Go Geisha!"), they found themselves attempting to deep-fry pork strips with no directions whatever.

The dieting stories ranged widely as well, from relatively sensible to far-fetched to wild-eyed, but on this terrain Helen was at home. All the weight-loss tips blazed with her verve and confidence no matter whose byline was on the article. Eat everything, absolutely everything, on Saturday and Sunday, she urged in the first big diet story she chose for the magazine: "The Low Will-Power, High-Protein Diet (that allows for binges and slide-backs)." Fudge, cinnamon buns, heaps of vanilla ice cream on apple pie, "English muffins dripping with butter, candy bars at the movies"—pack them in all weekend. Then plunge to some 650 calories' worth of raw vegetables and lean protein on Monday and practice self-denial nearly as rigorously throughout the rest of the week. Another story exulted in "the incredible, intoxicating joy of *tasting*" and encouraged readers to have just a single bite of whatever looked delicious to them. Soon they would reach their daily calorie limit, but without ever feeling deprived. "A sip of your husband's gin and tonic won't cost more than 20 calories and a bite of his pizza, 40 . . . one French fried potato (2 by 1/2 by 1/2 inches) 19 1/2 . . . . It's not difficult at all, especially carrying one of the new, more complete, calorie counters." Helen celebrated a diet based on the principles of hatha yoga; she celebrated never eating enough ("When you're full, you know you've been naughty"); she celebrated every artificial sweetener on the market, advising readers to ignore the health warnings from "overconscientious food and medical columnists"; and she celebrated weight-loss drugs. ("Ask your doctor about Bamadex Sequels, a prescription pill for appetite control that's mildly tranquilizing. Sometimes it *does* seem as if you'll never lose those final three pounds, and you need *something* to calm your fears. . . .")

Real food or diet food, splurging or starving—no matter what was on the table, Helen made it a point of honor to cast her public relationship with food in rapturous terms. Everything she ate had to be *"delicious"* or *"scrumptious"* or *"luscious,"* especially when she was evoking a zero-calorie bouillon cube or a breakfast of protein powder stirred into diet orange soda. Again and again she described to readers and interviewers what she voraciously consumed each workday (tuna fish; cottage cheese with mozzarella chopped into it; one apple) or ate on vacation ("an incredible salad bar I simply rolled *around* in every night"). A writer from *Esquire* once asked her for a Christmas recipe, and she said she had invented a new version of hot buttered rum: "I substitute fake ingredients for all of the fattening ones, and it's delicious."

Skinny Hot Buttered Rum

Into a mug or cup put:
 1 tablespoon "butter" made from Butter Buds
 1 packet of Equal
 1 oz. rum
Put a teaspoon into the mug. Fill to the brim with boiling
 water. Add a few cloves on top. Savor.

Back when she wrote *Sex and the Single Girl,* Helen was forty years old, five feet four inches, and slim, accustomed to a carefully monitored regimen of diet and exercise that kept her at 109 pounds. As soon as she started work at *Cosmopolitan,* however, it was apparent that she was a middle-aged woman in the land of the young, and vigilance was the price of survival. She decided she could afford fifteen hundred calories a day and not a single extra; if she gained a pound, she imposed a drastic calorie reduction or a total fast for at least a day. Exercise began first thing in the morning—"Thirty minutes on the body and 20 on the face"—and continued later in the day, whenever she had time to do a few leg lifts. "Age to me is a disease to be fought back like cancer, multiple sclerosis and typhoid," she told a reporter. "I'll do anything if it works." Her weight dropped to 105, then 97; when it reached 95 her hair started falling out. "I may have carried it 'too far,'" she admitted in her second-to-last memoir, *The Late Show,* and called herself, at the age of seventy, "a grown-up anorectic." The term "grown-up" would have been harder for her to utter than the word "anorectic." As she once remarked, "I think you may have to have a tiny touch of anorexia nervosa to maintain an ideal weight . . . not a *heavy* case, just a little one!" Nonetheless, she allowed the scale to creep back up to 102. But eating normally never became a habit. A reporter who treated her to a champagne cocktail one afternoon described what it was like for Helen to confront an article of food that threatened to make her fat. "She carefully fished out the calorie-laden brandy-soaked sugar lump, took a couple of polite sips, praised it extravagantly as the most *delicious* thing she'd ever had, and went back to Perrier water."

Helen loved the way she looked: her flat stomach and tiny dress size made up for every brownie she didn't eat. It was impossible for her to believe that she might have been badly served by decades of calorie counting and several rounds of plastic surgery, even when she read harsh remarks about her looks in the press. "Her face is strangely pinkish and immobile, and her sticklike arms make you wonder if she hasn't rather overdone the dieting," a reporter observed in 1980. *USA Today* once published the results of a survey in which respondents named the famous people whose looks they most admired and least admired. On the list of the least admired, the top four were Janet Reno, Roseanne Barr, Tipper Gore, and Helen. She was enraged—couldn't anyone recognize self-discipline? When friends begged her to eat more, when doctors urged her to gain a few pounds, when strangers came up to her in the street and told her she looked skeletal, she concluded they were jealous. "I get seriously aggravated by people who hate me because I'm thin," she complained. "I think I'm an affliction in some people's lives." She resented being teased for constantly ordering plain broiled fish in restaurants or refusing to taste the birthday cake at an office party. Helen rarely expressed vituperation in print about anyone; she made a habit of being nice to people under nearly all circumstances. But at the thought of hostesses trying to force her off her diet, she erupted. "Mostly the pushers are your 'friends,'" she wrote bitterly. "'For God's sake, have a roll and butter, have dessert . . . you can *afford* it!' Listen, if you 'afforded' it, you would be fat like they are." Once, she wrote, a hostess handed her a cup of Sanka and waited until she finished it before announcing with a chortle that Helen had just consumed some chocolate chips, which had been slipped into her cup back in the kitchen. Remembering this betrayal, Helen was still livid. "Bitch!"

Not many women with such a profound case of the jitters around food would have decided to write a four-hundred-page cookbook; and to give Helen credit, she resisted at first. Early in 1962 she was waiting for the publication of *Sex and the Single Girl* and conferring with her publisher, Bernard Geis, on what she should do next. Her first thought was to follow up her advice for single girls with a book of advice aimed at men—*How to Love a Girl*—because the prospect of becoming famous as an expert on sex and relationships appealed to her. Geis was more interested in a book about lesbians, however, so she duly called a few doctors to question them about the topic. They told her, she reported, that lesbianism was "one of the most difficult human

aberrations to treat—virtually impossible." It didn't occur to
Helen to seek out any actual lesbians, and the notion faded away.
For a while she considered a book based on the work of Dr.
George Watson, who specialized, as she put it, in "treating *emo-
tional* problems through diet." Helen was a grateful patient of
Watson's and later featured him in a *Cosmopolitan* article, but she
couldn't persuade him to collaborate on a book.

Ultimately she chose a near repeat of her first book and produced *Sex and the Office*, a guide to the possibilities of the work-
place as an arena for flirtation, dating, and having affairs. The
book came out in the fall of 1964 with an ambitious first printing
of seventy-five thousand copies, but it proved to have much less
appeal than *Sex and the Single Girl*. The haste and lack of editing
were apparent, and Helen's chirpy narration became tiresome as
she went on and on about the erotic potential of lunch dates,
"peek-a-boo necklines," and office decor. Sales were disappoint-
ing, but she was under contract for one more project with Geis,
and this time he wanted her to try a cookbook. Helen was dubi-
ous, but Geis was sure they could make money if they came up
with a "lulu of a cookbook," written for the *Single Girl* readership
and packed with "sexy innuendos." Neither of them envisioned
Helen as the author—she didn't have the skills or the desire to
write recipes, and she was already engrossed in *Cosmopolitan*—so
they hired a professional cookbook writer named Margo Rieman
to produce the recipes and the text. Helen would step in later and
contribute whatever she wanted by way of personality, and the
two would share credit equally as coauthors.

As it turned out, Helen hated being ghostwritten. She liked
Margo's recipes well enough, so much so that she gave her a
column in *Cosmopolitan* called "The 5-Minute Gourmet," but she
couldn't stand disappearing from view in a book published un-

der her own name. Deep in the job of transforming *Cosmopolitan,* she was reveling in her all-but-patented prose style, and the new circulation figures proved that readers loved it, too. There was no need to retreat from the spotlight just because she didn't have any professional expertise in the kitchen. And she was very fond of the creature known as "Helen Gurley Brown"—it was getting to be second nature.

Helen attacked the manuscript as energetically as if recipes were sex tips and her readers were desperate newlyweds. Queries about ingredients, quantities, timing, and directions flew off to the editor of the book, and pages went back and forth covered in scribbles. She was anxious about rice—why on earth was it showing up so often when she herself never ate it? The recipe better be "the best in the world!" She was anxious about boiled shrimp, which also appeared often, sometimes with a basic recipe affixed and sometimes not. Fix it! In the end she rewrote the entire text, and the book became *Helen Gurley Brown's Single Girl's Cookbook*. As Helen put it in the introduction, "Margo allowed me to take her wonderful recipes—which numerous reliable people have said are some of the best they've ever used—and present them to you in *my* words."

Helen Gurley Brown's Single Girl's Cookbook was published in 1969—her fourth book in seven years and the only one she ever wrote that wasn't based on her own life or some fantastic riff on it. Perhaps for that reason, much of the text was sensible, even useful, to a degree unknown in the rest of her writing. Typically Helen wrote as if she kept a mirror propped up on the typewriter by way of research, but the cookbook was far more demanding. She had to project herself into a different frame of mind, absorbing details on topics she rarely thought about. "It is for new-girl cooks," she told her editor, and she was determined to give them recipes that would be so clear, manageable, and reliable that nobody could fail. This, of course, was a traditional mandate for a cookbook, but it was a novelty for Helen. All her teaching thus far had been aimed at helping women refashion their bodies and tune their emotions according to fantasies she herself provided. Now she had to help them focus outside themselves, directing their minds and hands toward a goal that couldn't be reached by charm alone. For once, she had to work in the real world.

The book began with basic recipes requiring minimal technique, such as hamburgers, green salads, béchamel sauce, and lamb chops, and then expanded into a more elaborate repertoire including yeast rolls, chicken Kiev, *vitello tonnato*, and roast goose. Helen included lists of pantry staples and kitchen equipment; she had separate chapters on cheeses, eggs, and Thanksgiving dinner; there was a cocktail section; and there was a chapter on what to serve the man you don't want around anymore (liver, kidneys, and sweetbreads). Many of the recipes were arranged in menus, with carefully worked-out game plans letting the cook know when to start marinating the fruit in Cointreau, when to trim the asparagus, when to make the sauce for the veal, when to finish the asparagus, and when to summon everyone to the table. In its own way, the book was an old-fashioned kitchen bible. The instructions were clear to the point of obsessive, and no anxious cook could possibly feel abandoned in the kitchen. ("Tear off two sheets of wax paper about 12 inches long and lay one of them on a flat surface. Sprinkle with about 1 teaspoon of flour and spread this around with your fingers. Place ball of dough in center of floured paper and pat it out to a flattish circle about 1/2 inch thick. . . .")

This extraordinary degree of precision was applied to every

recipe in the book, from scrambled eggs to "Pressed Beef in Red-Wine Jelly." Any cookbook writer would have been proud of such an achievement, but for Helen it was only the beginning. Which was unfortunate, because she had little else to bring to a cookbook, once she had insisted on perfect clarity throughout. Helen was too nervous around food to develop a coherent gustatory approach, and the book suffered from the same mood swings that characterized the recipes in *Cosmopolitan*. A cook who mastered the homemade pastry for cocktail-sized savory turnovers, for instance, was advised to fill them with canned deviled ham. One dinner menu, "for the girls," included a throwback to 1950s faux-fancy entertaining that had the cook spreading undiluted cream of mushroom soup on slices of white bread, rolling them up, and baking them. But on the very next page came another dinner menu, also for the girls, featuring a recipe that could have come from *Gourmet—bagna cauda*, a warm dip made with butter, olive oil, garlic, and anchovies, served with crudités. The hummus recipe ("Garbanzo Dip"), which called for a little fresh mint, was well ahead of its time; the candied yams were free of marshmallows; and "Mama's Noodles" were made by hand. In an era when many food writers confined themselves to familiar, easily obtainable ingredients, Helen called for oxtails, veal knuckles, and cardamom pods; and she advised her cooks to invest in good knives, peppercorns, real butter, and a wire whisk. Meanwhile she put a package of dry onion-soup mix into her hamburgers, she made an hors d'oeuvre with canned Vienna sausages heated in bottled barbecue sauce, and for a summer dessert she mixed maraschino cherries, crushed pineapple, and miniature marshmallows into cooked rice.

But if the recipes ran amok, the voice was pure Helen. Throughout the manuscript she splashed the italics, the endearments, and the innuendos that had become the fundamentals of her written personality. "This darling cookbook" . . . "These dear little blender breakfasts" . . . "Go! Go! Go! We have *confidence* in you!" "Let *other* girls broil him a steak and slice a few tomatoes; he can do *that* himself. You're out to rapture him with golden Chicken Paprikash gurgling in its pot and maybe even *capture* him by the time he's through the Lemon Chiffon Crème."

Bernard Geis bought national advertising and mailed out a mortar and pestle with every review copy, but *Helen Gurley Brown's Single Girl's Cookbook* never attracted the excitement or even the respect Helen had hoped it would win. Maybe it was the mishmash of recipes, maybe it was the haze of flirtatious prose, or maybe women just didn't trust Helen as a cook to see them through. Women who liked personality-drenched cookbooks were buying *The Graham Kerr Cookbook,* by the Galloping Gourmet, which was based on Kerr's TV series and became the best-selling cookbook of the year. And women who wanted to learn to cook bought *Craig Claiborne's Kitchen Primer,* also published that year, which explained in simple steps how to prepare very good versions of classic dishes. The reviews were positive but perfunctory: *Publishers Weekly* called the book "lively and practical," and the *Chicago Tribune* noted "clear directions and some very easy-to-get-down recipes." Other reviewers joked about the writing, and one complained that there was no layer of pecan halves on top of the pecan pie. Helen never again published outside her comfort zone.

A writer from the *National Catholic Register* once asked Helen if *Cosmopolitan* encouraged women to think of themselves as sex objects. "I hope so," said Helen. "It's wonderful to be a sex object.

I can't think of anything more agreeable." But it was 1981 when she fielded this question, and she didn't sound girlish any longer; she sounded out of touch. During the next couple of decades, other women's magazines ran stories on AIDS, rape, and sexual harassment, but Helen couldn't bear the idea of associating sex with anything negative. She had put the sexual revolution at the center of her career, and as far as she was concerned, a bed with a man in it was still a precious thing. "I think date rape is *highly* overrated and exaggerated," she told a reporter, and when she was asked how she would deal personally with someone who sexually harassed her, she said, "Flattery, flattery, flattery. 'You're fabulous and so attractive . . . but I don't like it when you rub up close to me.' " By the time she turned seventy, newcomers such as *Allure* and *Marie Claire* were competing vigorously for readers and advertisers she had once controlled with ease. In January 1996, Hearst announced a change at the top of the magazine. Helen would surrender her job to Bonnie Fuller, the editor of *Marie Claire,* and accept a new title: editor in chief of *Cosmopolitan's* international editions. "Age gets all of us," Helen told *Modern Maturity*—not a magazine she would have courted back in her prime—but she continued working nearly to the end of her life, at a salary of $2 million a year, turning out three more books on the typewriter that had served her faithfully. She never switched to a computer.

The news of Helen's death set off a controversy that would have delighted her. Boomers and millennials, journalists and academics, her critics and her admirers—everyone jumped in to argue about whether or not Helen Gurley Brown had been a feminist. Helen certainly thought she was. She published *Cosmopolitan's* first article on the women's movement in 1970, a piece by Vivian Gornick, who was at the start of her literary career and already one of the best-known feminist social critics in New York. Gornick's essay had appeared a year earlier in the *Village Voice,* and Helen, who may have sensed that terms like "pippy-poo" would not do any favors to a story hailing the feminist revolution, worked over the prose with a relatively restrained hand. She did drop the title chosen at the *Voice:* no piece running in *Cosmopolitan* was ever going to be called "The Next Great Moment in History Is Theirs." Helen's version became "The Women's Liberation Movement!" But a single astute article could not outweigh an editorial philosophy focused exclusively on pleasing the male; and feminist attacks on the magazine kept up for decades. Even so, Helen always spoke positively about the movement. When an interviewer wanted to know her reaction to "militant feminism," she said she approved of it and was grateful to the rabble-rousers. "I think the militant feminists are the ones who got us this far," she said. "If they had been Southern belles the whole thing would not have happened. I give them total credit." Equal pay, equal opportunity, birth control, abortion, affordable child care—there was nothing in the feminist agenda she didn't support with her whole heart, except what she insisted on seeing as hostility toward men. "And perhaps that's where we and Women's Lib part company," she wrote in 1970. "We are pleasing men not because they DEMAND it or to get anything material from them but because we adore them, love to sleep with them, want one of our own, and there aren't enough to go around!"

Helen was nearly fifty when she made this declaration—too old to change a belief that had sustained her personally and was giving her a glorious career. She still enjoyed being a girl; in fact, she had no idea how to be a woman, and she didn't want to find out. Gloria Steinem, who was always Helen's favorite feminist, begged her once to say something strong and positive about herself—not coy, not flirtatious, but something that reflected the serious, complicated person who was in there, under the wig and makeup. Gloria had glimpsed that person and wanted her to speak out. Helen tried her best, she really did. "I'm skinny!" she exclaimed. "I'm skinny!"

Afterword

Ever since I began working on this book, I've been aware of all the food stories that will never be told. The women in these pages were prominent in their time, and they're still visible in ours; but most women don't live that way. They never attract public attention, they don't leave boxes of their personal papers to delight historians, and unless they happen to be unusually captivated by cooking and eating, they don't write food memoirs. Culinary historians looking back at the first decades of the twenty-first century will be blessed with vast quantities of material to study, thanks to blogs and social media, but all that material will still reflect only the lives of a certain swathe of active and self-promoting food lovers. What about everyone else? I'm thinking about women who don't contribute to online recipe forums, who would be astonished at the idea that anybody was interested in the spaghetti they put in front of the family the other night, who think home life belongs at home, not out in public. And what about mediocre cooks, reluctant cooks, wildly conflicted cooks? What about the legions of women in every generation who believe that the whole topic of food is unimportant? Theirs are the food stories I wish I knew.

Here's one I do know, because it's my own. Maybe it seems jarring for a food writer to class herself with the innumerable silent women I've just mentioned, the ones who never bother to notice their relationship with food or simply back away from the whole subject. But my food story takes place well before I started writing professionally about life in the kitchen. I had always been fascinated with food, but there came a moment when I realized I was obsessed with it. No, I didn't have an eating disorder. I had a cooking disorder.

Perhaps you're familiar with the way culinary memoirs often devote a few pages to the author's lifelong obsession with food. She'll explain how she grew up with a discerning palate, a wondrous instinct for inventing recipes, a sense of joyful adventure at the very thought of a meal to be prepared. Well, my obsession was marked by none of those helpful attributes; I don't have them even now. When I was obsessed—a feverish few months that began shortly after I got married—the pleasures of cooking were not only absent, they were inconceivable. Cooking for fun? Why not gravedigging for fun? I flailed away in the kitchen day after day for reasons entirely unrelated to dinner. I was trying to be married, that was all, and I didn't know any other way to go about it.

Cooking never bothered me until after the wedding. Living with Jack beforehand, I cooked whatever I felt like making, we ate it uncritically, and that was that. But once we were actually married, this excellent system collapsed without warning. It was as if another woman had suddenly shown up and seized control of the kitchen. I never encountered her anywhere else; but every day, when it came time to think about dinner, she materialized at my side and stayed right there at the kitchen counter with me, anxiously paging through recipes. Where on earth did they come from? I had never cooked such things in my life; they had names like "Skillet Supper" and "Italian Salad Boat." Students of witchcraft would have identified her immediately as a diabolical familiar—the devil, that is, in a very good disguise—but unfortunately I didn't know any students of witchcraft. It took a while before the grim truth began to seep across my consciousness. Here in my own home, brutally determined to undermine my convictions, my politics, my instincts, and my sacred honor, was a wife.

A wife! Doomed creature from a bygone era, wrapped in somebody else's name, committed to somebody else's dreams, humbly contributing her mite to the vast female substructure that kept the patriarchy flourishing. Away, away! But apparently I had invited her in. Readers of a certain age will recognize the 1970s. The women's movement was in flower, and I was a glad devotee, but these were early days, and we really hadn't figured it all out. Getting married seemed harmless enough: Jack and I would simply reinvent the ancient institution, just as we had come up with our own wedding ceremony. And in most regards, we did manage to arrange domestic life along lines that suited both of us. I was the cook, while Jack took over dishwashing, laundry, anything outdoors, anything to do with the car, all the heavy lifting, and later on a lot of child care—a pretty equitable division of labor, we both felt, in light of centuries of female oppression. Possibly I held this view more strongly than he did. At any rate, the arrangement has lasted a good long time, but it was no help in the beginning, especially after we moved to India.

I had known, of course, that married life was going to snatch me up from my job, my friends, and my beloved Cambridge apartment and drop me in a town some ninety miles from Delhi, and I hoped I was prepared. Jack, a graduate student in religion who was studying Hinduism, would be doing the research for his dissertation; and since I was a writer, surely I would write. I packed books, notebooks, and a portable typewriter. But I wasn't the only one packing for a year in India—my diabolical familiar was getting ready for the trip as well, and her list was longer than mine. I wish now I had kept it, if only to see what the handwriting looked like. She and I pushed a grocery cart around the Star Market, collecting provisions for the wildly irrelevant vision of domesticity that was clawing its way out of my subconscious—namely, life in a split-level suburban home, circa 1955. Up and down the aisles we went, filling the cart with cake mixes, bouillon cubes, lasagna noodles, giant plastic bottles of salad oil, and bags of a dry, soy-based product that looked like dog food but was meant for vegetarian cooking, which I planned to use in pasta sauces and faux sloppy joes.

The thing is, I didn't make sloppy joes, faux or otherwise, before I got married. Before I got married I cooked with meat, not soy chunks, unless I was cooking for vegetarians, in which case I made pesto. Before I got married I was so viscerally opposed to cake mixes I was certain I would be struck by lightning if I ever so much as reached for one. Bouillon cubes? Before I got married I bought a chicken if I wanted broth for a recipe, and if the recipe called for anything more elaborate by way of a liquid, I looked for a different recipe. Most of these totems of midcentury American kitchen life, which I lugged ten thousand miles and unpacked in an apartment near where the god Krishna spent his childhood, had never appealed to me in any way, at least when I was in my right mind. Clearly I wasn't.

Moving to a foreign country had undone me; and I don't mean India, I mean marriage. That's the foreign country that should have required a visa and a phrase book. There was nothing in wifedom that was familiar. I didn't speak the language, I didn't know the customs, I didn't know what to wear. Did wives travel in blue jeans on a sixteen-hour flight to Delhi, or did they go out and buy polyester bell-bottoms with a matching top suitable for Mother's Day brunch in a retirement community? My guess was wrong. What did a wife do when the clerk at American Express in Delhi refused to issue half the traveler's checks in her husband's name and half in hers, because this could be done only for married couples, and the proof of marriage was a shared name, which ours wasn't? Perhaps a wife was supposed to step back from the window with a polite nod, acknowledging the existence of cultural differences. Or perhaps she was supposed to grab the bars separating her from the clerk and shriek in despair, "Do you think I'd even be here if I weren't married?" Again, I guessed wrong. India was hardly irrelevant to my anomie as a wife, but most of the reasons why I seemed to be inhabited by another person could be traced directly to the ring on my finger. Sometimes I was surprised to see it there, since to my knowledge I didn't own any gold rings. One of our first errands in India was to go to the jeweler's, to get my ring made smaller, because for a few heart-stopping minutes during our honeymoon it had gotten lost in the sand.

All I knew for certain about being married was that the two people involved were supposed to have dinner together, and this portentous meal soon became the focus of my fretful days. What did married people eat if they lived in India? I didn't have the slightest idea. Please understand: we ate lots of Indian food everywhere we traveled in India, and I loved all of it without exception—I loved the food in restaurants, I loved the street food, I loved the meals we were served in people's houses, I loved the alley storefronts where a cook dished out scrumptious little mixtures of vegetables and a boy handed them around on saucers. In Delhi we went to a Chinese restaurant, which was also Indian except for the names of the dishes, and I loved that, too. But it was hard to become comfortable with the notion that because we were making our home in India, this was a cuisine that qualified as home cooking. At some mysterious level of propriety, Indian food didn't count. Those abundantly flavorful meals with their unfamiliar scents and textures seemed irrelevant to the project that my diabolical familiar was directing from her perch in the kitchen: to understand myself as an American wife.

So I made spaghetti with soy-chunk sauce, and I made toasted cheese sandwiches using tinned, processed cheese and the flabby white bread called "double roti." I cut up cabbage, carrots, and tomatoes, soaked them for hours in an iodine solution to kill the bacteria, and made them into big salads that tasted of iodine. I made soup with the bouillon cubes, though every time I used a bouillon cube I had to be extremely careful about disposing of the tiny foil wrappers, because each one had a minuscule picture of a chicken on it. We lived in a compound surrounding a busy temple, where the faithful were going in and out all day and everyone was a vegetarian—as were we at the time, except for the bouillon cubes. My husband was terrified of getting caught and would have much preferred plain water in the soups, but I had a dim sense that if I gave up the bouillon cubes, and the acrid, chemical flavor they imparted, I would be lost forever. I used to shred the wrappers into slivers and deposit them one by one in the garbage bag, trying to keep them separate so that nobody could possibly get the idea that they once belonged together. The bag was destined for the courtyard downstairs, where a cow would eat the garbage, but often she left scraps of food and paper scattered across the ground, and I didn't want to take any chances. Sometimes I thought about waiting in the courtyard to make sure she finished off all the foil—we occasionally saw part of a blue air letter from home hanging from her mouth—but I never did. I was a little afraid of her.

I studied Hindi, I tried to write, but the prospect of making dinner hovered over each day like a thundercloud that refused to break. I didn't know if I should be proud of my accomplishments in synthetic cuisine or apologize for them. Jack never complained—he was raised to appreciate other people's cooking, and he loyally did—but I noticed we were both eating large quantities of applesauce. This I made all the time, since it was easy to do on the kerosene burner that was my stove, and the accompaniment was always Gluco biscuits, a packaged cookie with an oddly addictive lack of flavor. Thanks to Glucos and applesauce, which stood in for either dessert or a side dish, the meals I was turning out did have the patina of dinner; but if this was dinner in wifedom, I wondered if we would be better off elsewhere.

What rescued me, and possibly us, was the fact that we had no refrigerator. Every day I had to restock our supply of butter, milk, and fresh produce, which meant that every day I had to go to the bazaar. These excursions into unmediated India could be nerve-racking—I had to speak Hindi in the bazaar, as well as dodge the cows and monkeys—but open-air food markets are powerful places. They can break down your resistance like a smile and a wave from a baby. The arrays of fresh produce were modest in this one, for it was a small bazaar, and its practicality appealed to me. No towering displays, just a scattering of the very local fruits and vegetables brought in that morning. The women selling produce sat alongside their eggplants and tomatoes and cauliflowers, listening impassively as I stumbled through my request, and always tossed a big bright chili into the bag as a lagniappe. The spices were the most aromatic I had ever used, the yogurt tasted better than any I had ever eaten, and over time this delicious bounty edged its way into my imagination. I stopped making the pallid soups and salads that had become my tormented specialty and started to cook real food.

Cautiously, I made a vegetable curry; even more cautiously, a pot of chickpeas for which I had to soak the dried beans— something I thought happened only in communes in Vermont, but there I was doing it. And perfectly! I was elated by my success. The recipes came from the Time-Life *Cooking of India*, which I had packed in a rare moment of optimism, and Time-Life was very good at writing recipes that worked. That's what I wanted, something that worked—not necessarily authentic, just something that didn't pick too many fights with India. I never tried the tricky ones, not the homemade cheese or the deep-fried breads or the syrupy, pretzel-shaped sweets called *jalebis*. I didn't want to fail. It was as if India, marriage, and I were wobbling into the future on a unicycle, and I had no wish to threaten our precarious sense of balance.

What I appreciated most about the Time-Life cookbook was that it was written for women who bought their eggplants and cauliflowers in American supermarkets and were unlikely ever to set foot in an Indian bazaar. This made me feel a little superior, which was a nice change from my usual state of confusion and defeat, while at the same time allowing me to identify with those busy, faraway women back home, heating their ghee and measuring their spices. We were all American wives, we were all using the same cookbook, we were all making the same dinner. It was very reassuring.

Food talks, and that's when I heard it for the first time, standing over the kerosene burner in my Indian kitchen. The cake mixes and bouillon cubes chattered away in a language I never understood, but my semi-Indian cooking spoke up in elementary Hindi, exactly my level. I made Time-Life's *"Mung ki*

Dal" and *"Dahi Vadda"* again and again, and they always assured
me that wifedom wasn't really a new planet, it was more like a
new neighborhood. By contrast I could sense that my chapatis,
the whole-wheat flatbreads that are a staple in North India, were
sneering at me. The ones I made were leathery, and although I
tried and tried—I even took a lesson from a chapati expert—I
never caught on. We ate them anyway, but they were emblems
of failure, and I didn't want anything to do with failure. I quit
trying and started buying half a dozen chapatis to go at the
Shyam Hotel, which wasn't a hotel at all but an extremely humble storefront with five tables and a rat; it was the only restaurant in our part of town. "To go" was not a concept the cook had
heard before, but he made chapatis for me, and I kept them
warm in the tin box that sat on the kerosene burner and passed
as an oven. Problem solved.

Shortly before leaving India, I astonished myself by mastering the little deep-fried jumbles of vegetables called *pakoras,* popular everywhere in India. I was so thrilled with this achievement
that I served them to an Indian neighbor, who came back the
next day with a batch of her own. These, she explained, were
pakoras. Of course she was right. I was happy to eat them; they
were infinitely better than mine, and I wrote down the recipe,
though I knew I would never use it. If I ever made *pakoras* again,
they would have to come from Time-Life and my own two
hands, as best they could. I was starting to understand home
cooking. The important word was "home."

ACKNOWLEDGMENTS

This book began during a fellowship year at the Dorothy and Lewis B. Cullman Center for Scholars and Writers at the New York Public Library. My experience with paradise has been limited, but it's hard to believe there's another realm quite like the Cullman Center, which Jean Strouse and her staff run as if it were an organic farm, tending each crop of fellows with labor-intensive care until at the end of the year we are harvested, gently but firmly, and sent to market. It is a pleasure to add my own expressions of gratitude to the many already heaped up in honor of the CSW. At the heart of the fellowship, of course, are the library's incomparable holdings, and I'm grateful to curators and librarians across the building who helped me take advantage of the collections, including Jay Barksdale, Elizabeth Denlinger, Anne Garner, Isaac Gewirtz, Matt Knutzen, and Maira Liriano. Throughout this project I've drawn on Rebecca Federman's deep knowledge of the NYPL and the skill and imagination she applies to opening up its resources.

The Jerwood Centre in Grasmere, next door to Dove Cottage, holds the preeminent archive of materials relating to the Wordsworths and their circle. With the help of the curator, Jeff Cowton, and the assistant curator, Rebecca Turner, I spent blissful days there puzzling over the handwriting in Dorothy Wordsworth's unpublished journals and studying the family's manuscript recipes. Two renowned scholars of British cuisine, C. Anne Wilson and Peter Brears, kindly responded to my queries with valuable information on Lake District culinary practices and how to track them down. I'm also grateful for the long-distance help supplied by Frances Lansley in the West Sussex Record Office of the National Archives and Janice Bailey at the Whitwick Historical Group.

Every visit to the Schlesinger Library is revelatory, and I'm always glad for the chance to thank its librarians for their ideas and guidance. Thanks as well to Virginia Lewick at the Franklin D. Roosevelt Presidential Library in Hyde Park, Karen Kukil at the Sophia Smith Collection at Smith College, to the staff in the Archives and Modern Manuscripts division of Special Collections at the Bodleian Library, and to the very patient staff of the copy center in Humanities Reading Room I at the British Library, whose quick help with baffling technology pulled me back from outright hysterics on several occasions.

Rosa Lewis's cooking—indeed, all the high-end cooking in the Edwardian era—posed a number of mysteries, and I'm grateful to Cathy Kaufman for a discussion early on that helped me start working my way through them. A series of enlightening e-mail exchanges with Stephen Schmidt, whose scholarship is known for its depth and precision, was a highlight of my research. With his help I was able to correct errors and reconsider crucial points in both the Rosa Lewis and the Dorothy Wordsworth chapters. The culinary historian Ivan Day, legendary for his hands-on understanding of the English kitchen across centuries, welcomed me to his home in the Lake District and responded to a torrent of questions about Dorothy Wordsworth and Rosa Lewis with an even greater torrent of fascinating insights and references. It was like sitting across the table from the British Library, except that the British Library never took me to lunch and drove me well out of its way to my B&B, all the while explaining fine points of local history, geography, botany, and literature.

Yvonne Cocking, who has spent more time in the Barbara Pym

archives than anyone except maybe Barbara Pym, has been an unfailing source of wisdom on all aspects of Pymiana. Tom Sopko, North American Organizer of the Barbara Pym Society, came to my aid several times with his wide-ranging knowledge of Pym's life and work. Katharine Whitehorn, author of the bed-sitter classic *Kitchen in the Corner* (1961), treated me to a cascade of memories from that era; and Luke Gertler walked me through Pym's last London residence, now his home, beautifully evoking her years there as well as his own.

Although I ended up differing from the late Angela Lambert on the question of Eva Braun's character, Lambert's scrupulously researched biography, *The Lost Life of Eva Braun*, was one of my most trusted sources for the Braun chapter. Through the kindness of Deirdre Bryan-Brown—whom I first met in the Barbara Pym Society—I was able to contact Lambert's daughter Carolyn Butler, who did me the enormous favor of gathering her mother's research notes, packing them into a huge suitcase, and allowing me to borrow them. Anja Schüler offered many thoughtful suggestions for the Braun chapter, and the tireless Carla Stockton took on a slew of research tasks for both the Braun and the Helen Gurley Brown chapters. Many thanks to Ingrid MacGillis for quickly delivering an expert translation of Therese Linke's memoir. Dr. Axel Drecoll at the Institut für Zeitgeschichte in Munich graciously drew from his deep, detailed knowledge of Obersalzberg to answer my questions and offer numerous suggestions for further research. My pursuit of Eva Braun was aided in a thousand ways by Ursula Heinzelmann, who shared with me her own work on German culinary history and helped me across many barriers of language and culture. I'm especially grateful for one particular mitzvah, performed in July 2015, when she accompanied me through Munich and into the library at the Institut für Zeitgeschichte, advising and translating at every step.

In the last few years I've delivered papers airing some of the ideas in these chapters at meetings of the Barbara Pym Society and the Oxford Symposium on Food & Cookery. My thanks to the generous and very knowledgeable members of both these organizations for their feedback.

As always, I count myself the luckiest of writers to be guided by a peerless agent, Amanda Urban, and an editor who somehow manages to be brilliant, relentless, and endearing all at once, Wendy Wolf. My husband, Jack Hawley, has been the guardian angel of this project since I dreamed it up nearly a decade ago. He never objected to the constant, ghostly presence of my six ladies at the dinner table; on the contrary, if they sat there silent and infuriating, as was often the case, it was he who invariably persuaded them to open up and reveal a few secrets. Our daughter, Nell, who knows me pretty well by now, quickly discerned what I was going to need in order to survive the writing of this book and set me up with Netflix and her favorite online exercise videos. Finally, I want to thank some world-class listeners—Rebecca Federman, Melody Lawrence, Sara Paretsky, Susan Pelzer, Susan Riecken, Jean Strouse, and Barbara Wheaton—for the gift of being there.

NOTES

Introduction

2 **which was fatal:** Notable exceptions include the work of Susan Strasser (*Never Done: A History of American Housework*, 1982) and Ruth Schwartz Cowan (*More Work for Mother: The Ironies of Household Technology*, 1983).

5 **Nell B. Nichols:** "Nell B. Nichols' Food Calendar," *Woman's Home Companion*, May 1953, 107.

5 **"had a laugh":** Mabel Dodge Luhan, *Intimate Memories*, 89.

6 **"numerous trivial details":** William Knight, ed., *Journals of Dorothy Wordsworth*, vii.

7 **"People blame one":** Barbara Pym, *No Fond Return of Love*, 169.

9 **"While we were at Breakfast":** Pamela Woof, ed., *The Grasmere and Alfoxden Journals*, Grasmere Journal entry March 14, 1802, 78.

9 **only a "day laborer":** "A Plate of Sandwiches," *New York Times*, June 10, 1894.

9 **"What you call 'premier'":** Mary Lawton, *The Queen of Cooks—And Some Kings*, 91.

10 **"dog-like attachment":** Quoted in Victoria Glendinning, *Anthony Trollope*, 334.

10 **"He might have been happier":** Eleanor Roosevelt, *This I Remember*, 349.

11 **"Today finished my 4th novel":** MS Pym 45, Oct. 10, 1954, Papers of Barbara Mary Crampton Pym, Bodleian Library, University of Oxford, Oxford, UK.

Dorothy Wordsworth

16 **"wild and startling":** Thomas De Quincey, *Recollections of the Lakes and the Lake Poets*, 134.

18 **"impossible to describe":** Dorothy Wordsworth to Jane Pollard, April 21, 1794, Ernest de Selincourt and Chester L. Shavers, eds., *The Letters of William and Dorothy Wordsworth*, vol. I, 114.

18 **"rambling about the country":** DW to Mrs. Crackanthorpe, ibid., 117.

19 **"thick":** Pamela Woof, ed., *The Grasmere and Alfoxden Journals*, Grasmere Journal entry Jan. 16, 1803, 137.

21 **"*May 14 1800*"**: Ibid., 1.

23 **More than two centuries:** Peter Brears, who has conducted extensive research on the cooking at Dove Cottage, takes a different view. Citing several examples of Dorothy's "culinary disasters" in his *Cooking and Dining with the Wordsworths* (23), he concludes that she was able to prepare plain, basic dishes but lacked the skills for anything more challenging.

24 **"my saddest thoughts":** Woof, ed., Grasmere Journal entry May 16, 1800, 2.

25 **"We had ate up":** Ibid., Jan. 27, 1802, 59.

25 **"We got no dinner":** Ibid., June 12, 1802, 108.

25 **"Wm was composing":** Ibid., Aug. 23, 1800, 17.

25 **"Coleridge obliged to go":** Ibid., Sept. 1, 1800, 19.

26 **"I baked pies":** Ibid., Dec. 23, 1801, 52.

26 **"Priscilla drank tea":** Ibid., Dec. 2, 1800, 34.

26 **"We had Mr Clarkson's":** Ibid., Jan. 24, 1802, 58.

26 **"We had pork":** Ibid., Feb. 11, 1802, 66.

26 **"I made bread":** Ibid., May 29, 1802, 102.

26 **"I threw him the cloak":** Ibid., June 14, 1802, 109.

27 **"Oh the darling!":** Ibid., March 4, 1802, 74.

27 **"How glad I was":** Ibid., March 7, 1802, 119.

27 **"There was a sky-like":** Ibid., July 8, 1802, 119.

28 **"I looked at everything":** Ibid., [Oct. 1802], 126.

28 **Examined under infrared light:** Ibid., 265.

28 **"I kept myself as quiet":** Ibid., 126.

29 **"Dear Mary had never seen":** Ibid., 128.

29 **"melted away":** Ibid., 129.

29 **"I cannot describe":** Ibid., 132.

29 **"Again I have neglected":** Ibid., Jan. 11, 1803, 135.

29 **"nice":** Ibid., 137.

30 **"Intensely cold":** Ibid., Jan. 16, 1803, 137.

30 **"Monda":** Ibid., [Jan. 17, 1803], 137.

31 **"There are not many places":** William Wordsworth to Lord Lonsdale, [March] 1828, Ernest de Selincourt and Alan G. Hill, eds., *The Letters of William and Dorothy Wordsworth*, vol. V, 595.

31 **a "fireside companion":** DW to Mary Laing, June 3, 1828, Ernest de Selincourt and Alan G. Hill, eds., *The Letters of William and Dorothy Wordsworth*, vol. IV, 611.

31 **"in a sharp and cold":** John Nichols, *The History and Antiquities of the County of Leicester*, vol. 3, part 2, 1112.

33 **"Five weeks have I been here":** DW to Jane [Pollard] Marshall, Dec. 26, 1828, de Selincourt and Hill, eds., *Letters*, vol. IV, 697.

33 **"A gloomy morning":** DW unpublished journal, Nov. 25–30, 1828, DCMS 104.10, Jerwood Centre, Wordsworth Trust, Grasmere, UK.

33 **"It may be called":** DW to Marshall.

33 **"I am more useful":** Ibid.

34 **"an honest good creature":** DW to Maria Jane Jewsbury, May 21, 1828, de Selincourt and Hill, eds., *Letters,* vol. IV, 606.

34 **"all sorts of nice things":** DW to Catherine Clarkson, April 24, 1814, Ernest de Selincourt, Mary Moorman, and Alan G. Hill, eds., *The Letters of William and Dorothy Wordsworth,* vol. III, 137.

34 **"She will be a right":** DW to Jewsbury.

34 **"Dined on black puddings":** DW unpublished journal, Jan. 13, 1829.

35 **"Rabbit pie":** Ibid., Dec. 25, 1828.

35 **"our homely Westmoreland":** DW to Jewsbury.

36 **"Fill the skins":** Hannah Glasse, *The Art of Cookery,* 249.

36 **"so ill manufactured":** Mary Radcliffe, *Domestic Cookery,* 115.

36 **"Merry Andrew":** Austin Dobson, ed., *Selected Poems of Matthew Prior,* 65.

36 **"Moggy":** Philip Breslaw, *Breslaw's Last Legacy,* 114.

37 **"savoury and piquant":** John Totter Brockett, *Glossary,* 39.

37 **"Black puddings are not bad":** Georgiana Hill, *The Breakfast Book,* in Kaori O'Connor, *The English Breakfast,* 115.

38 **"I can walk 15 miles":** DW to William Jackson, Feb. 12, 1828, de Selincourt and Hill, eds., *Letters,* vol. IV, 580.

38 **"excruciating torture":** WW to Jackson, April 10, 1829, de Selincourt and Hill, eds., *Letters,* vol. V, 63.

39 **"child-like feebleness":** Mary Wordsworth to Henry Crabb Robinson, July 4, 1836, Ernest de Selincourt and Alan G. Hill, eds., *The Letters of William and Dorothy Wordsworth,* vol. VI, 275.

40 **"faintness and hollowness":** WW to Robinson, July 6, 1835, ibid., 75.

40 **"Let that pass":** Woof, ed., Grasmere Journal entry May 31, 1802, 103.

40 **"It drew tears":** DW to Robinson, May 2, 1829, de Selincourt and Hill, eds., *Letters,* vol. V, 71.

41 **"Wm & Mary left us":** Quoted in Robert Gittings and Jo Manton, *Dorothy Wordsworth,* 269.

41 **"It will please Aunty":** Mary Wordsworth to Mary Hutchinson, Nov. 11, 1850, Alan G. Hill, ed., *Letters of William and Dorothy Wordsworth,* vol. VII, 291.

41 she said she was **"ill-used":** Mary Wordsworth to Marshall, [December] 1835, Mary E. Burton, ed., *The Letters of Mary Wordsworth,* 140.

41 **"You see":** Ibid.

42 **"she was sure":** WW to Robinson, Nov. 25, 1835, de Selincourt and Hill, eds., *Letters,* vol. VI, 121.

42 **"If I ask":** WW to Samuel Rogers, Sept. 26, 1835, ibid., 97.

42 **"This is an *intolerable*":** Mary Wordsworth to Dora Wordsworth, Aug. 14, 1837, Burton, 164.

43 **"I have been perfectly"**: DW to Catherine Clarkson, April 27, 1830, de Selincourt and Hill, eds., *Letters,* vol. VI, 75.

43 **"I wish you could"**: Mary Wordsworth to Marshall.

44 **"I feel my hand-shaking"**: WW to Robinson, July 6, 1835, de Selincourt and Hill, eds., *Letters,* vol. VI, 75.

44 **"She is . . . for a *short space*"**: Mary Wordsworth to Robinson.

44 **"Wakened from a wilderness"**: DW to Dora Wordsworth, March 20, 1837, in Jiro Nagasawa, "An Unpublished Dorothy Wordsworth Letter of 20 March 1837," *Notes and Queries* 48 (June 2001): 121.

Rosa Lewis

46 **"England's greatest woman chef"**: "England's Greatest Woman Chef," *Daily Mail,* Feb. 25, 1909.

46 **"the greatest woman cook"**: "Cookery Best Paid Profession in the World," *Daily Sketch,* June 13, 1914.

46 **"When you cook a quail"**: "British Queen of Cooks Advises Plain Cooking," *New York Times,* Jan. 16, 1927.

47 **"Rosa Lewis, cook!"**: Mary Lawton, *The Queen of Cooks—And Some Kings,* 54.

47 **"She began life"**: Ibid., xi.

48 **"Once, when I went out"**: Ibid., 38.

48 **"travesty"**: "World-Famous Cook," *Daily Mail,* Aug. 24, 1925.

50 **"Her life is a solitary one"**: Isabella Beeton, *Beeton's Book of Household Management,* 1001.

51 **"if cold meat"**: Ibid., 1002.

51 **"a little needlework"**: Ibid., 1005.

51 **"washer-up"**: Lawton, 6.

51 **"I worked in their family"**: Ibid., 9.

52 **"For an Englishwoman"**: Ibid.

52 **"I learnt to think"**: Ibid.

52 **"Just one of a number"**: Ibid., 10.

52 **"My family did not know"**: Ibid., 4.

54 **"I went off to church"**: Ibid., 16.

54 **"I took *full* charge"**: Ibid., 44.

55 **"I used to go"**: Ibid., 51.

55 **"I furnished the linen"**: Ibid., 79.

56 **"So I put my shoulder"**: Ibid., 21.

57 **"One King leads"**: Ibid., 67.

57 **"Woman Cook's Triumph"**: "Foreign Office Dinner," *Daily Telegraph,* Feb. 20, 1909, 14.

57 **"I was at the top"**: Lawton, 86.

58 **"What is to become of me?"**: George Bernard Shaw, *Pygmalion,* edited by L. W. Connolly, 93.

58 **"I was overwhelmed"**: Lawton, 7.

58 **"If you had a round back"**: Ibid.

59 **"She was one of the most perfect"**: Ibid., 11.

59 **"Lord Ribblesdale was the most"**: Ibid., 100.

59 **"boughten"**: Ibid., 124.

59 **"people used to lie under"**: Ibid., 164.

60 **"I was smartly dressed"**: Ibid., 43.

61 **"Although I was a servant"**: Ibid., 183.

61 **"Mrs. Charlotte"**: Ibid., facing 84.

61 **"My cook photographed"**: Ibid. 83.

62 **"Then I made all the gentry"**: Ibid.

62 **"the other side of life"**: Ibid., 84.

62 **"very ugly"**: Ibid., 165.

62 **"pure and classical parlance"**: Lynda Mugglestone, *Talking Proper: The Rise of Accent as Social Symbol,* 212.

63 **"insufferably vulgar"**: Ibid., 93.

64 **"Nothing more plainly shows"**: *How to Dine, or Etiquette of the Dinner Table,* 12.

64 **"They need not necessarily"**: Lady Colin Campbell, ed., *The Etiquette of Good Society,* 135.

64 **"Soup will constitute"**: *How to Dine,* 8.

65 **"Fish should be eaten"**: A Member of the Aristocracy, *Manners and Tone of Good Society,* 93.

65 **"No age, since that of Nero"**: Harold Nicolson, "The Edwardian Weekend," in *The Age of Extravagance,* Mary Elisabeth Edes and Dudley Frasier, eds., 247.

65 **"A guest never eats"**: *Party-giving on Every Scale, or The Cost of Entertainments,* 183.

66 **"piquant savories"**: Ibid., 207.

66 **"Ample choice"**: Campbell, 132.

67 **"I still remember"**: Consuelo Vanderbilt Balsan, *The Glitter and the Gold,* 83.

67 **"very ragged"**: Anthony Trollope, *Miss Mackenzie,* 97.

68 **"thick and clotted"**: Ibid.

68 **"so fabricated"**: Ibid., 99.

68 **"After the little dishes"**: Ibid., 101.

68 **"Why tell of the ruin"**: Ibid.

68 **"Her place in the world"**: Ibid., 102.

68 **"the ordinary Englishman"**: Ibid., 102.

69 **"a by-word of ridicule"**: Charles Elmé Francatelli, *The Modern Cook,* vi.

70 **"A good woman cook":** Lawton, 91.

71 **"M. Escoffier holds":** Nathaniel Newnham-Davis, *The Gourmet's Guide to London*, 19.

71 ***"Baisers de Vierge":*** Ibid., 20.

71 **"one of the few Frenchmen":** Lawton, 91.

71 **"I did the buying myself":** Ibid., 52.

72 **"Whatever I got":** Ibid., 53.

72 **"What I have always done":** Ibid., 13.

72 **"just the same as if":** Ibid., 14.

73 **"Good cooking really came":** Ibid., 89.

73 **"You don't want to know":** Ibid., 90.

73 **"And I don't like anything":** Ibid., 89.

73 **"Englishwomen seem to be":** "England's Greatest Woman Chef."

73 **"To cook, to a Frenchman":** "Cookery Best Paid Profession in the World."

74 **"Your American darkies":** Lawton, 92.

75 **"the most wonderful":** Ibid., 63.

75 **"There is probably no man":** "Hors d'Oeuvre," *Food and Cookery*, July 1900, 196.

76 **"an unconscious mockery":** Jane Ridley, *The Heir Apparent*, 445.

76 **"Do you know":** "Cookery Best Paid Profession in the World."

78 **"Into the tea-room":** Newnham-Davis, 314.

78 **"Mrs. Lewis lays it down":** Ibid., 315.

78 **"one of those delicious":** Ibid.

79 ***"Pouding de Cailles":*** Charles Herman Senn, *The New Century Cookery Book*, 541. I am indebted to Ivan Day for tracing Rosa's signature dish back to Senn.

80 **"Life became the War":** Lawton, 85.

81 **"Every man who left":** Ibid., 180.

81 **"a nice, damp plum-cake":** Charles Lister, *Letters and Recollections*, 222.

82 **"I can not get":** Lawton, 206.

82 **"There is nothing":** Ibid., 180.

82 **"The young bloods":** Ibid., 179.

82 **"The only thing":** Ibid., 180.

83 **"Sables of Sin":** Ibid., 197.

83 **"wearing a bile-green coat":** Joseph Bryan III, " 'Orrible Woman," *New Yorker*, Sept. 16, 1933, 23.

83 **"had suddenly decided":** Anthony Powell, *Messengers of Day*, 51.

84 **"an irascible, scowling":** Daphne Fielding, *Mercury Presides*, 171.

84 **"cherrybum":** Theodora FitzGibbon, *With Love*, 50.

84 **"after a court ball":** Fielding, *Mercury*, 172.

84 **"You don't know":** Powell, 135.

85 **"Game Pie":** FitzGibbon, 48.

85 **"the most remarkable woman":** Bryan, 23.

86 **"You all know Lord Thingummy"**: Evelyn Waugh, *Vile Bodies*, 43.

86 **"The food at Shepheard's"**: Ibid., 112.

87 **"the greatest people"**: Lawton, 205.

88 **"I *wish* I hadn't"**: Isabella Gardner to George Peabody Gardner and Rose Grosvenor Gardner, October 1937, quoted in Marian Janssen, *Not at All What One Is Used To: The Life and Times of Isabella Gardner*, 42.

89 **"We were supposed to have"**: Lawton, 54.

90 **"many other families"**: "Rosa Lewis funeral," in "Tanfield's Diary," *Daily Mail*, Dec. 4, 1952.

Eleanor Roosevelt

91 **"Victuals to her"**: James Roosevelt and Sidney Shalett, *Affectionately, F.D.R.*, 238.

91 **"I am sorry"**: Eleanor Roosevelt to the *Ladies' Home Journal*, Sept. 29, 1939, quoted in Joseph Lash, *Eleanor and Franklin*, 456.

92 **"sick-looking"**: Alonzo Fields, *My 21 Years in the White House*, 46.

92 **"infinitely superior"**: Hiram Johnson to son, April 1, 1933, quoted in Frank Freidel, *Franklin D. Roosevelt: Launching the New Deal*, 285.

92 **"We had a rainwater"**: Ernest Hemingway to Mrs. Paul Pfeiffer, Aug. 2, 1937, in Carlos Baker, ed., *Ernest Hemingway: Selected Letters, 1917–1961*, 460.

94 **"I suppose one ought"**: Harold L. Ickes, *The Secret Diary of Harold L. Ickes*, 248.

94 **"traditionally American"**: "Roosevelts Hosts at State Dinner," *New York Times*, Nov. 17, 1933.

94 **"Gentlemen, let us adjourn"**: William Harlan Hale, "An Attack Without Mercy," *Washington Post*, Nov. 18, 1933.

95 **"light American wines"**: Catherine MacKenzie, "Simple Fare for the White House," *New York Times*, Dec. 9, 1934.

95 **"The sherry was passable"**: Ickes, 248.

95 **"abominable"**: Diary, Nov. 20, 1933, box 1, Victoria Henrietta Kugler Nesbitt Papers, 1933–1949, Manuscript Division, Library of Congress, Washington, DC.

98 **"absolutely self-forgetful"**: Eleanor Roosevelt, "My Day," Sept. 1, 1936.

98 **"How I wish"**: Eleanor Roosevelt to Lorena Hickok, April 8, 1934, box 1, Lorena Hickok Papers, Franklin D. Roosevelt Presidential Library, Hyde Park, NY.

99 **"She so often said"**: Eleanor Roosevelt, *This Is My Story*, 46.

99 **"an almost exaggerated idea"**: Ibid., 98.

100 **"knowledge and self-confidence"**: Ibid., 145.

100 **"I was simply petrified"**: Ibid., 141.

100 **"He thought I was"**: Ibid., 162.

101 **"What she wanted":** Eleanor Roosevelt, "I Remember Hyde Park," *Mc-Call's*, Feb. 1963, 73.

103 **"Few pictures":** Blanche Wiesen Cook, *Eleanor Roosevelt*, vol. 1, 235.

103 **"Religion was of the utmost":** Lash, 333.

104 **"I looked at everything":** Eleanor Roosevelt, *Story*, 173.

106 **"darky":** See Cook, vol. 2, 439.

106 **"I think much can be done":** Eleanor Roosevelt, "If You Ask Me," *Ladies' Home Journal*, Dec. 1941, 48.

106 She was **"shocked":** Eleanor Roosevelt, *Story*, 180.

107 **"she-males":** Lash, 358.

107 **"I prefer doing my politics":** Ibid.

107 **"You have heard politics":** Ibid., 357.

107 **"During this time":** Cook, vol. 1, 333.

109 **"I would not be in this field":** Flora Rose to Eleanor Roosevelt, March 9, 1934, box 602, Anna Eleanor Roosevelt Papers, Franklin D. Roosevelt Presidential Library, Hyde Park, NY.

111 **"I can remember exactly":** Theodore Harris, *Pearl S. Buck*, 290.

112 **"her disdain for any interest":** Lash, 456.

113 **"good":** "7 1/2 Cent Economy Luncheons Served to the Roosevelts," *New York Times*, March 22, 1933. See also the menu for Tuesday, March 21, 1933, "Luncheon," in box 5, Nesbitt Papers.

114 **"The turmoil in my heart":** Eleanor Roosevelt, *This I Remember*, 74–75.

114 **"a real job":** Ibid., 76.

115 **"Her vision shaped":** Cook, vol. 2, 30.

116 **"a godsend":** Henrietta Nesbitt, *White House Diary*, 18.

116 **"I don't want":** Ibid., 20.

116 **Mrs. Nesbitt didn't know":** Lillian Rogers Parks and Frances Spatz Leighton, *The Roosevelts: A Family in Turmoil*, 30.

116 **"Fluffy":** Ibid., 70.

117 **"dingy":** J. B. West with Mary Lynn Kotz, *Upstairs at the White House*, 27.

117 **"Father never told me":** James Roosevelt with Shalett, *Affectionately*, 382.

118 **"Of course, Henrietta":** Parks and Leighton, 69.

119 **"We leaned on salads":** Henrietta Nesbitt, *The Presidential Cookbook*, 124.

120 **"I am doing away":** Alice Rogers Hager, "The Vibrant First Hostess of the Land," *New York Times*, May 14, 1933.

120 **"For Chinese people":** Nesbitt, *White House Diary*, 74.

121 **"cornbreads and gumbos":** Ernestine Evans, memo to Mary Chamberlain, n.d., box 3, Nesbitt Papers.

121 **"a special sort of patriotism":** Sheila Hibben, *National Cookbook*, x.

122 **"Father, who would have been":** Elliott Roosevelt with James Brough, *A Rendezvous with Destiny*, 46.

122 **"some of that big white asparagus":** Grace Tully, *F.D.R., My Boss*, 114.

123 **"Laughing, FDR said she ought to send":** Parks and Leighton, 70.

123 **"I had to do a little":** Eleanor Roosevelt, "My Day," Feb. 27, 1937.

123 **"in a tizzy":** Nesbitt, *White House Diary*, 185.

123 **"When he said":** Ibid., 185–86.

124 **"I remember one day":** Bernard Asbell, ed., *Mother and Daughter: The Letters of Eleanor and Anna Roosevelt*, 177.

124 **"Eleanor and the President":** Parks and Leighton, 219.

125 **"They had the most separate":** West with Kotz, 23.

125 **"secret paradise":** Doris Kearns Goodwin, *No Ordinary Time*, 385.

126 **"ER's Revenge":** Cook, vol. 2, 52.

127 **"After all, when one travels":** Eleanor Roosevelt, "My Day," March 28, 1938.

127 **"We went to a marvellous":** Asbell, ed., 117.

127 **"delicious Arab dinner":** Eleanor Roosevelt, "My Day," Feb. 15, 1952.

127 **"The French don't like":** Ibid., May 3, 1951.

128 **"There is one art":** Ibid., Nov. 5, 1948.

128 **"She had no idea":** "Oral History Interview with Mrs. Marguerite Entrup," Eleanor Roosevelt Oral History Transcripts, Franklin D. Roosevelt Presidential Library, Hyde Park, NY.

129 **"We all became":** Eleanor Roosevelt, "My Day," Jan. 14, 1936.

130 **"I did the ironing":** Eleanor Roosevelt to Hickok, Sept. 9, 10, and 11, 1936, box 4, Hickok Papers.

130 **"On the whole":** Eleanor Roosevelt, *This I Remember*, 350–51.

Eva Braun

132 **"I could never imagine":** Gitta Sereny, *Albert Speer: His Battle with Truth*, 508.

132 **"She was of course very feminine":** Ibid., 193.

132 **"Eva Braun radiated":** Albert Speer, *Inside the Third Reich*, translated by Richard and Clara Winston, 484.

134 **"Oh that girl":** Sereny, 532.

134 **"The Führer repeatedly":** Lizzie Collingham, *The Taste of War*, 156.

135 **"I'm sitting down":** Sarah Helm, *Ravensbrück*, 126.

137 **"celibate":** Janet Flanner, "Führer," part 1, *New Yorker*, Feb. 29, 1936, 20.

137 **"Evi Braun":** "Hitler's Girl Takes His Picture," *Life*, Nov. 6, 1939, 27.

137 **"sources inside Germany":** Richard Norburt, "Is Hitler Married?," *Saturday Evening Post*, Dec. 6, 1939, 14.

138 **"Obviously not good":** "Hitler's Girl."

139 ***"Guten appetit"*:** Interview with Franziska and Fritz Braun, Sept. 4, 1948, 26, Justice Michael A. Musmanno Collection, University Ar-

chives and Special Collections, Gumberg Library, Duquesne University, Pittsburgh, PA.

140 **"who volunteered"**: Ibid.

140 **"We come from a decent"**: Ibid., 1.

140 **"I disliked politics"**: Ibid., 2.

140 **"That was in 1933"**: Ibid., 3–5.

141 **"Is it true that you"**: Ibid., 1.

142 **"I am so infinitely happy"**: Diary of Eva Braun, Feb. 18, 1935, National Archives at College Park, College Park, MD.

142 **"mortally unhappy"**: Ibid., March 4, 1935.

142 **"seriously ill"**: Ibid., March 11, 1935.

143 **"Agreed that he's been busy"**: Ibid., May 28, 1935.

143 **"Her name is WALKURE"**: Ibid., May 10, 1935.

143 **"decisive"**: Ibid., May 28, 1935.

144 **"The weather is gorgeous"**: Ibid., May 10, 1935.

146 **"On the terrace"**: Albert Speer, *Spandau: The Secret Diaries,* translated by Richard and Clara Winston, 129.

146 **"a hand-painted flower pattern"**: Traudl Junge, *Until the Final Hour,* translated by Anthea Bell, 64.

147 **"Two orderlies"**: Ibid., 65.

147 **"nothing extravagant"**: Quoted in Margret Nissen, *Sind Sie die Tochter Speer?,* 25. I am grateful to Carla Stockton for translating portions of this book.

148 **"Hitler himself would have"**: Junge, 70.

149 **"stew Sundays"**: Ursula Heinzelmann, *Beyond Bratwurst,* 260.

150 **"delicate stomachs"**: Junge, 58.

150 **"Here on the Berghof"**: Ibid., 73.

151 **"the summer residence"**: Speer, *Spandau,* 129.

151 **"How nouveau riche"**: Ibid., 131.

151 **"Most gracious and respected"**: Ibid.

152 **"The idea of a caviar-eating Leader"**: Speer, *Third Reich,* 128.

153 **"my spies"**: William L. Shirer, *Berlin Diary,* 243.

153 **"Even in his meatless"**: Ignatius Phayre [George Fitz-Gerald], "At Home with Hitler," *Homes & Gardens,* Nov. 1938, 194.

153 **"He is not indifferent"**: Hedwig Mauer Simpson, "Herr Hitler at Home in the Clouds," *New York Times Magazine,* Aug. 20, 1939, 267.

154 **"trailing pink begonias"**: George Ward Price, *I Know These Dictators,* 30.

154 **"the greatest German"**: Stella Rudman, *Lloyd George and the Appeasement of Germany, 1919–1945,* 227.

154 **"slices of cold ham"**: Thomas Jones, *A Diary with Letters, 1931–1950,* 249.

155 **liver dumplings**: Therese Linke, unpublished memoir, Institut für Zeitgeschichte, Munich. I am grateful to Ingrid MacGillis for translating this manuscript.

155 **"sour"**: Heinz Linge, *With Hitler to the End*, translated by Geoffrey Brooks, 38.

155 **"For me, sweets"**: Ibid., 133.

156 **"very thin pastry"**: Christa Schroeder, *He Was My Chief*, translated by Geoffrey Brooks, 119.

156 **"She answered"**: Interview with Traudl Junge, March 21, 1948, 4, Musmanno Collection.

156 **"the Italian way"**: Ibid., 7.

157 **"She hated fat women"**: Junge, 66.

157 **"Eva Braun cast me"**: Ibid., 47.

159 **"had to make do"**: Speer, *Spandau*, 55.

159 **"Torrents of champagne"**: Bella Fromm, *Blood and Banquets*, 134.

160 **"Dinner started"**: Ibid., 239.

160 **"It's like a liquid symbol"**: Janet Flanner, "A Reporter at Large," *New Yorker*, Dec. 7, 1940, 59.

160 **"huge trucks"**: Harry Flannery, *Assignment to Berlin*, 166.

161 **"For Ribbentrop"**: "More Loot from France," *Observer*, Sept. 8, 1940.

161 **"The Germans who are there"**: Flanner, "Reporter at Large," 57.

161 **"Every little bureaucrat"**: Quoted in Roger Moorhouse, *Berlin at War*, 96.

162 **"wisely"**: Marie Vassiltchikov, *Berlin Diaries, 1940–1945*, 122.

162 **"After a fist fight"**: Ibid., 164.

162 **"empty rooms"**: Marianne Feuersenger, *Mein Kriegstagebuch*, 152. I am grateful to Ursula Heinzelmann for translating portions of this book.

163 **"all needed big houses"**: Speer, *Third Reich*, 217.

164 **"She had a very natural"**: Linge, 39.

164 **"rather strict"**: Interview, 10, Musmanno Collection.

164 **"She opened a file"**: Quoted in Anna Maria Sigmund, *Women of the Third Reich*, 167.

166 *"Deutschland, Deutschland"*: Album 6, Eva Braun's Photo Albums, 1913–1944, National Archives at College Park, College Park, MD.

167 **"I shan't go on living"**: Eva Braun to Adolf Hitler, quoted in Angela Lambert, *The Lost Life of Eva Braun*, 395.

167 **"Everything is kept secret"**: Quoted in ibid., 337.

168 **"silvery blue brocade"**: Junge, 159.

169 **"Children, I wish you"**: Henrik Eberle and Matthias Uhl, eds., *The Hitler Book*, translated by Giles MacDonogh, 258.

169 **"I want to be"**: Junge, 177.

169 **"I cannot understand"**: Eva Braun to Herta Schneider, quoted in Lambert, 426.

169 **"Why do so many more"**: Speer, *Third Reich*, 484.

169 **"the only person"**: Ibid.

170 **"Unfortunately my diamond"**: Eva Braun to Gretl Fegelein, quoted in Lambert, 430.

170 **"the Fuhrer's favourite":** Junge, 187.
171 **"We just thought":** Helm, *Ravensbrück*, 617.

Barbara Pym

173 **"[We] stopped at a beautiful":** Julia Child to Avis DeVoto, March 4, 1953, Julia Child Papers, Schlesinger Library, Radcliffe Institute for Advanced Studies, Harvard University, Cambridge, MA.
174 **"faded lettuce":** P. Morton Shand, *A Book of Food*, 13.
174 **"Our Cooking":** "Lambs' Tails and Hop-Tops," *Manchester Guardian*, March 29, 1932.
174 **"It was a time":** Quoted in Michael Bateman, *Cooking People*, 156.
176 **"Soup, jelly":** MS Pym 53, March 1, 1961, Papers of Barbara Mary Crampton Pym, Bodleian Library, University of Oxford, Oxford, UK.
177 **"In the dining-room":** Barbara Pym, *Some Tame Gazelle*, 13.
177 **"Boiled Chicken with Special Sauce":** Helen Simpson, *The Cold Table*, 92.
178 **"stringy cabbage":** Pym, *Gazelle*, 206.
179 **"Life's problems":** Barbara Pym, *No Fond Return of Love*, 13.
179 **"tame":** John Betjeman, "In London, SW 1," *Daily Telegraph*, March 14, 1952.
180 **"tragic":** See Nicola Shulman, "To Marry or to Smoulder Gently," *Times Literary Supplement*, Dec. 25, 1987, 1420; Hilary Laurie, "An Indexer Observes," *Times Literary Supplement*, July 29, 1988, 832; Margaret Bradham, "Lonesome Piners," *Times Literary Supplement*, Sept. 8, 1989, 967; Lorna Sage, review of *Less Than Angels*, *Observer*, Aug. 8, 1993.
180 **"wanly Christian":** John Updike, "Lem and Pym," *New Yorker*, Feb. 26, 1979, 115.
181 **"*11 March 1938*":** MS Pym 103, March 11, 1938.
181 **"the loveliest cocktail":** Ibid., 102, Nov. 25, 1933.
181 **"huge toast sandwiches":** Ibid., 101, March 5, 1938.
181 **"We had eggs":** Ibid., 103, March 5, 1938.
182 **"Our greater English poets":** Pym, *Gazelle*, 81.
183 **"snatched kisses":** MS Pym 110, Sept. 17, 1944.
184 **"There is so much":** Pym to Henry Harvey, Feb. 20, 1946, quoted in Hazel Holt and Hilary Pym, eds., *A Very Private Eye*, 251.
185 **"More household detail":** MS Pym 3, [1945].
185 **"but the food isn't bad":** Ibid., 102, March 29, 1934.
185 **"Two women at my table":** Ibid., 40, [1948].
185 **"This middle-aged lady":** Ibid., 41, [1950].
186 **"The back view":** Ibid., 43, [1952–1953].
186 **"In the hotel":** Ibid., 40, Sept. 27, 1948.
186 **"Later (in Lyons)":** Ibid., 65, Dec. 12, 1967.
186 **"What is this":** Ibid., 41, [1950].

186 **"Dear Colleague"**: Ibid., 45, [1954].

186 SECRET LOVE: Ibid., 48, Oct. 5, 1956.

186 **"and he didn't like it"**: Ibid., 49, Aug. 8, 1957.

187 **"Often it is just"**: Ibid., 98, "The Novelist's Use of Every-day Life," [1950s].

187 **"Hazel and I"**: Ibid., 60, Dec. 27, 1964.

188 **"Food—a fresh salad"**: Ibid., 40, [1948].

188 **"impoverished gentlewomen"**: Barbara Pym, *Excellent Women*, 12.

189 **"I washed a lettuce"**: Ibid., 156.

189 **"How one learns to dread"**: Elizabeth David, *Summer Cooking*, 26.

190 **"I went upstairs"**: Pym, *Excellent Women*, 174.

190 **"curried whale"**: Ibid., 102.

190 **"a very nice bird"**: Ibid., 254.

191 **"After the service"**: Ibid., 134.

191 **"a *woman's* meal"**: Ibid., 174.

191 **"Why is it that *men*"**: Pym to Robert Smith, Dec. 8, 1963, MS Pym 162/1.

191 **"quite extraordinary deadness"**: A. N. Wilson, introduction to Pym, *Excellent Women* (Penguin), xv.

191 **"is regarded as an extraordinary"**: Ibid., xiii.

192 **"Man fussing about wine"**: MS Pym 40, [1948].

192 **" 'It might,' he said seriously"**: Pym, *Excellent Women*, 67.

192 **"mousy"**: Ibid., 7.

192 **"I sat down"**: Ibid., 14.

193 **"This uncompromisingly English"**: Evelyn Board, *The Right Way to His Heart*, 71.

194 **"sometimes smelled of garlic"**: Barbara Pym, *Less Than Angels*, 26.

194 **"Oh, what joy"**: Ibid., 104.

194 **"to perfection"**: Pym, *No Fond Return of Love*, 144.

195 **"like *Americans*"**: Barbara Pym, *An Unsuitable Attachment*, 30.

195 **"boiled baby"**: Pym, *No Fond Return of Love*, 95.

195 **"How would she eat"**: MS Pym 50, April 8, 1958.

196 **"a dry sausage roll"**: Ibid., 49, March 14, 1957.

196 **"delicious creamy cake"**: Ibid., 62, Oct. 26, 1965.

196 **"Macaroni Bolognaise"**: Ibid., 45, Oct. 11, 1954.

196 **"Tio Pepe, ravioli"**: Ibid., 61, March 30, 1965.

196 **"gorgeous roast beef"**: Ibid., 47, Oct. 7, 1955.

196 **"We had much congenial talk"**: Ibid., 77, March 3, 1977.

196 **"I am writing"**: Pym to Robert Smith, Sept. 29, 1974, MS Pym 162/2.

196 **"fish fingers"**: MS Pym 65, Aug. 18, 1968.

196 **"Miracle Whip??"**: Ibid., 66, [1970].

197 **"Vin rouge"**: Ibid., 60, [1956].

197 **"Coke, Beaujolais"**: Ibid., 65, Aug. 18, 1968.

197 **"veal escalopes"**: Ibid., 48, [1956].

197 **"Pesto Alle Genovese"**: Ibid., 79, June 24, 1978.

197 **"We ate kipper paté"**: Ibid., 77, April 23, 1977.

198 **"Sunday—eggs and bacon"**: Ibid., 75, Feb. 22–28, 1976.

198 **"our Indian cooking"**: Pym to Robert Smith, May 11, 1978, MS Pym 162/2.

198 **"all those Sundays"**: MS Pym 40, [1949].

199 **"Tin fruit"**: Ibid., 49, Jan. 1957.

199 **"Steak, etc."**: Ibid., 60, Feb. 2, 1965.

199 **"Here, she knew"**: Barbara Pym, *Jane and Prudence*, 198.

200 **"where great joints"**: Barbara Pym, *A Glass of Blessings*, 98.

201 **"The first picture"**: Raymond Postgate, ed., *The Good Food Guide, 1951–1952*, 25.

201 **"*Real* cream"**: Ibid., 70.

201 **"*real* coffee"**: Ibid.

201 **"real mayonnaise"**: Ibid., 47.

201 **"duckling which really is"**: Ibid., 59.

201 **"home-cured mild sweet"**: Ibid., 144.

201 **"good, plain English"**: Ibid., 99.

202 **"the best place for ravioli"**: Ibid., 185.

202 **"the authentic, best *cuisine*"**: Ibid., 198.

202 **"Food rich, substantial"**: Ibid., 184.

202 **"an excellent little restaurant"**: Ibid., 183.

202 **"smorrebrod"**: Ibid., 187.

202 **"Pekinese chicken noodle"**: Ibid., 185.

202 **"Arroz alla Valenciana"**: Ibid., 196.

202 **"Apfel strudel"**: Ibid., 186.

202 **"They were only tolerable"**: Raymond Postgate, ed., *The Good Food Guide, 1963–1964*, xii.

203 **"roast woodcock"**: Postgate, ed., *Guide, 1951–1952*, 153.

203 **"splendidly cooked chateaubriand"**: Ibid., 47.

203 **"first-class French chef"**: Ibid., 164.

203 **"delicious jugged hare"**: Ibid., 113.

203 **"unexpectedly high quality"**: Ibid., 25.

203 **"only French butter"**: Postgate, ed., *Guide, 1963–1964*, 423.

203 **"Several of us"**: Wren Howard to Pym, March 19, 1963, MS Pym 164.

204 **"was really run down"**: Nicholas Wroe, "Talent Spotter," *Guardian*, March 12, 2005.

204 **"For my first seven years"**: Tom Maschler, *Publisher*, 64.

204 **"I have got a new typewriter"**: Pym to Robert Smith, May 24, 1963, MS Pym 162/1.

205 **"mild novels"**: Ibid., June 11, 1963, MS Pym 162/1.

205 **"so well written"**: Ibid., March 24, 1970, MS Pym 162/2.

205 **"I am bound to admit"**: Ibid., Sept. 14, 1971, MS Pym 162/2

205 **"perfection of taste"**: Ibid., Jan. 26, 1970, MS Pym 162/2

205 **"in perfect taste"**: Ibid., March 24, 1970, MS Pym 162/2.

205 **"accomplished"**: Ibid., Nov. 6, 1970, MS Pym 162/2.

205 **"it was 'virtually impossible'"**: Ibid., March 7, 1972, MS Pym 162/2.

205 **"They are all like SHEEP"**: Ibid., Dec. 3, 1969, MS Pym 162/1.

205 **"a delicious book"**: Review by Siriol Hugh-Jones, *Tatler*, Feb. 1, 1961, in Yvonne Cocking, *Barbara in the Bodleian*, 163.

205 **"amusing"**: Marie Hannah, "Trouble Brewing," *Times Literary Supplement*, Nov. 18, 1955, 685.

206 **"My new novel"**: Pym to Smith, Jan. 23, 1964, MS Pym, 162/1.

206 **"I have finished"**: Ibid., Sept. 26, 1967, MS Pym 162/1.

206 **"I am trying"**: Ibid., April 2, 1968, MS Pym 162/1.

206 **"Lunch at the Royal"**: MS Pym 65, July 31, 1968.

206 **"Is there a rather good"**: Ibid., 69, April 9, 1971.

206 **"I think, why"**: Ibid., 70, May 10, 1972.

207 **"What is wrong"**: Ibid., 68, Nov. 9, 1970.

207 **"'Notebook of an unsuccessful'"**: Ibid., 68, Sept. 6, 1970.

207 **"a failing novelist"**: Ibid., 69, Nov. 10, 1971.

207 **"an unpublished novelist"**: Ibid., 76, Dec. 13, 1976.

207 **"Miss Pym (a failure)"**: Ibid., 59, [1964].

207 **"charlatan"**: "Reputations Revisited," *Times Literary Supplement*, Jan. 21, 1977, 66.

208 **"almost any contemporary"**: Ibid.

208 **"Young girls in love"**: Ibid.

208 **"my name appeared"**: MS Pym 76, [Jan. 1977].

208 **"Hilary and I invented"**: Quoted in Hazel Holt, *A Lot to Ask*, 254.

209 **"I sometimes think"**: A talk to the Senior Wives Fellowship, United Reform Church Hall, Headlington, May 15, 1978, MS Pym 98.

210 **"(*Finstock*. Barn Cottage Restaurant . . .)"**: Pym to Smith, July 15, 1977, MS Pym 162/2.

210 **"awful good food guide"**: MS Pym 77, March 7, 1977.

210 **"tasting, sampling"**: Barbara Pym, *A Few Green Leaves*, 10.

210 **"That celery"**: Ibid., 25.

211 **"Leonora could see"**: Barbara Pym, *The Sweet Dove Died*, 155.

212 **"I've just eaten"**: MS Pym 82, Nov. 21, 1979.

Helen Gurley Brown

214 **"Never did write"**: Handwritten note, Nov. 20, 2000, box 35, folder 11, Helen Gurley Brown Papers, Sophia Smith Collection, Smith College, Northampton, MA.

214 **"David is a motion picture producer"**: Helen Gurley Brown, *Sex and the Single Girl* (hereafter *SASG*), 3.

216 **"There's nothing left"**: Nora Ephron, "'If You're a Little Mouseburger,

Come with Me. I Was a Mouseburger and I Will Help You,' " in *Wallflower at the Orgy*, 21.

216 **"I like it with a light cream sauce"**: "Feedback," *Bon Appetit*, April 1989, 150.

216 **"Eating is sexy"**: "The Low Will-Power, High-Protein Diet," *Cosmopolitan*, Aug. 1965, 37.

216 **"If I eat"**: Felicity Green, "Helen Gurley Brown, Six-O and Still Going Strong," *Daily Express* (London), Feb. 26, 1982.

217 **"struggling"**: Helen Gurley Brown, *Helen Gurley Brown's Single Girl's Cookbook* (hereafter *Cookbook*), 5.

217 **"a pretty good cook"**: Brown, *SASG*, 143.

217 **"Lots of canned sausages"**: Ibid., 152.

217 **"Skinny to me"**: Manuscript, *I'm Wild Again*, n.d., box 31, folder 7, Brown Papers.

217 **"Heaven!"**: Helen Gurley Brown, *I'm Wild Again*, 156.

218 **"He makes me feel"**: Manuscript, n.d., box 35, folder 12, Brown Papers.

218 **"beautiful pearls"**: Manuscript, 1962–1963, box 35, folder 10, Brown Papers.

220 **"People would walk"**: Brown, *SASG*, 169.

221 **"Have half mid-morning"**: Ibid., 173.

221 **"like Gandhi"**: Ibid., 169.

222 **"Candy is a damned fine stripper"**: Manuscript, 1962–1963, box 35, folder 10, Brown Papers.

222 **"Suffice it to say"**: Brown, *SASG*, 170.

222 **"Whatever your age"**: Green, "Helen Gurley Brown."

222 **"If you are already"**: Brown, *SASG*, 178.

223 **"the weirdies, the creepies"**: Ibid., 18.

223 **"The fact is, you vote"**: Valerie Groves, "All You Need Is Brains," *Standard* (London), Feb. 25, 1982.

223 **"We health nuts"**: Brown, *SASG*, 177.

223 **"I diet every day"**: Ibid., 179.

223 **"particularly happy"**: Manuscript, 1962–1963, box 35, folder 10, Brown Papers.

224 **"I'm a *wife*"**: Ibid.

224 **"MY WHITE KNIGHT"**: Manuscript, 1962–1963, box 35, folder 9, Brown Papers.

224 **"I am not your truly liberated"**: Diana Lurie, "Living with Liberation," *New York*, Aug. 31, 1970, 22.

226 **"She's most pleased"**: "Perspectives," *House Beautiful*, March 1972, 28.

226 **"I take good care"**: Ibid.

226 **"When she receives"**: Chris Welles, "Soaring Success of the Iron Butterfly," *Life*, Nov. 19, 1965, 66.

226 **"I'm the geisha girl":** Chris Barnett, "The Movie Mogul and 'That Cosmo Girl,'" *Mainliner*, July 1980, 56.

227 **"Money is sexy":** Elin Schoen, "Seven Two-Career Couples," *New York*, Oct. 25, 1976, 40.

228 **"Don't you like me anymore?":** Manuscript, 1962–1963, box 35, folder 10, Brown Papers.

228 **"I said, 'That's my *book*!'":** Brown to Bernard Geis, Oct. 10, 1962, box 19, folder 2, Brown Papers.

228 **"We had bloody battles":** Ibid.

229 **"In other words":** Ibid.

230 **"I can't cook":** Manuscript, n.d., box 25, folder 2, Brown Papers.

230 **"(They assume I *have* . . .)":** Ibid.

231 **"failing with the never-fail":** Brown, *SASG*, 143.

231 **"a pretty good cook":** Ibid.

231 **"fabulous little dinners":** Ibid., 154.

231 **"Rumanian gypsy music":** Ibid., 151.

231 **"a hearty little breakfast":** Ibid., 152.

231 **"Rosa Rita frozen":** Ibid., 148.

231 **"Or use canned tomatoes":** Ibid., 154.

232 **"borrowed heavily":** Ibid., 155.

232 **"Marinated Vegetable Platter":** Ibid., 163.

232 **"Foamy Vanilla Sauce":** Ibid., 158.

233 **"It's a chance for everybody":** Manuscript, "The Single Girl," box 35, folder 3, Brown Papers.

234 **"to say some of the things":** Manuscript, "Frankly Female," box 35, folder 3, Brown Papers.

234 **"soothing, soporific talk":** Manuscript, "The UNWIND UP," box 35, folder 3, Brown Papers.

234 *Cook's on the Fire*: Manuscript, "TV format," box 35, folder 3, Brown Papers.

235 *"Femme"*: Manuscript, "A Proposal for a New Magazine," 13, box 37, folder 2, Brown Papers.

235 **"fight against aging":** Ibid., 14.

235 **"The Men in Your Life":** Ibid., 15.

236 **"a superbly eligible man":** Ibid, 16.

236 **"New Yorker size":** Ibid., 5.

236 **"Great Stars":** *Cosmopolitan*, July 1962; August 1962; June 1960.

237 **"I always knew":** "How to Reposition a Publication," *Media Management Monograph*, no. 18, Feb. 1980, 4–5.

237 **"one of the fastest":** Welles, "Soaring Success," 65.

238 **"Every new paragraph":** "*Cosmopolitan*'s Ubiquitous Editor," *Media People*, Fall 1983.

238 **"You and I are such"**: Helen Gurley Brown, "Step into My Parlor," *Cosmopolitan*, March 1975, 6.

238 **"If Mrs. Brown"**: Quoted in "*Playboy* Interview: Helen Gurley Brown," *Playboy*, April 1963, 56.

239 **"italics, exclamation points"**: Ephron, " 'If You're a Little Mouseburger,' " 17.

239 **"I would say the writing"**: "*Cosmopolitan*'s Ubiquitous Editor."

239 **"Let's just say"**: "*Playboy* Interview," 56.

240 **"Cooking *is* part of wooing"**: Brown, *SASG*, 140.

241 **"sinful," "naughty"**: Helen Gurley Brown, *Having It All*, 121–26.

241 **"Poulet Negresco"**: Manuscript, 1962–1963, box 35, folder 9, Brown Papers.

241 **"I have dumped"**: Brown, *Having It All*, 114.

242 **"Passionate Antipasto Party"**: *Cosmopolitan*, July 1966, 96.

243 **"hearty open-faced steak Tartare"**: Ibid., March 1966, 72.

243 **"Exotic East Indian Meat Loaf"**: Ibid., April 1972, 38.

243 **"easy feast"**: Memorandum to "Barbara Ann," Aug. 25, 1975, box 42, folder 5, Brown Papers.

243 **"Go Geisha!"**: *Cosmopolitan*, Jan. 1975, 16.

244 **"The Low Will-Power"**: Ibid., Aug. 1965, 37.

244 **"English muffins dripping"**: Ibid.

244 **"the incredible, intoxicating joy"**: Gael Greene, "Forbidden Fruit for Indulgent Dieters," *Cosmopolitan*, Dec. 1965, 24.

244 **"When you're full"**: Joan Dunn, "Dieter's Notebook," *Cosmopolitan*, Feb. 1970, 46.

244 **"overconscientious food and medical"**: Ibid., March 1968, 44.

244 **"Ask your doctor about Bamadex"**: Ibid., Jan. 1966, 23.

245 **"an incredible salad bar"**: Brown, "Step into My Parlor," *Cosmopolitan*, Jan. 1978, 6.

245 **"I substitute fake ingredients"**: *Esquire*, Nov. 1984, C24.

245 **"Thirty minutes on the body"**: Green, "Helen Gurley Brown, Six-O," 15.

245 **"Age to me is a disease"**: Pamela Coleman, "Things I Wish I'd Known at 18," *Sunday Express* (London), Sept. 4, 1983.

246 **"I may have carried it"**: Helen Gurley Brown, *The Late Show*, 264.

246 **"I think you may have to have"**: Brown, *Having It All*, 129.

246 **"She carefully fished out"**: Audrey Slaughter, "In Her Own Image," *Sunday Times* (London), Dec. 28, 1980.

246 **"Her face is strangely"**: Ibid.

247 **"I get seriously aggravated"**: Nancy Lloyd, "Helen Gurley Brown," *Modern Maturity*, May–June 1997, 56.

247 **"Mostly the pushers"**: Brown, *The Late Show*, 191.

247 **"Bitch!"**: Brown, *Having It All*, 112.

247 *How to Love a Girl:* Brown to Bernard Geis, March 5, 1962, box 19, folder 2, Brown Papers.

248 **"peek-a-boo necklines":** Helen Gurley Brown, *Sex and the Office,* 24.

248 **to try a cookbook:** By the time the cookbook was finally published in 1969, it had become Helen's fourth book with Geis. In 1966 he brought out, in cooperation with Avon Books, *Helen Gurley Brown's Outrageous Opinions,* a collection of syndicated newspaper columns that Helen had written between 1963 and 1965.

248 **"lulu of a cookbook":** Bernard Geis to Margot Reiman Martin, June 22, 1963, box 19, folder 8, Brown Papers.

249 **"the best in the world!":** Memorandum, "Notes on Single Girl's Cookbook," box 25, folder 1, Brown Papers.

249 **"Margo allowed me to take":** Brown, *Cookbook,* 4.

249 **"It is for new-girl cooks":** Brown to Jackie Farber, Oct. 13, 1968, box 19, folder 2, Brown Papers.

250 **"Tear off two sheets":** Brown, *Cookbook,* 174.

251 **"for the girls":** Ibid., 145.

251 **"Garbanzo Dip":** Ibid, 188.

251 **"Mama's Noodles":** Ibid, 209.

252 **"This darling cookbook":** Ibid., 57.

252 **"These dear little blender breakfasts":** Ibid., 71.

252 **"Go! Go! Go!":** Ibid., 196.

252 **"Let *other* girls":** Ibid., 195.

252 **"lively and practical":** *Publishers Weekly,* Feb. 13, 1969, 62.

252 **"clear directions":** Gloria Levitas, "Summer Eating," *Book World* (*Chicago Tribune*), July 6, 1969, 5.

252 **"I hope so":** "Dialogue," *National Catholic Register,* March 29, 1981, 5.

253 **"I think date rape":** Bob Frost, "Interview," *West* (*San Jose Mercury News*), Oct. 31, 1993.

253 **"Flattery, flattery":** Lloyd, "Helen Gurley Brown."

253 **"Age gets all of us":** Ibid.

254 **Helen's version became:** Vivian Gornick, "The Next Great Moment in History Is Theirs," *Village Voice,* November 27, 1969; Gornick, "The Women's Liberation Movement!" *Cosmopolitan,* April 1970, 140.

254 **"militant feminism":** "Ten Questions We Finally Got the Nerve to Ask Helen Gurley Brown," *Madison Avenue,* September 1985.

254 **"And perhaps that's where":** Brown, "Step into My Parlor," *Cosmopolitan,* June 1970, 6.

255 **"I'm skinny!":** Transcript of interview by Gloria Steinem for ABC/Hearst, "In Conversation with Helen Gurley Brown," 1985, box 16, folder 5, Brown Papers.

BIBLIOGRAPHY

Libraries and Archives

Journals of Dorothy Wordsworth
  Jerwood Centre, the Wordsworth Trust, Grasmere, UK
Anna Eleanor Roosevelt Papers
Eleanor Roosevelt Oral History Transcripts
Lorena Hickok Papers
  Franklin D. Roosevelt Presidential Library, Hyde Park, NY
"My Day"
"If You Ask Me"
  Eleanor Roosevelt Papers Project, Digital Edition
Victoria Henrietta Kugler Nesbitt Papers, 1933–1949
  Manuscript Division, Library of Congress, Washington, DC
Interrogations of Hitler Associates
  Justice Michael A. Musmanno Collection
  University Archives and Special Collections
  Gumberg Library, Duquesne University, Pittsburgh, PA
Diary of Eva Braun
Eva Braun's Photo Albums, 1913–1944
  National Archives at College Park, College Park, MD
Papers of Barbara Mary Crampton Pym
  Bodleian Library, University of Oxford, Oxford, UK
Julia Child Papers
  Schlesinger Library, Radcliffe Institute for Advanced Studies,
    Harvard University, Cambridge, MA
Helen Gurley Brown Papers
  Sophia Smith Collection, Smith College, Northampton, MA

Other Sources

Aly, Gotz. *Hitler's Beneficiaries: Plunder, Racial War, and the Nazi Welfare State.*
  Translated by Jefferson Chase. New York: Metropolitan, 2007.
Asbell, Bernard, ed. *Mother and Daughter: The Letters of Eleanor and Anna
  Roosevelt.* New York: Coward, McCann and Geoghegan, 1982.

Baker, Carlos, ed. *Ernest Hemingway: Selected Letters, 1917–1961.* New York: Scribner, 1981.

Balsan, Consuelo Vanderbilt. *The Glitter and the Gold.* London: Heinemann, 1953.

Barker, Juliet. *Wordsworth: A Life.* New York: Ecco, 2005.

Bateman, Michael. *Cooking People.* London: Leslie Frewin, 1966.

Beeton, Isabella. *Beeton's Book of Household Management.* London: S. O. Beeton, 1861.

Board, Evelyn. *The Right Way to His Heart.* Kingswood, Surrey: Elliot Right Way Books, 1952.

Braun, Eva. Diary of Eva Braun. [Eva Braun's Diary with English Translation.] Record Group 242. National Archives, College Park, MD.

———. Eva Braun's Photo Albums, 1913–1944. Record Group 242. National Archives, College Park, MD.

Brears, Peter. *Cooking and Dining with the Wordsworths.* Ludlow: Excellent Press, 2011.

Breslaw, Philip. *Breslaw's Last Legacy.* London: Printed for T. Moore, 1784.

Brockett, John Trotter. *A Glossary of North Country Words.* Vol. 1. Newcastle upon Tyne: E. Charnley, 1846.

Brown, David. *Let Me Entertain You.* New York: William Morrow, 1990.

Brown, Helen Gurley. *Having It All.* New York: Simon and Schuster, 1982.

———. *Helen Gurley Brown's Outrageous Opinions.* New York: Avon Books, 1966.

———. *Helen Gurley Brown's Single Girl's Cookbook.* New York: Bernard Geis, 1969.

———. *I'm Wild Again.* New York: St. Martin's Press, 2000.

———. *The Late Show.* New York: William Morrow, 1993.

———. *Sex and the Office.* New York: Bernard Geis, 1964.

———. *Sex and the Single Girl.* New York: Bernard Geis, 1962.

———. *The Writer's Rules.* New York: William Morrow, 1998.

Bryan, Joseph III. " 'Orrible Woman." *New Yorker,* September 16, 1933, 23.

Burton, Mary E., ed. *The Letters of Mary Wordsworth.* Oxford: Oxford University Press, 1958.

Campbell, Lady Colin, ed. *The Etiquette of Good Society.* London: Cassell and Company, 1893.

Cocking, Yvonne. *Barbara in the Bodleian.* Oxford and Boston: Barbara Pym Society, 2013.

Collingham, Lizzie. *The Taste of War.* New York: Penguin Press, 2012.

Cook, Blanche Wiesen. *Eleanor Roosevelt.* 3 vols. New York: Viking, 1992–2016.

Cooper, Artemis. *Writing at the Kitchen Table.* New York: Ecco Press, 2000.

Davenport, Walter. "The Cook's Day Out." *Collier's,* March 5, 1927, 26.

David, Elizabeth. *Summer Cooking.* 1955. Reprint, New York: New York Review Books, 2002.

De Quincey, Thomas. *Recollections of the Lakes and the Lake Poets.* Edinburgh: Adam and Charles Black, 1862.

de Selincourt, Ernest. *Dorothy Wordsworth.* Oxford: Clarendon Press, 1933.

de Selincourt, Ernest, and Alan G. Hill, eds. *The Letters of William and Dorothy Wordsworth.* Vol. IV, *The Later Years: Part I, 1821–1828.* 2nd rev. ed. Oxford: Clarendon Press, 1978.

———. *The Letters of William and Dorothy Wordsworth.* Vol. V, *The Later Years: Part II, 1829–1834.* 2nd rev. ed. Oxford: Clarendon Press, 1979.

———. *The Letters of William and Dorothy Wordsworth.* Vol. VI, *The Later Years: Part III, 1835–1839.* 2nd rev. ed. Oxford: Clarendon Press, 1982.

de Selincourt, Ernest, Mary Moorman, and Alan G. Hill, eds. *The Letters of William and Dorothy Wordsworth.* Vol. III, *The Middle Years: Part II, 1812–1820.* 2nd rev. ed. Oxford: Clarendon Press, 1969.

de Selincourt, Ernest, and Chester L. Shaver, eds. *The Letters of William and Dorothy Wordsworth.* Vol. I, *The Early Years: 1787–1805.* 2nd rev. ed. Oxford: Oxford University Press, 1967.

Dobson, Austin, ed. *Selected Poems of Matthew Prior.* London: Kegan Paul, Trench and Co., 1889.

Driver, Christopher. *The British at Table, 1940–1980.* London: Chatto and Windus, 1983.

Drummond, J. C., and Anne Wilbraham. *The Englishman's Food.* Introduction by Tom Jaine. London: Pimlico, 1991.

Eberle, Henrik, and Matthias Uhl, eds. *The Hitler Book.* Translated by Giles MacDonogh. New York: Public Affairs, 2005.

Ephron, Nora. *Wallflower at the Orgy.* New York: Viking, 1970.

Escoffier, A. *A Guide to Modern Cookery.* 1907. Reprint, Provo, UT: Repressed Publishing, 2013.

Fest, Joachim. *Inside Hitler's Bunker.* Translated by Margot Bettauer Dembo. New York: Picador, 2004.

Feuersenger, Marianne. *Mein Kriegstagebuch.* Freiburg: Herder, 1982.

Fielding, Daphne. *The Duchess of Jermyn Street.* London: Penguin Books, 1978.

———. *Mercury Presides.* New York: Harcourt, Brace and Co., 1955.

Fields, Alonzo. *My 21 Years in the White House.* New York: Coward-McCann, 1960.

FitzGibbon, Theodora. *With Love.* London: Century, 1982.

Flannery, Harry. *Assignment to Berlin.* New York: Alfred A. Knopf, 1942.

Francatelli, Charles Elmé. *The Modern Cook.* London: Richard Bentley, 1846.

Freidel, Frank. *Franklin D. Roosevelt: Launching the New Deal.* Boston: Little, Brown and Co., 1973.

Fromm, Bella. *Blood and Banquets.* Garden City, NY: Garden City Publishing Co., 1944.

Garrett, Theodore Francis, ed. *The Encyclopædia of Practical Cookery.* London: L. Upcott Gill, 1897.

Gittings, Robert, and Jo Manton. *Dorothy Wordsworth.* Oxford: Clarendon Press, 1985.

Glasse, Hannah. *The Art of Cookery, Made Plain and Easy.* London: Printed for W. Strahan, J. and F. Rivington, 1774.

Glendinning, Victoria. *Anthony Trollope.* New York: Alfred A. Knopf, 1993.

Goodwin, Doris Kearns. *No Ordinary Time.* New York: Simon and Schuster, 1994.

Gornick, Vivian. "The Next Great Moment in History Is Theirs." *Village Voice,* Nov. 27, 1969.

———. "The Women's Liberation Movement!" *Cosmopolitan,* April 1970, 140.

Görtemaker, Heike B. *Eva Braun: Life with Hitler.* New York: Alfred A. Knopf, 2011.

Haber, Barbara. *From Hardtack to Home Fries: An Uncommon History of American Cooks and Meals.* New York: Free Press, 2002.

Harris, Theodore. *Pearl S. Buck.* 2 vols. New York: John Day, 1969–1971.

Harrison, Michael. *Rosa.* London: Corgi, 1977.

Heinzelmann, Ursula. *Beyond Bratwurst.* London: Reaktion Books, 2014.

Helm, Sarah. *Ravensbrück.* New York: Doubleday, 2014.

Hibben, Sheila. *The National Cookbook.* New York: Harper and Brothers, 1932.

Hill, Alan G., ed. *The Letters of William and Dorothy Wordsworth.* Vol. VII, *The Later Years, Part 4: 1840–1853.* Oxford: Clarendon Press, 1993.

Hill, Georgiana. *The Breakfast Book.* London: Richard Bentley, 1865. Reprinted in *The English Breakfast,* by Kaori O'Connor. London: Bloomsbury, 2013.

Holt, Hazel. *A Lot to Ask.* New York: Dutton, 1991.

———, and Hilary Pym, eds. *A Very Private Eye.* 1984. Reprint, London: Grafton, 1985.

How to Dine, or Etiquette of the Dinner Table. London: Ward, Lock, and Tyler, 1879.

Ickes, Harold L. *The Secret Diary of Harold L. Ickes.* New York: Simon and Schuster, 1953.

James, Kenneth. *Escoffier: The King of Chefs.* London and New York: Hambledon and London, 2002.

Janssen, Marian. *Not at All What One Is Used To: The Life and Times of Isabella Gardner.* Columbia: University of Missouri Press, 2010.

Johnston, Kenneth R. *The Hidden Wordsworth.* New York: W. W. Norton and Co., 1998.

Jones, Thomas. *A Diary with Letters, 1931–1950.* London: Oxford University Press, 1954.

Junge, Traudl. *Until the Final Hour.* Edited by Melissa Müller. Translated by Anthea Bell. London: Weidenfeld and Nicolson, 2003.

Kladstrup, Don and Petie. *Wine & War.* New York: Broadway Books, 2002.

Knight, William, ed. *Journals of Dorothy Wordsworth.* London: Macmillan and Co., 1904.

Lambert, Angela. *The Lost Life of Eva Braun.* New York: St. Martin's Press, 2006.

Lash, Joseph. *Eleanor and Franklin.* New York: W. W. Norton and Co., 1971.

Lawton, Mary. *The Queen of Cooks—And Some Kings.* New York: Boni and Liveright, 1925.

Leslie, Anita. *Edwardians in Love.* London: Hutchinson, 1972.

Linge, Heinz. *With Hitler to the End.* Translated by Geoffrey Brooks. London: Frontline Books, 2009.

Linke, Therese. Unpublished memoir. Munich: Institut für Zeitgeschichte, n.d.

Lister, Charles. *Letters and Recollections.* London: T. F. Unwin, 1917.

Long, Ava, with Mildred Harrington. "Presidents at Home." *Ladies Home Journal,* September 1933, 17.

———. "Three a Day in the White House." *Ladies Home Journal,* December 1935, 19.

Luhan, Mabel Dodge. *Intimate Memories.* Edited by Lois Palken Rudnick. Albuquerque: University of New Mexico Press, 1999.

MacDonogh, Giles. "Otto Horcher, Caterer to the Third Reich." *Gastronomica* 7, no. 1 (Winter 2007): 31–38.

Maschler, Tom. *Publisher.* London: Picador, 2005.

Masters, Anthony. *Rosa Lewis: An Exceptional Edwardian.* London: Weidenfeld and Nicolson, 1977.

A Member of the Aristocracy. *Manners and Tone of Good Society.* 13th ed. London and New York: Frederick Warne and Co., 188–.

Mennell, Stephen. *All Manners of Food.* London: Basil Blackwell, 1985.

Merrill, Flora. *Kippy of the Cavendish.* New York: R. M. McBride, 1934.

Moorhouse, Roger. *Berlin at War.* New York: Basic Books, 2010.

Mugglestone, Lynda. *Talking Proper: The Rise of Accent as Social Symbol.* 2nd ed. Oxford: Oxford University Press, 2003.

Nagasawa, Jiro. "An Unpublished Dorothy Wordsworth Letter of 20 March 1837." *Notes and Queries* 48 (June 2001): 121.

Nesbitt, Henrietta. *White House Diary.* New York: Doubleday, 1948.

———. *The Presidential Cookbook.* New York: Doubleday, 1951.

Newnham-Davis, Nathaniel. *The Gourmet's Guide to London.* New York: Brentano's, 1914.

Nichols, John. *The History and Antiquities of the County of Leicester.* Vol. 3, part 2. London: John Nichols, 1800.

Nicolson, Harold. "The Edwardian Weekend." In *The Age of Extravagance.* Edited by Mary Elisabeth Edes and Dudley Frasier. London: Weidenfeld and Nicolson, 1955.

Nissen, Margret, with Margit Knapp and Sabine Seifert. *Sind Sie die Tochter Speer?* München: Deutsche Verlags-Anstalt, 2005.

O'Donnell, James P. *The Bunker.* Boston: Houghton Mifflin, 1978.

Owings, Alison. *Frauen.* New Brunswick, NJ: Rutgers University Press, 1993.

Parks, Lillian Rogers, and Franzes Spatz Leighton. *The Roosevelts: A Family in Turmoil.* Englewood Cliffs, NJ: Prentice-Hall, 1981.

Party-giving on Every Scale, or The Cost of Entertainments. London: Frederick Warne and Co., 188–.

Postgate, John, and Mary. *A Stomach for Dissent: The Life of Raymond Postgate, 1896–1971.* Keele, England: Keele University Press, 1994.

Postgate, Raymond, ed. *The Good Food Guide, 1951–1952.* London: Cassell and Co., 1951.

———. *The Good Food Guide, 1963–1964.* London: Consumers Association and Cassell, 1964.

Powell, Anthony. *Messengers of Day.* New York: Holt, Rinehart and Winston, 1978.

Price, George Ward. *I Know These Dictators.* New York: Henry Holt and Co., 1938.

Pym, Barbara. *Excellent Women.* 1952. Reprint, New York: Plume, 1988.

———. *A Few Green Leaves.* 1980. Reprint, New York: Perennial Library, 1981.

———. *A Glass of Blessings.* 1958. Reprint, New York: Perennial Library, 1981.

———. *Jane and Prudence.* 1953. Reprint, New York: Perennial Library, 1982.

———. *Less Than Angels.* 1955. Reprint, New York: Perennial Library, 1982.

———. *No Fond Return of Love.* 1961. Reprint, New York: Perennial Library, 1984.

———. *Some Tame Gazelle.* 1950. Reprint, New York: Dutton, 1983.

———. *The Sweet Dove Died.* 1978. Reprint, New York: Perennial Library, 1980.

———. *Quartet in Autumn.* 1977. Reprint, New York: Perennial Library, 1980.

———. *An Unsuitable Attachment.* 1982. Reprint, New York: Perennial Library, 1983.

Radcliffe, Mary. *A Modern System of Domestic Cookery.* Manchester: J. Gleave, 1823.

Ridley, Jane. *The Heir Apparent.* New York: Random House, 2013.

Roosevelt, Eleanor. *This Is My Story.* New York: Harper and Bros., 1937.

———. *This I Remember.* New York: Harper and Bros., 1949.

Roosevelt, Elliott, with James Brough. *A Rendezvous with Destiny.* New York: Putnam, 1975.

Roosevelt, James, and Sidney Shalett. *Affectionately, F.D.R.* New York: Harcourt, Brace, 1959.

Rudman, Stella. *Lloyd George and the Appeasement of Germany, 1919–1945.* Newcastle upon Tyne: Cambridge Scholars Publishing, 2011.

Scanlon, Jennifer. *Bad Girls Go Everywhere.* New York: Oxford University Press, 2009.

Schroeder, Christa. *He Was My Chief.* Translated by Geoffrey Brooks. London: Frontline Books, 2009.

Schultz, Gladys, and Daisy Gordon Lawrence. *Lady from Savannah.* New York: Lippincott, 1958.

Senn, Charles Herman. *The New Century Cookery Book.* London: Spottiswoode, 1901.

Sereny, Gitta. *Albert Speer: His Battle with Truth.* New York: Alfred A. Knopf, 1995.

Shand, P. Morton. *A Book of Food.* New York: Alfred A. Knopf, 1928.

Shaw, George Bernard. *Pygmalion.* Edited by L. W. Connolly. London and New York: Bloomsbury, 2008.

Shirer, William L. *Berlin Diary.* New York: Alfred A. Knopf, 1941.

Sigmund, Anna Maria. *Women of the Third Reich.* Richmond Hill, ON: NDE Publishing, 2000.

Simpson, Helen. *The Cold Table.* London: Jonathan Cape, 1935.

Speer, Albert. *Inside the Third Reich.* Translated by Richard and Clara Winston. New York: Macmillan, 1970.

——. *Spandau: The Secret Diaries.* Translated by Richard and Clara Winston. New York: Macmillan, 1976.

Stratigakos, Despina. *Hitler at Home.* New Haven, CT: Yale University Press, 2015.

Sweet-Escott, Thomas Hay. *Society in London.* London: Chatto and Windus, 1885.

Swift, Jonathan. *Polite Conversation.* London: Printed for Joseph Wenman, 1783.

Trollope, Anthony. *Miss Mackenzie.* 1865. Reprint, New York: Dover, 1986.

Trubek, Amy. *Haute Cuisine.* Philadelphia: University of Pennsylvania Press, 2000.

Tschumi, Gabriel. *Royal Chef.* London: William Kimber, 1954.

Tully, Grace. *F.D.R., My Boss.* New York: Scribner's, 1949.

Vassiltchikov, Marie. *Berlin Diaries, 1940–1945.* New York: Alfred A. Knopf, 1987.

Waugh, Evelyn. *Vile Bodies.* 1930. Reprint, Boston: Little, Brown and Co., 1977.

West, J. B., with Mary Lynn Kotz. *Upstairs at the White House.* New York: Coward, McCann and Geohegan, 1973.

Wilson, A. N. Introduction to *Excellent Women,* by Barbara Pym. New York: Penguin, 2006.

Wilson, Frances. *The Ballad of Dorothy Wordsworth.* New York: Farrar, Straus and Giroux, 2008.

Woof, Pamela, ed. *The Grasmere and Alfoxden Journals,* by Dorothy Wordsworth. Oxford: Oxford University Press, 2002.

Wordsworth, Dorothy. Journal, 1828–1829. Dove Cottage manuscripts (DCMS). Jerwood Centre, Grasmere, Cumbria.

INDEX

Page numbers in *italics* refer to photo captions.